COMMON ERA

COMMON ERA

BEST NEW WRITINGS ON RELIGION

VOLUME ONE

EDITED BY STEVEN SCHOLL

WHITE CLOUD PRESS
ASHLAND, OREGON

99 98 97 96 95   5 4 3 2 1

Cover Design by Daniel Cook
Cover illustration, "Masked Volcano" © Betty LaDuke
Printed in the United States of America

01 00 99 98 97 96 95   1 2 3 4 5

LIBRARY OF CONGRESS CATALOGING IN PUBLICATION DATA

Common era : best new writings on religion / edited by Steven Scholl.
p.   cm.
Includes bibliogprahical references
ISBN 1-883991-12-9
1. Religion. 2. Religions. I. Scholl, Steven, 1954-   .
BL25.C56 1995
200--dc20
95-2883
CIP

Table of Contents

Introduction   ix
STEVEN SCHOLL

1. Dialogue Among the World's Religions   1
   PAUL KNITTER

2. Let There Be Light   11
   BILL MOYERS

3. The Vomit of a Mad Tyger   30
   ALLEN GINSBERG

4. Anchored in a Different Place:
   Human Rights, Democracy and Transcendence   47
   VACLAV HAVAL

5. Ecopsychology and the *Anima Mundi*   54
   THEODORE ROSZAK

6. Deep Politics and Grace: A Postmodernist Viewpoint   69
   MATTHEW FOX

7. Liberating Sexuality: Tantra Talk   73
   MIRANDA SHAW

8. The Caravan of Summer   82
   PETER LAMBORN WILSON

9. Pity and Terror in Waco   93
   JAMES S. GORDON

10. Does A Global Village Warrant a Global Ethic? An analysis
    of *A Global Ethic*, the Declartion of the 1993 Pariliament
    of the World's Religions   99
    JUNE O'CONNOR

11. Bosnia: Some Religious Dimensions of Genocide in Bosnia   114
    MICHAEL A. SELLS

12. Return of the Sacred 127
JERRY MANDER

13. Dharma, Democracy, and the Information Highway 139
MITCHELL KAPOR

14. A Path Uncovered 156
DAVID A. COOPER

15. Grace in the Midst of Failings 161
ROSEMARY RADFORD RUETHER

16. Comparativism in a World of Difference: The Legacy of
of Joseph Campbell to the Postmodern History of Religions 168
DAVID MILLER

17. Border Crossings 178
LAUREL THATCHER ULRICH

18. A Faith to Move Mountains: Shaking the Foundations
of Power in Mexico 186
JEFF SHRIVER

19. From Yale to Jail: David Dellinger's Quest for Justice 195
GEORGE HOWLAND, JR.

INTRODUCTION

We live in the Common Era, a time of acceleration, chaos, collaboration, new visions, destruction, creation, sober reflection and ecstatic wonderment. It is now commonplace for commentators to note that we are witnessing the death of an old order and the birth of a new world order, though these same commentators differ radically as to what that might mean and in which direction we should be heading. The role of religion in this process is fundamental. The world's religions are now pivotal players on the world stage and must be involved participants whether we are dealing with solving the political crises of India, the Middle East, and Bosnia or formulating changes in health care and welfare.

Common Era is an attempt to look back at recent writings in the field of religion to further reflection on the spiritual and religious dimensions at play in our worlds. By worlds I mean the overlapping realms of politics, culture, literature, mysticism, theology, economics, ethics, etc. Each yearly edition of *Common Era* will take a broad look at the various forms of religious expression from an ecumenical and multicultural bias. To pick and choose "the best" of anything is, naturally, an artificial exercise to some degree. In choosing "the best new writings on religion" for the previous year, I have labored to find works that are representative of trends in religious life as reflected in media coverage on religious topics. In 1994 there was, for example, numerous responses to the 1993 Parliament of World Religions; growing interest in Buddhism, particularly

Tibetan Buddhism and tantric practices; and reflections on the ecological dimensions of life on earth and the role religion may yet play in restoring the natural order of things. These subjects are represented admirably in *Common Era* with contributions from Vaclav Havel, Allen Ginsberg, Bill Moyers, Miranda Shaw, Theodore Roszak, Jerry Mander, June O'Connor, David Miller, Mitchell Kapor, and Matthew Fox .

I have also been struck in my reading by the personal dimensions of religious experience in our time. As the anthology evolved, I found more and more that I was being drawn toward writings that revealed personal stories of faith and commitment. Rosemary Radford Ruether and Laurel Thatcher Ulrich describe with passion and wisdom how two feminist religious scholars maintain faith in their churches (Roman Catholic and Mormon respectively); George Howland, Jr. brings us David Dellinger's lifelong quest for justice rooted in his deep religious faith; while Ginsberg's remarkable autobiographical essay illuminates the spiritual quest of one of America's greatest poetic voices. Paul Knitter, who opens the book with a profound reflection on dialogue among the world's religions, also adds a very personal dimension to our discussions when he describes some of the existential dimensions of interfaith dialogue.

David Cooper and Peter Lamborn Wilson explore the mystical side of religion in their respective essays. Cooper uncovers the ancient Jewish path of mysticism while Wilson brilliantly contrasts our modern disease of tourism with the wandering Sufi mystics of Islam.

The political dimension of faith and religion is amply represented in these pages. Jeff Shriver's journey to Chiapas, Mexico uncovers the story of a revolution from the perspective of the biblical call for social justice. Michael Sells painstakingly recounts the religious dimensions of genocide in the continuing tragedy of Bosnia. Sells article also brought to my attention an organization that is working to save Bosnian culture from "ethnic cleansing" and provide relief to the victims of this program of genocide. The Community of Bosnia Foundation has been formed to preserve the magnificent cultural legacy of the multi-religious community of Bosnia through publication of books and monographs on art and architecture, translations of Bosnian literature, and memoirs of concentration camp survivors. This work is crucial to the morale of the one million Bosnians in exile and to the memory of a multi-religious Bosnia, a memory the "ethnic cleansers" want to efface.

To aid in this much needed effort, royalties from *Common Era* will be directed to the Community of Bosnia Foundation and I encourage your support of this effort. For more information, contact The Community of Bosnia Foundation, c/o The Religion Department, Haverford College, Haverford, PA 19041-1392. E-mail address: msells@haverford.edu. In this small way it is my hope that *Common Era* will serve the common good.

Steven Scholl
Ashland, Oregon

DIALOGUE AMONG THE WORLD'S RELIGIONS†

by PAUL F. KNITTER

from DIALOG

Anyone who has had the privilege of engaging in interreligious dialogue might find the following description appropriate: interreligious dialogue is the confrontation with utter, bewildering, often threatening *differences* and at the same time, the *trust* that such differences are, for the most part, friendly rather than hostile, fruitful rather than barren. In dialogue one faces the utterly other and trusts that one can speak to, learn from, even work with that other. Within the heart of dialogue, therefore, there beats a deep act of faith and trust.

Unpacking this description, I find four essential ingredients in the mix that is dialogue: differences, trust, witnessing, and learning.

DIFFERENCES

ANYONE WHO BEGINS AN INTERRELIGIOUS conversation with the announcement of how much we have in common or that we are really saying "the same thing in different words" has done just that—only begun the conversation. Such announcements, though they may have their element of truth, can be maintained only on the surface of dialogue; they begin to fade away as one goes deeper into the experience, the beliefs and practices, and the historical development of the different religious traditions.

Like a newly married couple growing out of the first stages of infatuation into real living together, partners in religious sharing, as they get to know each other, soon arrive at the existential realization of how bewilderingly different they are. What had been initially experienced as similarities now become differing, even opposing, faces. The Tao and God, Zen meditation and Christian prayer, Jesus and Buddha, *avidya* and original sin—become as different as they once were similar. One gradually becomes aware of the naiveté and the downright danger of proclaiming a "common essence" or a "common core" within all the religions of the world.

Given my own experience of dialogue and thanks to the chidings of my postmodern friends, I have realized over the past years that I, like many proponents of religious pluralism, have too hastily hoisted the banner of "pluralism," before sufficiently recognizing the reality of "plurality." We pluralists have been too quick to propose an "ism" or a system on the vast, buzzing array of plurality; and in so *proposing* we have *imposed*. David Tracy's admonition, arising out of his own experience of religious otherness, rings true: "pluralists, the vaunted defenders of difference, can become the great reductionists—reducing differences to mere similarity, reducing otherness to the same, and reducing plurality to my community of right-thinking competent critics. In this light, there is truth in Simone de Beauvoir's bitter charge that 'pluralism is the perfect ideology for the bourgeois mind.'"[1]

TRUST

AND YET, THOUGH WE STARE at each others' religious traditions across differences that seem incommensurable, though we well realize the difficulty of understanding and the danger of judging another person's religious beliefs and practices, we find ourselves borne or grasped by a suspicion, a hope, a resolve that we *can* speak to each other across our religious barriers, that it is worthwhile, even necessary, to do so. This is, indeed, an act of faith. It is a deep-seated feeling which seems to be given to us or to take hold of us; we find ourselves believing in something which, though rooted in experiential evidence, goes beyond that evidence. It is similar to Luther's "*trotzdem*," his "despite all that": despite the stark differences between religions, we believe that the sheer actuality of *plurality* can lead to the inter-relatedness of *pluralism*. There is *life* in the differences. In speaking to each other across our gaps, we can come closer.

2

In fact, it seems that this coming closer, this conversation with those who are genuinely different, is an indispensable condition for growing in the understanding of reality, in the pursuit of truth. If, as we are told nowadays, there is no absolute criterion of truth given to us from above, if there is no foundation outside the fluctuations of history for evaluating the many forced options that face our world, then we must plunge into the conversation, listen to each others' differences, and in this engagement, fashion, step by difficult step, our understanding of reality. In order to "grow in wisdom and truth before God and our fellow human beings," we must talk to each other. In order to enrich and save our world we must embrace plurality.

In the ebb and flow of conversing, with all its complexity and dangers, we can create, not foundations, but "shaky common ground." Not with pre-packaged methods or systems but by genuinely trying to "pass over" to the otherness of the other, by stretching our own visions and paradigms, we can establish new, shared ground on which we *can* truly understand another culture or religion, and they us. The gap of incommensurability *can* be bridged—but the bridge will never be set in cement; it will, rather, sway in the wind and have to be frequently reconstructed or torn down to be rebuilt at a better crossing. Just how these bridges are built and how this common shaky ground is discovered cannot be stated in advance of the conversation. It can be discovered, created, maintained only in the act and process of dialogue.

WITNESSING

IN INTERRELIGIOUS DIALOGUE WE CONFRONT otherness as something we want not only to embrace but also to address. Ideally, we come to the conversation from a position of richness, not impoverishment—that is, we speak to each other out of our own religious experience. We speak because we have discovered something of value—the pearl of great price. As Raimundo Panikkar has continuously insisted, in order to have religious encounter, we must speak from religious experience—or at least from religious quest. Such "subjective" contents and perspectives are not to be cut out and packed in some kind of deep-freeze "*epoché*" but, rather, are to be poured, warm and bubbling, into the conversation.[2] The "object" of dialogue is approached through a meeting of "subjects."

And because we speak out of our different religious experiences and convictions, we will seek not only to explain but to *persuade*. If genuinely experienced, religious truth, like all truth, can never be only "for me."

3

If it is, it is somehow diluted or not yet fully grown. A quality of "universal relevance" is ingredient to every encounter with or revelation of the Ultimate; what one has seen, felt, been transformed by—can also so affect others. All interreligious dialogue, therefore, is animated by a certain missionary élan. We want our partners to see what we have seen; we want their lives to be touched and transformed as ours have been. Yes, let me use the offensive word: we want to *convert* our partners.

But the conversion that is sought is not one of "winning over" but of sharing. This is a big difference—between saving from damnation and sharing the light. This distinction is based on the difference between religious truth experienced as "universally relevant" and as "one and only." Authentic religious experience naturally includes, I suggest, the former quality, not the latter. When experienced, truth is always felt to be *universal*; it is not necessarily felt to be *singular* or *final*. Therefore, what animates me in the dialogue is not the conviction that you are lost without my understanding of truth, but that there *is* something missing in your life until you have seen what I have seen. You can be different, richer, if I can pass on to you what has been passed on to me.

LEARNING

BUT THE DIALECTICAL PENDULUM SWINGS BACK, and just as much as we desire to witness and convert, we feel the need to be witnessed to and, yes, converted by our partners. Witnessing will go astray unless it is accompanied by listening and learning. This need to learn from others is rooted in the same "trust," described above, that the "other" has words of life to speak to us. But it is also rooted in and demanded by our own religious experience. In Christian terms, to experience the living God is not only to experience a truth and a power that is "universally relevant," to be proclaimed to all the nations; it is also to fall into the embrace of a Mystery that will always and enticingly be more than what we have experienced. To experience this Mystery of God authentically is to know for sure that we are experiencing it only *partially*. All religious traditions seem to bear witness to this aspect of religious experience—that God, Allah, Brahman, Sunyata, the Tao—can never be known *in toto* (totally) but only *in parte*. And if only partially, then we must be open to discovering "other parts"; we must look through other windows out onto the universe of Truth and Mystery. As wonderful as is the view from our window, it impels us to look through others.

4

The need to learn from others is also fostered by our postmodern awareness of the dangers of all truth claims. Thanks to progenitors of the "hermeneutics of suspicion" such as Nietzsche, Freud, Marx, we have come to realize the limits and the corruptions of reason and the human heart; in our noblest and most reasoned efforts to know the truth and fashion our world, in every effort to interpret the revelation given us by God, there is the worm of *ideology*—the ever lurking propensity to use our "truth" as a means of assuring our own advantage or control over that of others. Ideology stalks our noblest ideals and projects. As Walter Benjamin has said, "Every work of civilization [we could add, every work of religion] is at the same time a work of barbarism."[3]

Therefore, we need others. We need the insights and perspectives of others who look at the world differently than we do, who can look at our visions of truth from a critical standpoint outside our circle, who perhaps can tell us how our "truth" has excluded or victimized them. We must, again, *learn* from others, so they can point out our distortions, our self-centered abuse of the truth that has been given us. Without conversation with others, we cannot protect ourselves against the ideological abuse of our own truth.

CROSSING A THEOLOGICAL RUBICON

I SUSPECT THAT MANY CHRISTIANS would want to affirm the kind of dialogue just described. They view it as something rewarding—both for the community of nations and for their own faith-lives. But the rewards of such dialogue are coupled with demands. In affirming and engaging in a dialogue that truly embraces the rich diversity of other religious ways and in trying to open themselves to learn from that diversity, Christians can feel themselves called, or pushed, beyond their traditional theological models for understanding other religions. In contemporary theological jargon, a number of Christians are stepping beyond past models of "exclusivism" (other religions are false) and of "inclusivism" (other religions may be true but Christianity, because of Christ, is the truest and the fulfillment of all others) and are exploring a "pluralistic" theology of religions. This pluralist model affirms the possibility that other religions may have just as valid and important a role to play in God's plan of salvation as does Christianity. Only with such a model, so it seems, can Christians avoid forcing the truth of other religions into their own standards; only with such a model can Christians be ready to learn "brand new things" that they haven't encountered in their own religion.

But such a pluralistic move appears, even to those who are making it, a dangerous theological Rubicon, a crossing over into something that is so new it may destroy their Christian identity. The primary problems have to do with Christology: on the other side of the Rubicon, it seems that Jesus loses the pivotal place he has always played in Christian life and worship; he becomes "one among many" religious figures and saviors.

I would like to suggest how recent developments in the theology of religions can help Christians explore possibilities of a pluralistic view of the world of religions. What has been called a *soteriocentric* or *salvation-centered* approach to other believers can help Christians explore the other side of the Rubicon without losing their Christian compass.

Especially in its Roman Catholic expression, mainline Christian theology of religions over the past decades has undergone an evolution that seems to point in the direction of what I am calling a salvation-centered model. In the 1960s and early '70s (in Vatican II and in the World Council of Churches), there was a move from *ecclesiocentrism* (or exclusivism) to *christocentrism* (or inclusivism) in the churches' approach to other faiths. Theologians no longer talked about the church as the "necessary means of salvation" or of the need to make all peoples members (manifest or latent) of the church. The universal, cosmic Christ was the principle of salvation.[4] In the '70s and early '80s some theologians began to move from christocentrism to *theocentrism* (or pluralism). They no longer insisted on Jesus Christ as the one mediator—or "constitutive cause"—of all salvation, which meant they no longer had to posit a hidden activity of the cosmic Christ within all other religions or to surreptitiously identify authentic believers in other traditions as "anonymous Christians." God, not necessarily Jesus Christ, was the center of the salvific universe.[5]

More recently, a number of theologians are taking a further step. Aware of the christological problems in theocentrism, aware too of the amazingly diverse ways of speaking about God or the Ultimate (or of not speaking of God at all as in Buddhism), aware, even more soberingly, of the mounting human and ecological suffering that afflicts our world, some proponents of interreligious dialogue have been urging a salvation-centered or "globally responsible" foundation or starting point for interfaith encounter.[6] In this approach, the primary (but not the exclusive) concern and guideline for speaking with or assessing other religious traditions is not how they might be made members of the Christian community, not how they can be brought to confess the Lord Jesus as their one and only savior, not even whether they affirm the reality of God. Rather, the foundation for a Christian view of and relationship with other religious believers is whether and how they are fostering the well-being of humans and of the earth, how they are confronting and assessing the ills of hunger, exploitation, ecological devastation. In Christian terms, such an approach might be called "Kingdom-centered"; the framework and foundation for a Christian approach to and dialogue with other religious traditions is the Kingdom of God in its this-wordly manifestation—that vision of a world in which all may have life and have it more abundantly (John 10:10).

Such a salvation-centered approach to other believers enables Christians to carry on a dialogue in which they can effectively embrace the diversity of religious perspectives in the hope that such diversity will contribute to eco-human well-being. It will also be a dialogue in which Christians can truly witness and learn—one in which, although they affirm the validity of other religions, they do not lose their moorings in the Gospel of Jesus. In such a salvation-centered dialogue, while Christians may not be proclaiming that Jesus is the only Lord and Savior, they *are* announcing the Good News of how Jesus' view of the Kingdom can promote the well-being of all creatures; and this Good News is not just interesting, it makes demands, it calls for commitment to the values of the Kingdom. But at the same time, in such a Kingdom-centered dialogue, Christians will be genuinely open to and ready to learn how the visions and values of other religions can promote *soteria* or eco-human well-being.

In such a salvation-centered relation with other believers, Christians continue to make *universal* claims about Jesus' vision for the well-being or salvation of the world. The values of mutuality and justice that are intrinsic to his message are meant not just for Christians but for all peoples; all peoples can be "saved" by encountering and accepting this message. But at the same time, Christians will be open to the *universally* relevant and saving messages of, perhaps, Buddha or Muhammad or Lao Tzu—and how their visions might add to, clarify, give new direction to what Christians know of the Kingdom of God through Jesus. In other words, in a soteriocentric theology of religions, Christians continue to announce that Jesus is *really* and *universally* "Savior." But they do not insist that he is *solely* or *definitively* Savior. They are open to the possibility of other words and other stories that will enhance and expand, maybe even correct, their vision of the Kingdom.

7

More personally, in this form of dialogue, Christians remain *fully*, even *absolutely* committed to Jesus as Savior and Son of God. But at the same time, paradoxically, they know that the vision he gives of God and of the Kingdom is *relative*, that is, *limited*. And they know this not because of some postmodern announcement of the socially mediated nature of all knowledge but because of what Jesus himself has made known to them: that "the Father is greater than I" (John 14:28), that the Spirit will have further truth to make known to them (John 14:26), and especially that the Kingdom of God is an *eschatological reality*. Though always "already," the Kingdom is also always "not yet." Because of the "already" Christians are fully committed to this Kingdom and passionately represent it in the dialogue; but because of the "not yet" they are also humbly, readily open to other manifestations of that Kingdom—to other understandings of what makes for human and ecological well-being. *Soteria* or the Kingdom of God, therefore, serves Christians as a criterion for understanding and judging other traditions but never in a definitive, or absolute way. It requires Christians always to be open to and stand criticized by how others understand and judge them.

Such a pluralistic, salvation-centered understanding of other religions is, I suggest, more faithful to what we can know of Jesus' own view of himself. Whatever Jesus' self-understanding was, it took shape in relation—and in subordination—to his commitment to God's Kingdom. Scholars tell us that we perhaps come closest to Jesus' own sense of identity and mission when we view him as a prophet—as a servant of the Kingdom. Yet he also seems to have understood himself as the *eschatological* or final prophet.[7] This underlines what is otherwise evident in the Gospels—that Jesus felt his message and role was essential to bringing about this Kingdom, that people had to "take sides" on what he was announcing. Still, this does not mean that he was setting himself above the Kingdom or that he was limiting to himself possibilities of knowing and working for the Kingdom. As Jon Sobrino and Juan Luis Segundo insist, we are doing Jesus a disservice, to say the least, when we so absolutize him as to distract from our own responsibilities to work for and to recognize the Kingdom of God wherever it might be.[8]

After the resurrection when the proclaimer rightfully and necessarily became the proclaimed, Christianity became exposed to the danger of a "Jesusolatry" or a "christological reduction" that reduces God and the Kingdom of God to Jesus and the church.[9] If Jesus is so absolutized, Christian existence is understood primarily as a confession of or a relationship with Jesus rather than as a commitment to working for the King-dom. We forget that Jesus "does not himself exhaust the totality of mediation of the will of God" and does not "represent the accomplish-ment of God's final will."[10] In our full commitment to him, we must be open to other expressions, other possibilities of realizing human well-being and liberation.

This, I believe, is one of the most urgent, difficult, and rewarding challenges facing Christians today: to be as fully committed to Jesus and his Good News of salvation as they are open to the Good News that may be waiting for them in other religious communities.

NOTES

† This essay adapts and expands my contribution to *Death or Dialogue: From the Age of Monologue to the Age of Dialogue*, by Leonard Swidler, John B. Cobb, Jr., Paul F. Knitter, Monika K. Hellwig (Philadelphia: Trinity Press International, 1990) 19-44.

1. David Tracy, "Christianity in the Wider Context: Demands and Transformations," *Religion and Intellectual Life* 4 (1987) 12.

2. R. Panikkar, *The Intrareligious Dialogue* (New York: Paulist, 1978).

3. David Tracy, *Plurality and Ambiguity: Hermeneutics, Religion, Hope* (New York: Harper & Row, 1987) 69.

4. Paul Knitter, *No Other Name? A Critical Survey of Christian Attitudes toward World Religions* (Maryknoll: Orbis, 1985) 121-130.

5. Ibid., 145-204; John Hick, *God and the Universe of Faiths* (New York: St. Martin's, 1973).

6. Hans Küng, *Global Responsibility: In Search of a New World Ethic* (New York: Crossroad, 1991); Aloysius Pieris, *An Asian Theology of Libera-tion* (Maryknoll: Orbis, 1988); Paul F. Knitter, "Dialogue and Liberation: Foundations for a Pluralist Theology of Religions," *The Drew Gateway* 58 (1988) 1-53.

7. Edward Schillebeeckx, *Jesus: An Experiment in Christology* (New York: Seabury, 1979) 154-229, 441-515.

8. Jon Sobrino, *The True Church and the Poor* (Maryknoll: Orbis, 1984) 43; Juan Luis Segundo, *The Historical Jesus of the Synoptics* (Maryknoll: Or-bis, 1985) 186f.

9. Jon Sobrino, *Jesus in Latin America* (Maryknoll: Orbis, 1987) 20; id., 41.

10. Sobrino, *The True Church*, 41-42.

PAUL F. KNITTER is Professor of Theology at Xavier University in Cincinnati, Ohio. He is the author of **No Other Name? A Critical Survey of Christian Attitudes Toward World Religions**; *co-editor with John Hick of* **The Myth of Christian Uniqueness: Toward a Pluralistic Theology of Religions**; *co-author with John Cobb and Monika Hellwig of* **Death or Dialogue: From the Age of Monologue to the Age of Dialogue**.

Reprinted from *Dialog*, 2481 Como Ave., Saint Paul, MN 55108-1496. Subscription: $22/year.

LET THERE BE LIGHT

by BILL MOYERS

from RELIGION AND VALUES IN THE PUBLIC LIFE

I want to share with you some of the reasons why it seems to me no beat in journalism is more important than religion.

On a recent Friday night, I awoke after midnight and could not get back to sleep. Turning on the bedside radio for company, I found myself listening to a call-in show devoted mainly to current events. The discussions were so perfunctory that they had the effect on me of a sedative, and I began to drift back into unconsciousness. But then a plaintive voice caught my ear, and I heard a young man telling the host, "This is my birthday. Here I am three hours into my eighteenth year, and I need help to know how to live in a world that is disintegrating."

The host was momentarily taken aback, so he tried a wise crack. "No," the young man persisted, "I'm really serious. I'm scared. I'm starting my eighteenth year in a world that makes no sense to me."

"Are you thinking about checking out?" the host blurted. There was a long pause before the young man answered: "I don't know. I

This essay originally was delivered as the keynote address to the Religion Newswriters Association.

don't want to. All I know is this world I'm living in is a shambles, and I don't know how to put it together."

Other callers chimed in to talk about how awful things are, and the young man's voice was soon lost in the chorus. Whether he got any help from that exchange among disembodied strangers in the night, I cannot report. But as I lay there thinking about him, Gabriel's line from "Green Pastures" came to me: "Everything that's tied down is coming loose." I thought of the chaos in the lives of the characters my wife and I had just seen in Tony Kushner's play, "Angels in America," where disease, madness and cynicism make wrecks of health, hope and love. Remembering Stephen Mitchell's new translation of the Book of Job, I got out of bed to find it in my study and reflected for awhile on the story of another man in another time whose world came apart without rhyme or reason.

I looked at my desk, piled high with research for a series we are producing about violence, and I could see the titles of comic books promulgating a paranoid view of reality. With names like "Swamp Thing," "War of the Worlds," "The Warlock Five," "The Avengers," "Shattered Earth," "Gun Fury," "The Huntress," and "The Blood Sword," these comic books portray a society where young boys find in the initiation of violence their only protection against enemies plotting their doom. In their pages and in their video counterparts are the stories feeding the generation of that midnight caller whose confession of despair had been offered earnestly but vainly to a talk show host. Shortly before dawn I drifted into sleep again, still thinking of that young man's lament: "I am starting my eighteenth year in a world that makes no sense to me. . . .I don't know how to put it together again."

Such lamentations are deep currents running throughout the liberal West today. Our secular and scientific societies are besieged by violence, moral anarchy, and purposelessness that have displaced any mobilizing vision of the future except hedonism and consumerism.

It is this aspect of modernism that the Islamic world has taken note of and to which it has sworn enmity. The scholar Bernard Lewis says the principal function of government in the Islamic world is to enable the individual Muslim to live a good Muslim life; this is "in the last analysis, the purpose of the state." With our traditions of individualism, religious pluralism, and the neutral state, Americans reject that role for government as strenuously as Muslims deplore the moral squalor of Times Square. Yet Hillary Clinton brought 15,000 people to their feet in Austin, Texas, when she talked about the politics of meaning, and while Beltway pundits hooted and dismissed her remarks, callers to radio talk shows across the country were far more sympathetic and supportive. There is a widespread sense in the country that everything that is tied down is coming loose.

Something is happening in America that is worthy of the sharpest reporting and analysis we can bring to it. Millions of Americans are searching for some clearer understanding of the core principles of religion and how they can be applied to the daily experience of living as well as to humanity's common destiny on this planet. The Gallup organization reports that more Americans today say religion plays a role in their lives than did in 1987. Church attendance by teenagers is up, and other surveys report that even among people who reject organized religion there is a yearning for spiritual connections. Craig Dykstra writes in *Theology Today:*

> Something interesting is happening. Religious searching is going public today, and people seem to want to talk about God. Recent novels, magazine stories, and newspaper articles increasingly reflect a more serious attention to religious matters. What, if anything, it all will amount to is unclear. Are there cues here that some sort of religious awakening is just over the horizon? Who knows. But it makes sense to pay attention.

We should not be surprised that some people take comfort from "old-fashioned religion." Edith Hamilton writes in her classic study of ancient Greece that "when the world is storm-driven and the bad that happens and the worse that threatens are so urgent as to shut out everything else from view, then we need to know all the strong fortresses of the spirit which have been built through the ages."

For others, the Rock of Ages has been chipped away, and they are looking for new ground to stand upon. Thomas Berry writes about this in his interpretation of the importance of religious narrative. "Story" is the plot we assign to life and the universe, our basic assumptions and fundamental beliefs about how things work, a world view, the paradigm that instructs us. Berry says we are in trouble just now because we are in between stories. "The old story—the account of how the world came to be and how we fit into it—sustained us for a long period of time. It shaped our emotional attitudes, provided us with life purpose, energized action. It consecrated suffering, integrated knowledge, guided education. We awoke in the morning and knew where we were. We could answer the questions of our children. Everything was taken care of because the story was there. *Now the old story is not functioning properly, and we have not yet learned the new . . . "*

For many, a new story is emerging from the coupling of East and West. In his monumental exploration of *The Religions of Man*, Huston Smith writes that authentic religion is "the clearest opening through which the inexhaustible energies of the cosmos can pour into human existence." Nothing can rival its power to touch and inspire the deepest creative centers of our being, he writes. From the perspective of history, the most important fact about the twentieth century may be "the meeting of East and West." "Meeting" is hardly the word for it. They are "being flung at one another, hurled with the force of atoms, the speed of jets, the restlessness of minds impatient to learn ways that differ from their own." And when historians look back upon our years "they may remember them not for the release of nuclear power but as the time in which all the peoples of the world had to take one another seriously, including our quest for meaning . . . "

In these insights—Edith Hamilton's, that in troubled times men and women seek to renew our understanding of the historical faiths; Huston Smith's, that migrations and the intermingling of cultures are producing a new religious dynamic; and Thomas Berry's, that we are between stories and cannot long survive without one—are rich grist for the journalist's mill.

I SEE EVIDENCE OF THIS RELIGIOUS STIRRING on many levels. At the Jewish Theological Seminary of America, for example, there is occurring what the *New York Times* called "the best conversation" in New York City. Once a month, under the tutelage of Rabbi Burton Visotzky, theologians, philosophers, linguists, novelists, historians, filmmakers and others meet to discuss, dissect and debate the Book of Genesis. If you walked in on this seminar, you would find some two dozen people seated around a bare table in an ordinary room, passionately talking about Adam and Eve, Noah's obedience, and Lot's daughters. You are likely to be stirred, as I was, by the capacity of these old biblical stories to still inspire the human imagination—to call us to wisdom, remind us of deep truths, and summon us to consider the boundaries of conduct.

It happens outside of established channels, too. Just the other day, I talked to a young professional woman who belongs to a study group in New York City that gathers informally but regularly to read and discuss the Bible. They are also working their way through Genesis, trying to apply its ancient insights to their own experience here on the shore of the twenty-first century. They ask themselves such questions as: Can you trust a God who asks a father to sacrifice his only son? What does it mean to trust what one cannot see? What today is obedience to the Word when the Word has to compete with MTV? And what about the great message of forgiveness in the story of Joseph? Why is forgiveness so hard for us? Is this unwillingness to repent and forgive at the heart of our social predicament today, our jugular politics, the collapse of our social contract?

This same young woman told me how a discussion about Noah and his sons and Lot and his daughters led her group into a spirited debate over whom to believe in disputes over sexual abuse. And the stories of Abraham, she said, prompted sustained debate over the nature of doubt, the definition of faith, and the meaning of God's promises to humanity today. As she told me of the group's attempt to work through the modern relevance of these biblical tales, I remembered a play from many years ago. Its premise was that the life-supporting systems of the earth were on the verge of collapse, and all the great minds of the world met at MIT to feed everything they knew into a computer. They hoped it would process all this data and provide a solution that would stave off calamity. After the last syllable of the final authority had been entered, the computer shuttered and blinked and beeped and then gave forth the answer:

"Honor thy father and thy mother . . ."
"You shall not kill . . ."
"You shall not commit adultery . . ."
"You shall not steal . . . "
"You shall not bear false witness . . ."
"You shall not covet . . ."

Then there was the experience of my televised interviews with Joseph Campbell on "The Power of Myth." As Campbell roamed the ancient religions of the world, retelling stories of creation, of sacrifice and bliss, of forbidden fruit and serpents, of love and betrayal, of death and redemption, people all over the country gathered around their television sets as if it were a tribal campfire where their elders told stories to explain the universe and their place in it.

Tens of thousands of people wrote me in response to the Campbell series. One of my favorite letters came from a man in Vermont. He wrote:

> One evening per week for the last half-dozen weeks, a group of us, mostly strangers to each other, have gathered in front of a television set to watch, and then discuss, the PBS series on "The Power of Myth." These shows have fascinated me not only because of their content. After all, as a scholar of myth I have been tracking Joseph Campbell and his ideas for twenty-five years, and I don't even agree with all of them. No, it is the *appeal* of these shows that has mainly intrigued me; the fact that stations have repeated the entire series so quickly, and especially the fact of the presence of those fifteen to twenty-five strangers, brought out of their homes every week to huddle around a video campfire in a room at the River Valley Playhouse in Putney. Several of the participants in our largely self-led discussions had never heard of Campbell until the TV series, but we find these episodes have supplied something which is generally lacking in our culture of getting and spending, commerce and computers, and unconvincing campaign promises. These stories [from the world's religions] speak to our yearnings, so much so that our weekly group (which just came together to share a common television set) will continue to meet in Putney, inspired to explore in greater depth the themes brought home to us by these programs. No doubt at times we will replicate the sometimes stale debate of college philosophy: the existence of God, the limits of language, the basis of an ethical life. But what will keep us meeting, I suspect, will not be such worthy arguments in their abstractness. Rather, it will be the connection Campbell has reminded us of between these philosophical conundrums and our most private, often irrational concerns.

When I think about all that is happening in the religious dimension, of the search for meaning and the appetite to connect, I am bewildered at the absence on television of any serious, ongoing, nonpartisan, democratic dialogue about religion and values.

Think about it. Just about every other human endeavor is the subject of continuing coverage by the media, even to saturation: economics, politics and government, business, foreign policy, sports, sex, cooking, consumer interests, physical fitness, movies and entertainment, war, crime, even wrestling. But religion as a crucial force in American life; as source of values and ideas reflecting different aspirations for a moral and political order; as the exercise of free men and women to bring form to their lives from the chaos around them; as the interpretation of experience itself—for this view of religion, there is on television no room at the inn.

IT IS NOT SURPRISING THAT SO MANY OF US remain religiously illiterate. Even if we are intimate with our own tradition, we know little about other faiths. Rarely do we ever even see or hear people of different faiths discussing ideas, interpreting events, and presenting issues from their religious perspectives. Broadcast journalists are especially out of the loop. When the Nieman Foundation at Harvard University devoted its journal to the theme "God in the Newsroom," one editor confessed: "Let's face it. The media don't handle religion well . . . Too many reporters, commentators and anchormen just don't know much about the subject and don't care." So religion is rarely afforded on television the time or format devoted to the rise and fall of the Dow-Jones index, the President's standing in the latest polls, today's Congressional scandal, or the latest antics of Hollywood celebrities.

Now I don't want to appear naive about this. Popular culture, including television, flourishes precisely because there exists a vast audience to feed it. Wealth, fame, sex and violence are for many the true gods of our secular age, with whom television offers daily communion. Cornel West says the market now defines our morality. The good is not what is true or beautiful. The good is what makes money.

But this reality makes all the more imperative the importance of our paying attention on television to religious affairs, to the philosophical and ethical challenges we must sort out as a society if we are to recover our moral gravity. Because television has become our all-encompassing environment, none of us can escape its pervasive presence any more than we can by closing our windows escape the air pollution that seeps undetected through the cracks. If you were trying to study the effects of television on society, it would be meaningless merely to count the number of sets per household and the total hours of viewing. That would be like trying to calculate the effects of the automobile on society by looking under the hood without taking into consideration the air pollution, road systems, gas stations and community relocations that resulted. What should be studied, rather than facts and figures, is the mix of programming that establishes the density, quality and character of the whole environment. In our environment today, you will look long and hard for even a pittance of non-fiction programming that addresses the yearning described by Saul Bellow's fictional character Herzog:

> The people who come to evening class are only ostensibly after culture. Their great need, their hunger, is for good sense, clarity, truth—even an atom of it. People are dying—it is no metaphor— for lack of something real when day is done.

So it is that in his 1993 best-seller, *The Culture of Disbelief,* Stephen Carter of Yale Law School observed that the dominant secular forces in American society act as though "religion is, like building model airplanes, just another hobby: something quiet, something private, something trivial—and not really a fit activity for intelligent, public-spirited adults." Roy Larson, who is spear-heading an effort to open a Center for Religion and the News Media at Northwestern University's Medill School of Journalism and Garrett-Evangelical Theological Seminary, says that what Carter writes about the ways "American law and politics trivialize religious devotion" could be applied with equal force to the media.

Thus, a reporter seeking a comment today on an issue such as assisted suicide or American intervention in Bosnia will ask an economist, politician, psychologist, sociologist, lawyer—almost anyone but a member of the clergy, or a philosopher, or an ethicist, or a theologian, even though life and death, right and wrong, war and peace are the very heart of religious concerns. Sometimes it appears that the "wall of separation" that is meant to keep the government from giving any specific religion a privileged position in American life is interpreted as a rampart dividing all of religion from the rest of American life.

Yet in a democracy we have a responsibility to discuss and debate our value systems in the "marketplace of ideas" because here our collective identity and our governing consensus and, indeed, our social peace are secured or lost. Once the marketplace of ideas was the marketplace. People would meet their neighbors in the street or store and hear the news. In late twentieth-century America, our television sets have become not only a place to shop, but a primary source of ideas and information about the world. News programs, entertainment programs and particularly commercials show us who is important, what is important, and how to live. We learn from television what "everyone is talking about." Not, however, if they are talking about religion.

IN PREPARATION FOR THIS GATHERING, I tried to imagine a television news program that would help to fill the void. It would be a conversation format, because talk is the ideal way to explore religion. The communications scholar Joshua Meyrowitz, stressing the need for more rational argument and social criticism on television, writes that "words can stand alone in the development of abstract ideas, while images and expressions cannot. One can picture two people eating together, but the concepts of 'kindness,' 'friendship,' and 'love' exist through language. One can show a picture of a big statue holding a torch, but the ideas of 'liberty,' 'freedom,' or 'democracy' need to be developed and debated through words." Anyone at home in religious discourse will hardly find this surprising, for "in the beginning was the Word."

In our television weekly we would certainty talk about news of the mind. Because ideas are experiences of the mind, we would turn to books that bring us news hot off the writer's imagination. Every week important books are published in the field of religion and culture. Only a few receive the attention of Stephen Carter's *The Culture of Disbelief,* but many are fertile sources of revelation, debate and discourse. For example, Eerdmans is publishing Ted Peters' new book on *Sin: Radical Evil in Soul and Society*. It is a fascinating book, employing a wealth of theology, philosophy and history mixed with everyday experience. When was the last time you heard sin discussed in the national discourse? Yet listen to Peters:

> The next decade will find our entire society wrestling with an unprecedented array of questions regarding the cultural, philosophical, and legal implications of genetic research and proposals for biological determinism. This should prompt theologians to open up discussion on a number of doctrinal fronts, especially the doctrine of sin. One obvious point of contact is the concept of inheritance. Christian and Jewish thinking about sin is steeped in the idea of inheritance. We will have to take a closer look at the idea that the propensity for sin originated with Adam and Eve and has been passed down congenitally from generation to generation.

For context, we would recall the Social Gospel ideas of that turn-of-the-century theologian Walter Rauschenbusch, who developed the notion of socially inherited sin, sins lodged in social customs and institutions and then absorbed by the individual. And we would invite Peters to engage with Elaine Pagels, whose book *Adam, Eve and the Serpent* explores what the old story of the Garden of Eden reveals about our attitudes toward sexuality, politics, suffering and guilt, not to mention the roles of men and women in society.

We would build one program around the debates generated by D.Z. Phillips in his book *From Fantasy to Faith*. Phillips is a Welsh philosopher of religion who uses modern writers to uncover what is distinctive about religious language. He asks four questions in the book that many are wrestling with in their search for meaning. Has the human race outgrown religion? What authority is left to the rules of morality without God? Must morality be religious? Can a religious perspective incorporate the fact of human suffering without explaining it away?

Or we would take Diane Eble's new book published by Zondervan, *Men in Search of Work and the Women Who Love Them.* When Eble's husband was laid off and could find no comparable job, she kept bumping into other people who were experiencing the pain, isolation and confusion that had invaded her household. Among people who had been laid off she found, behind all the statistics, flesh-and-blood human beings who were trying to cope with loss of self-esteem, loss of income, loss of social relationships. An article she wrote about them for a Christian magazine prompted such a response that she wrote this book to raise theological questions about a subject almost exclusively within the province of economists and politicians. In the midst of downsizing, leveraged buyouts, dislocation, declining family incomes and failing standards of living, ordinary citizens are asking: Why did God let this happen? Why is this situation continuing, despite our best efforts? Does this life offer us any kind of future, or should we just put all our hope in heaven? Should I pray for a specific job or just that God would provide for my needs? Imagine a discussion of these subjects with a group of unemployed whose belief system has crumbled under the weight of everyday experience. It is not the stuff of Oprah, Donahue or Geraldo, but that is the point.

Or consider the just-published *Cosmos Crumbling: American Reform and the Religious Imagination,* by the University of Texas historian Robert H. Abzug. He explores the religious roots of that peculiarly American variety of political and social action we have come to call "reform." Abolitionists stormed against the cruelties of slavery. Temperance zealots hounded producers and consumers of strong drink. Sabbatarians fought to make Sunday an officially recognized sacred day. Women's rights activists proclaimed the case for sexual equality. Abzug is especially concerned with the relation between the sacred and profane elements in reform. While most recent scholarship has concentrated on the socioeconomic and psychological interpretations of reform, giving a mostly perfunctory nod to "religion," Abzug maintains that we can only understand reformers if we try to comprehend the sacred significance they bestowed upon these worldly arenas. His book raises questions about the future of reform if the cosmology of religion, in which individuals are morally responsible agents accountable to God, continues to crumble. One can conjure up the names of a dozen prominent philosophers, historians and theologians who could gather to confront these questions.

ON THE OTHER HAND, THERE ARE PEOPLE who believe a whole new cosmology is arising—Brian Swimme and Thomas Berry, for example. Swimme is director of the Center for the Story of the Universe at the California Institute of Integral Studies in San Francisco; Berry is the historian of cultures educated at Catholic University of America and the author of *The Dream of the Earth*. In their new book, *Universe Story: From the Primordial flaring Forth to the Ecozoic Era,* they meld the findings of contemporary science with the religious search for meaning and call for a "new ecological imperative." Crippling the Earth's biodiversity, "we are deciding what species will live or perish, we are determining the chemical structure of the soil and the water, we are mapping out the areas of wilderness that will be allowed to function in their own natural modalities." This, say the authors, "is filled with risk and presumption, for the story of the Earth is also the story of the human." It is also the kind of thing that drives editor Robert Hartley of the *Wall Street Journal* to fits, and I would relish the opportunity to pit Swimme and Berry in a televised debate with Hartley, Richard John Neuhaus and Michael Novak.

Another week, we would bring together Andrew M. Greeley and Jacob Neusner to read biblical passages aloud and talk about them. A few years ago they wrote *The Bible and Us: A Priest and a Rabbi Read Scripture Together* to demonstrate how each interprets Scripture from his own faith's tradition. In so doing they revealed how to engage in a mutually respectful conversation—Jew to Catholic, Catholic to Jew. One reviewer wrote:

> Lucid, funny, tender, inspiring and intellectually challenging, this book offers readers more than the latest in biblical scholarship, though it serves that, too. It provides a front-row seat to a fascinating dialogue between two prominent men who take faith seriously . . . The rabbi and the priest also consider whether or not their two religions as *religions* can engage in dialogue. Neusner says no, the religions are too different. Greeley says yes, suggesting that the question of Jesus as Messiah be buried and a new Christology be developed, acceptable to both faiths . . . This is a rich fare that will satisfy the hungry reader.

A television program with them could be just as nutritious.

So could a conversation between Jonathan Sacks, Britain's chief rabbi; Hans Kung, the Catholic theologian; and Shabbir Akhtar, the Muslim philosopher. Their recent books appeared almost simultaneously, provoking a long essay in the *Economist* on "That Overarching Meaning" which each addresses in different ways. All are concerned with the loss of publicly acknowledged moral values in Western society, and their books prompted the *Economist* to wonder:

> Why do right and not wrong? The question seems too easy. If you do right you prosper; if you do wrong you pay for it with conscience, or in jail, or both. But then a second question arises: how do we know what right and wrong are? When parental slaps and teachers' lectures have faded out of memory, there is no longer much compelling reason to go one way rather than another. For some there remain the constraints of God, religion and the priests; but these have been fast disappearing. The certainty of salvation or damnation had this to be said for it: it gave human life a firm, if coercive, ethical framework, an overarching meaning. With that gone, or largely gone, it is no wonder that people cannot make up their minds about abortion, euthanasia, the limits of research or the care of the planet; it is no surprise that the New World Order, posited on some shining morality, is seen to be so much tosh. People do not even know why they live. All is adrift.

Alas, authors of books that address the black hole of disbelief that has opened in the modern world rarely show up on television. For broadcast executives, news of the soul is no news at all.

We would also treat popular culture on our show. Richard Brookhiser has written that "the artifacts of culture express the way we live." Some of them have the power to change our metaphors and thus to affect the way we live. So if our imaginary television program were on the air now, we would have to respond not only to new books but to movies and music.

"Schindler's List," for one, raises profound questions about the individual and the social order: Why do people do good things in bad times? How far does one go to compromise with evil in order to do good? Such a discussion could include Thomas Kenneally, the author of the book on which Steven Spielberg based his movie. It could bring in Philip Hallie, the scholar and philosopher who came home from World War II so disturbed at having killed other human beings that he has spent his life studying the nature of evil and how we respond to it. (He is also the author of a splendid book on the village of Le Chambon in southern France, whose Protestant residents risked their own lives to harbor Jewish families under the Nazi regime.) We could listen to the producer of the forthcoming documentary on Dietrich Bonhoeffer, the Christian pastor who went home to Germany during the war to oppose the Nazis although it meant almost certain imprisonment and death. Bonhoeffer's participation in the plot to assassinate Hitler also raises hard questions about just how far one's religious principles should lead one in opposition to evil, and just who today is paying what Bonhoeffer called "the cost of discipleship."

Another program might look at Hollywood's interest in Buddhism. Some of you may have seen the recent film based on the life of Tina Turner, "What's Love Got to Do With It?" It presents Buddhism in a positive light to American moviegoers. Another movie, "Little Buddha," intertwines the stories of Siddhartha and a Seattle boy who is supposedly the reincarnation of a Tibetan holy man. The movie portrays the precise moment when the young Buddha, sitting under a tree in northern India, experienced the "enlightenment" that enabled him to understand the secret of life in the universe. The theme is amplified as the movie progresses. In an interview, one of the screenwriters said that "Buddhism is increasingly intriguing to Western intellectuals. It is not a religion in the normal sense, since the higher power is within oneself. There is no god, so there is no deferral of responsibility to some omnipotent being. Buddhism lends itself to contemporary times because one does not rely on an external god for refuge." The director of the film, Bernardo Bertolucci, although not a Buddhist himself, says he is "fascinated by the fact that Buddhism is more a philosophy than a religion. Buddha said, 'Enough gods,' and put man in the center. That was so modern." Yes, and fashionable. Even current political rhetoric often has a Buddhist flavor—Al Gore's "cosmic meditations on the global ecosystem" and Ross Perot's "veneration of the wisdom of ordinary people." At last year's Academy Awards, actor Richard Gere asked a billion viewers to send a telepathic message urging the Chinese government to end its occupation of Tibet. So our broadcast would ask whether Buddhism really is gaining influence on modern culture and science, as Woody Hochswender argues in a recent *Harper's Bazaar* article, and how other faiths are responding. Our discussion would almost certainly include Steven Rockefeller, professor of religion at Middlebury College and himself a convert to Buddhism.

If our series had been on the air when "Thirtysomething" was the hot television show, we would have built a program around one episode in particular which arrested Craig Dykstra's attention sufficiently for him to write about it in *Theology Today*. In the episode, Michael, who works in advertising and is a few years over thirty, finds himself wandering into a synagogue service. He has not been anywhere near a synagogue for years, but when his wife and infant daughter are in an automobile accident he seems driven toward some deeper context within which to deal with the shakiness he feels. Synagogue is the only such place he knows. And to a friend who wonders what he is doing lurking around the edges of religion, he answers (with no small hint of ambiguity) "I don't know. I think maybe I believe." Just what does the post-baby boom generation believe in?

Or take an episode of "The Wonder Years," another popular show. Two young boys turn thirteen. For Paul, the rite of passage is marked by a joyous bar mitzvah during which he receives a Talmud that has been in the family for generations. For his friend Kevin, there is only a desultory little birthday party that does not seem to mean much to anyone. When he asks his mother, "Who are we?" she replies, "What?" "Well, Paul is Jewish. Who are we?" All Mom can come up with is a halting, complicated genealogy of Anglo-ethnic cross-breeding. And Kevin's disappointment shows that that is not good enough for him. I would like to hear that sequence interpreted by Dr. Irving Greenberg, the prominent Jewish thinker who has created a stir in Jewish circles by forcefully asking questions about the future of Judaism.

Sometimes we would take our cameras to where religion is revealed in art and conversation. Last fall, the gifted flutist, Eugenia Zuckerman, and the virtuoso harpsichordist, organist and pianist, Anthony Newman, gave three concerts in New York that explored, through music, documents and letters, the clash between religions and secular music in the eighteenth century. You couldn't attend without thinking of the clash between the Rev. Calvin Butts of the Abyssinian Baptist Church and Sister Souljah over rap and rock.

I haven't even touched on current events as a source of religious news which our mythical program might address. Even the agnostic cannot fail to notice that the headlines and airwaves are full of religion: Bosnia, Waco, the World Trade Center; priests arrested for pederasty and preachers for stealing from the collection plate; a pro-life activist charged with murder; Hindu-Muslim violence in India; more martyrs in Northern Ireland. There is a theme that binds these stories, especially when they are told in the truncated form of television news where the great enemy of understanding is brevity. The unspoken theme is that religion is up to no good; religion is a cloak for fanaticism and cupidity, is irrational and hypocritical; when it is not dangerous, religion is weird, talking about harmonic convergence or weeping statues.

I am exaggerating, of course, for emphasis. There is some superb and balanced coverage of religion in American journalism. But what religion coverage lacks as a whole is perspective, context and depth, not to mention a sensitivity to distinctions. On the World Trade Center bombing, for instance, some broadcast reporters routinely used the words "Arab" and "Muslim" or "fanatic" and "fundamentalist" as if they mean the same thing. They do not. Not only is such usage inaccurate, it is dangerous, demonizing an entire religion. The vast majority of Muslims around the world surely are as offended by violence committed in the name of Islam as most Christians are by the violence condoned by some Serbian Christians or by David Koresh.

There are plenty of other examples. You find them in Stephen Carter's book, in the recent study by The Freedom Forum first Amendment Center at Vanderbilt University entitled "Bridging the Gap: Religion and the News Media," and in the flow of events around us. The airwaves are so full of the shrill and off-putting cries of true believers or the confused and condescending commentary of the religiously tone-deaf that there is little room for the authentic voices of religiously engaged people to be heard. So our ears are not trained to hear. To take another big story: federal agents, in retrospect, acknowledged that one factor contributing to the Branch Davidian disaster was their not listening to the spiritual language, garbled as it was, being spoken inside the Ranch Apocalypse. Lawrence Sullivan of Harvard Divinity School was one of a panel of ten experts asked by the Justice and Treasury Departments to review their behavior in Waco. Sullivan, who is director of Harvard's Center for the Study of World Religions, wrote:

> Though the Branch Davidians may not, in everyone's view, typify religious life in many American communities, the response of public officials and federal law enforcement agencies may, in fact, reflect the marginal value assigned to religion as a public matter and the reduction of public religious convictions and actions to the realm of private readings, individual affairs, and even "unconventional" behaviors. . . .My reflections and recommendations do not call for greater piety or lament its absence. What is disconcerting is the lack of knowledge about the historical role of religion as a basic element constitutive of society—in molding personal identities, shaping social identity, generating community and goals, transmitting values, sharpening critical moral sense, challenging the status quo and questioning authority.

Of course, one of the barriers to understanding the role of religion is the sheer cacophony of tongues that speak of God—and for God. Until recently, our nation's religious and political discourse was dominated by white, male, Protestant, cultural conservatives of a European heritage. They did not have to contend in a serious manner with alternative cultures. Their core values remained not only intact, but largely unchallenged. Dissenting versions of American history, of the role of women, of cultural norms based upon race, language and ethnic tradition—none of these issues had truly penetrated to mainstream culture until the 1960s. Now American society is in the midst of a major upheaval that is directly related to the incredible diversity of our citizenry. The old "melting pot" is being supplanted by metaphors of "mosaic" or "tossed salad." America has become the meeting place for nearly all of the living religions of the world. We are home to more than 1500 different religious organizations—churches, sects, cults, temples, societies, missions—each seeking to be the place of expression of the primary religious allegiances and sentiments of its members and adherents. One has to wonder if it will be possible to develop a new cultural myth that combines this robust religious pluralism within the traditional American consensus that everyone belongs. If not, whose story will become the "official" one?

The struggle over this consensus is one journalists will be covering well into the next century. One of its most portentous skirmishes occurred recently when five white, male, well-off Republicans, clearly identified with the right wing of their churches and party, announced a new accord called "Evangelicals and Catholics Together." Pat Robertson and Charles Colson joined with conservative Roman Catholic leaders to declare a moratorium on proselytizing each other's flocks and on theological competition in order to advance a common agenda around conservative economics, nationalism, opposition to homosexuality and abortion, and public taxes for parochial schools. We have to wonder if any consensus can emerge unless conservatives learn to live with the pluralism of faith itself and liberals strive to nurture a compelling philosophy of public virtue. Without earnest and respectful civil dialogue, the culture war will continue with no quarter given, and our politics will be fought out along the fault lines of religion.

The most interesting stories of our time are indeed emerging in this intersection between the secular and the spiritual, between God and politics.

One story is the attempt to find a new vision for America which has the authority and power of a religious vision but which is inclusive, not sectarian. Something is emerging that is not yet articulated in public policy. It is hinted at in the ecological vision which people talked about once they had seen the earth from outer space, and it is implicit in the indisputable evidence of a shrinking world in which none of us can run or hide. But the ecological impulse has not moved yet from piety to policy, and the necessity for a new ethic of cooperation is threatened by the economics of competition, so this tale is not over. At its best, religion's great accomplishment has been to create social bonds based on love and justice and mutual respect rather than necessity and law. In a society essentially pluralistic and secular but containing diverse and strongly opinionated factions of the faithful, what gives us now an energizing and organizing vision?

The second story is the groping to rewrite our own history so that we can tell the truth about America and still be proud of the country. Dedicated to the proposition that all men are created equal, Americans violently dispossessed the Indian and nurtured slavery in the cradle of liberty. So what is the story we can write that does not deny our sin but does not end in cynicism? Somewhere between the righteous right and the critical left is a real country people can recognize and attempt to improve but which, nonetheless, provide the healthy ground for being honest with ourselves.

Also emerging is the question: How can we be properly enthusiastic—that is, filled with God—without denying mind or matter? What does it mean to be inspired? There is a hunger for a vision; otherwise, Jim and Tammy Bakker would not have been so successful, and the revelations about John F. Kennedy would have destroyed the hold his memory has over people. In other words, how is our pride to be justly sustained and our hunger suitably filled?

These are stories I would hope television will cover. Because these are questions all of us must address together.

So I end where I began. Considering the titanic forces of this century, it sometimes appears we are in a spiritual war of attrition, and one can understand the despair and fatalism expressed by the eighteen-year-old on the radio in the middle of the night. Walter Capps, professor of religious studies at the University of California at Santa Barbara, puts it this way:

There is tension in the air. There are dilemmas that remain unresolved. There is a mood of ambivalence. Previous confidences appear to be slipping, but the desire for spiritual certainty and collective self-confidence remains . . . What compelling religious values and spiritual vitality sustain America in this last decade of the twentieth century? What wellsprings of moral and spiritual vitality can still be tapped by a society wishing to recover from successive forms of collective trauma?

Contemporary American religion is at the crossroads because it is striving to address the perennial aspirations of the human spirit in accordance with the dictates of democracy and in light of specific challenges to the present generation. And what are the desires of the human spirit if not for compelling moral values, a sound historical orientation, and some reliable basis for discerning relationships between individuals and communities?

What journalist could ask for a bigger story? It is emerging just as many professional journalists sense that "religion is an invaluable window into the larger whole of society" and should be covered, as Roy Larson has urged, with greater depth and sophistication. I, for one, would not have you think I believe more and better coverage of religion on television alone is the answer, but it is a matter of faith to me that this medium can indeed honor that imperative of ancient scripture: Let There Be Light!

BILL MOYERS is a leading cultural commentator on the American scene. His numerous PBS series have explored the Power of Myth with Joseph Campbell, Religion in American Life, Watergate, and Violence. His latest book is **Healing and the Mind**.

Reprinted from *Religion and Values in the Public Life*, Harvard Divinity School, 45 Francis Avenue, Cambridge, MA 02138.

THE VOMIT OF A MAD TYGER

by ALLEN GINSBERG

from SHAMBHALA SUN

We'll begin at the beginning, because what I'd like to do is trace what spiritual inklings I had that led to interest in Tibetan Buddhism and guru relationship. I was in love with a high school fellow who went off to Columbia College when he graduated a half-term before me in Central High School in Paterson, New Jersey. So I decided to go to Columbia College instead of Montclair State Teachers College, where all my family had gone.

Out of some kind of devotion I broke away from the traditional pattern of my family but I didn't have money, so I had to take a scholarship entrance exam. On the ferry between Hoboken and New York I got down on my knees and made a vow that if I were admitted to Columbia, I would do everything I could to save mankind. It was a naive bodhisattva's vow out of fear of not getting into Columbia.

By the time I got into school, I ran into William Burroughs and Lucian Carr and Jack Kerouac. We became friends.

The conversation between 1945 and 1948 was recollections of our own childhood inklings, including the big question, "How big was the universe?" I think Kerouac and myself had a sense of panoramic awareness of the vastness of space. So the question, how big was the "Unborn" arose. Or how vast was the space we were in, and what was the mystery of the universe.

That led to a lot of conversations and inquiries with marijuana and wandering around the city considering the look of the buildings and the appearance of the facades of Times Square, particularly. Times Square seen as a stage set with a facade that could vanish at any second. That impression of the apparent material of the universe as "real," but at the same time "unreal" in some way or other, either because we were high, or because time would dissolve the "seen," or maybe some trick of the eyeball reveal the "facade" as empty.

So we began talking about what in 1945 we called a New Consciousness, or New Vision. As most young people probably do, at the age of 15 or 19, whether it's punk or bohemia or grunge or whatever new vision adolescents have, there is always some kind of striving for understanding and transformation of the universe, according to one's own subjective, poetic generational inspiration.

That led to an exploration of the otherwise rejected world of junkies around Times Square and underworld. The world of drugs—which had a slight effect in transforming consciousness or altering moods and was presumed to be a kind of artistic specimen trial—I found quite harmless and useful as an educational experience, though some of my contemporaries did get hung up, like Burroughs—although the main problem seemed to be alcohol more than any other.

IN 1948 I HAD SOME KIND OF BREAK in the normal modality of my consciousness. While alone living a relatively solitary vegetarian contemplative life, reading St. John of the Cross, Plotinus some, notions of "alone with the Alone," or "one hand clapping," or *The Cloud of Unknowing*, or Plato's *Phaedrus*, and William Blake, I had what was—for me—an extraordinary break in the normal nature of my thought when something opened up.

I had finished masturbating, actually, on the sixth floor of a Harlem tenement on 121st Street looking out at the roofs while reading Blake, back and forth, and suddenly had a kind of auditory hallucination, hearing Blake—what I thought was his voice, very deep, earthen tone, not very far from my own mature tone of voice, so perhaps a projection of my own latent physiology—reciting a poem called "The Sunflower," which I thought expressed some kind of universal longing for union with some infinite nature. The poem goes, *"Ah, Sunflower/Weary of time/Who counteth the steps of the sun/Seeking after that sweet golden clime where the traveler's journey is done/Where the youth pined away with desire/And the pale virgin shrouded with snow/Arise from their graves and aspire where my sunflower wishes to go."*

I can't interpret it exactly now, but the impression that I had at the time was of some infinite yearning for the infinite, finally realized, and I looked out the window and began to notice the extraordinary detail of intelligent labor that had gone into the making of the rooftop cornices of the Harlem buildings. And I suddenly realized that the world was, in a sense, not dead matter, but an increment or deposit of living intelligence and action and activity that finally took form—the Italian laborers of 1890 and 1910, making very fine copper work and roofcomb ornament as you find along the older tenement apartment buildings.

And as I looked at the sky I wondered what kind of intelligence had made that vastness, or what was the nature of the intelligence that I was glimpsing, and felt a sense of vastness and of coming home to a space I hadn't realized was there before but which seemed old and infinite, like the Ancient of Days, so to speak.

But I had no training in anything but western notions and didn't know how to find a vocabulary for the experience, so I thought I had seen "God" or "Light" or some western notion of a theistic center, or that was the impression at the time.

That got me into lots of trouble because I tried to explain it to people and nobody could figure out what I was saying. They thought I was nuts, and in a way, I was. Having no background and no preparation, I didn't know how to ground the experience in any way that either could prolong it or put it in its place, and certainly didn't know any teachers whom I could have consulted at Columbia University at the time, although D. T. Suzuki was there.

My first experience with Blake was quite heavenly but the second experience about a week later was just the opposite. At Columbia Bookstore looking around and thinking this and that, suddenly a sense of sea change of my consciousness overtook me again, and I got scared because everyone in the bookstore looked like some sort of wounded, neurotic pained animal with "marks of weakness and marks of woe" on their faces that Blake speaks of in "London."

A night later, wandering around the Columbia campus, it happened again with a poem called "The Sick Rose," which goes, *"Oh, rose, thou art sick/the invisible worm/that flies in the night/in the howling storm/has found out thy bed/of crimson joy/And his dark secret love/does thy life destroy."* And I had a sense of the black sky coming down to eat me. It was like meeting Yamantaka without preparation, meeting one of the horrific or wrathful deities without any realization that it was a projection of myself or my nature, and I tried to shut off the experience because it was too frightening.

By 1950 or 1951, because of those experiences, I was curious about the Tibetan thangkas which had the wrathful deities, but I had no idea what their functions were. I also began experimenting more with peyote and other psychedelics—mescaline and later LSD—to see if I could approximate the natural experience I'd had. My experience with them was very similar, although the natural experience was much more ample and left a deeper imprint on my nature, and it certainly turned me around at the age of 22.

BY 1956 THERE WAS SOME POETRY AND FAME. The impulse of my own poetry, Burroughs', and Kerouac's was still based on some kind of examination of the texture of consciousness. That was probably the key to why we were of interest to others. Kerouac, in spontaneous prose, trying to track his mind and give some imprint to the actual sequence of thought forms as they rose during the time of writing. Burroughs, similarly interested in alternative modes of consciousness, getting away from stereotyped mentality, experimenting a great deal with drugs, with psychoanalysis, with hypnoanalysis, with writing, and finally arrived at a kind of writing that was like the nature of his own mind, primarily visual.

I remember when talking with Burroughs once, I asked him what was he thinking of. He had his hands over his typewriter, hovering, ready to write something. "What are you thinking of?" And he said, "Hands pulling in nets from the sea in the dark." I said, "That's a very Blakian image of God the Fisher, or something." He explained that it was just the visual memory of fishermen on the beach at Tangiers, pulling in their nets at dawn. So Burroughs' thought-forms were primarily visual, whereas mine were more verbal, auditory, rhythmic.

So we were interested in the texture of consciousness and how to notate it on the page, preoccupations which go through to the present for everyone alive of that group.

By 1950 Kerouac had begun reading Buddhist texts, in reaction to our friend, Neal Cassady, who was involved with Edgar Cayce, a sort of "channeling" specialist somewhat famous in those years. Kerouac thought this was a crude provincial American "Billy Sunday in a suit," so maybe go back to the original text relating to metempsychosis and reincarnation. So Kerouac began reading Goddard's *Buddhist Bible*, which had samples of hinayana and mahayana texts, including Diamond Sutra, and some vajrayana texts, at least relating to Milarepa and others. And he laid that trip on me.

Now as an ex-Communist Jewish intellectual, I thought his pronouncement of the First Noble Truth, that existence was suffering, was some sort of insult to my left-wing background, since I was a progressive looking forward to the universal improvement of matters, if only through spiritual advancement. Kerouac's insistence was that existence contained suffering. I thought he was just trying to insult me, for some reason or other. It took me about two years to get it through my head that he was just telling me a very simple fact.

I still remember the first real dharma instruction I got from Kerouac, which was consistent with Burroughs' laconic cynicism and critique of "all apparent phenomena": "All conceptions as to the existence of the self, as well as all conceptions as to the non-existence of the self; as well as all conceptions as to the existence of a Supreme Self, as well as all conceptions as to the non-existence of a Supreme Self, are equally arbitrary, being only conceptions." That made quite a bit of sense, since Burroughs had already presented me with western semantics, Korzybski's book *Science and Sanity*, which had some similar insight.

The first time I heard the refuge vows was from Kerouac also, crooned like Frank Sinatra in a very beautiful way. So that imprinted itself on me, and I began going to the New York Public Library and looking at Chinese paintings of the S'ung Dynasty, interested in the vastness of the landscape scrolls, as correlating with the sense of vastness that I had already experienced.

IN 1962, AFTER A TRIP TO EUROPE, I went to India primarily to look for a teacher, because I realized I would have to get a teacher, or wanted one, or intuited that I needed one, or wasn't quite sure.

By then I was quite well-known as a poet, and I figured that the proper move, being now famous, would be to disappear into India for a couple of years and look for some wisdom, and also experience a different culture than the western culture, which I thought from the viewpoint of Spengler, the decline of the West, was perhaps exhausted of inspiration and it was time for a second religiousness, and so I went to look for a teacher. I went in company with Gary Snyder, who four years earlier had gone to Kyoto to study at the First Zen Institute at Daitoku-ji Monastery and had begun helping translate *Zen Dust*, a handbook of koans.

We went on a Buddhist pilgrimage to Sarnath, Sanchi, Ajanta, Ellora. In a cave at Ellora, Gary sat himself down and chanted the Prajnaparamita Sutra in Sino-Japanese, with echoes of the cave around, and that blew my mind. That was such an extended, long and obviously spiritual breath, vocalized, that I got really interested and began to ask him about what it meant and why he was doing it in Japanese, and what was the history of it.

In the course of our trip we went to visit the Dalai Lama and I was interested in what he thought of LSD. He asked me if with LSD I could see what was inside of a briefcase. And I said yes, because it is empty. And Gary said, "Oh, stop quibbling, Ginsberg. Give him an answer."

I went to Sikkim, just sightseeing, and wound up in Rumtek Monastery. I met the Karmapa lama and saw the Black Hat Ceremony, which came to mean a great deal to me much later on. And we also visited the Lamas' Home School at Dalhousie, where my later teacher, Chogyam Trungpa Rinpoche, was the director. Although I didn't have much conversation with him, Gary Snyder took a picture showing Peter Orlovsky leaning over, me looking on and Trungpa Rinpoche showing us a text that was on the altar.

I went on to Kalimpong to visit Dudjom Rinpoche, the head of the Nyingma School, and I brought him my problems with LSD, because I had a lot of bum trips. Every time I took acid or psychedelia, I would come back to "The Sick Rose," like some kind of monster, coming to eat me from an outside space. And he did give me a very good pith instruction, which I never forgot. It turned my mind around and made the world safe for my democratic thoughts: "If you see something horrible, don't cling to it, and if you see something beautiful, don't cling to it." That cut the Gordian knot that I'd inherited from too rash and untutored experiments with psychedelics.

On my way home I went to Japan and visited Gary, and sat at Temple Daitoku-ji, and actually did a short *sesshin* but didn't learn anything because I didn't get any real instructions. The problem I had in India was that I didn't know what to ask for. I went there looking for a teacher and I saw many swamis, but I didn't know enough to ask them for a meditation practice. Which was the simplest way in? What kind of meditation do you do, and can you suggest a practice? I just was too dumb to know that. I remember asking Dudjom Rinpoche for initiations, *wang*, as if I were trained enough or prepared for it, but I didn't ask him what kind of meditation should I practice meanwhile.

So ever since then, I have perhaps been overeager to teach meditation to people who are too dumb, like myself, to ask for it. It seems to me that in America it might be useful for people to be more forward. Usually, I understand, the proper etiquette is to wait until someone asks you three times. But you can always suggest to them that they might ask you three times.

IN 1968 I TRIED USING MANTRA CHANTING, which I had been dodging all the years from 1964 on, when I came back, usually Hari Krishna or OM SRI MAITREYA, a mixture of Hinduism and Buddhism, which I liked, without any instruction in how to do it. By 1968 I applied mantra chanting to situations of violence in Chicago, and I found that it worked on a limited scale. At least, it kept me safe and the people that were around me.

After I met Chögyam Trungpa, for the rioting after the bombing of Hanoi Harbor and the increased bombing under Nixon about 1972, he suggested using the mantra AH instead of OM, because OM was much too foreign sounding, while AH was just a good old American Fourth of July sound, like "Ah, fireworks." And also, it goes out as purification of speech and a measure of the breath. So I actually did try that.

By 1970 I met Swami Muktananda Paramahansa at an interesting meet with Ram Dass, Muktananda and Satchitananda, all of them sitting up on the altar at Universalist Church, Central Park. Swami M. invited me to come down to Dallas. I had nothing better to do, so I actually went down to Dallas, registered in the hotel where he was staying, and then he had the sense to say, "What kind of practice do you know, or do you have a practice?" I said, "No, I don't." He said, "Why don't you go to your room and sit and meditate using a mantra GURU OM at your heart level, using that on your breath."

So I was relieved. I had thought he was going to exploit me or parade me in front of his Dallas disciples as an asset of some sort, but instead he suggested that I go to my room and stay by myself and sit. And that as a tremendous relief, I suddenly realized that I had a practice finally.

I did that, and he would come in and check me out every once in a while. I think he comes from the same or related lineage as the vajrayana practitioners. I remember once he invited me into his room where he was having a darshan with some students and giving them chocolate cookies. Donald Duck was on the television and suddenly he turned and offered a cookie to Donald Duck. Somehow, I got the idea of emptiness out of that.

I RAN INTO THE TIBETAN LAMA Chögyam Trungpa in 1970 on the street, coming from a poetry book signing party on 47th Street. I had brought my poet father Louis to meet Snyder for the first time. So this was a big meeting, since it was already many years since my father had read Snyder's work and knew his influence on me.

My father was over 70 years old and couldn't move very well, it was a New York summer, really hot, and as we went out on the street toward the Port Authority to get him back to New Jersey, I realized that he was going to faint. We got to 43rd and 6th and I saw this Asian gent hailing a taxicab with a bearded friend, and so I stepped in front of them and said, "May I borrow your vehicle?" which was an odd word to use, you know, the three vehicles of Buddhism, but it was a word.

The friend, named Kunga Dawa, said, "Are you Allen Ginsberg?" and I said, "Yes." And he said, "OM AH HUM VAJR GURU PADMA SIDDHI HUM," the Padmasambhava mantra I'd learned the week before from Gary Snyder. Years later I said to Trungpa, "What did you think of that?" and he said he wondered whether I knew what I was talking about. So we exchanged addresses, and I got my father to the Port Authority in the cab.

About a month or two later, I got an invitation to visit with Trungpa Rinpoche at a tiny apartment on the Lower East Side. We sat down and Kunga Dawa, at Trungpa's side, offered me a joint of marijuana—skillful means, I thought—and I was amazed that Trungpa was that much of a bohemian, or that supple-minded. So I smoked a little—he didn't but Kunga did—and then he gave me his Sadhana of Mahamudra, which he offered as a poem for me to read and critique.

He asked me to read it aloud as a way of hooking me into his mind-beam. It's a very great poem, a long poem. The refrain, "In the slime and muck of the dark age, I still desire to see your face," is repeated over and over in different stanzas, which appealed to my romantic heart. And I really liked it, as both a religious document and as a poem, and went through the entire thing, which takes a half-hour, and made friends.

And a while later, in 1971, we had a really interesting meeting in San Francisco. I had made a date to meet at his motel. When I got there, everybody was late, and then I heard a noise outside, and I saw him with two disciples, stumbling totally drunk up the stairs. He was so drunk that his pants got caught on a nail and ripped. He got into the room, and his wife was angry at him, she had a new little baby. And pissed off that he was drunk in the middle of the afternoon.

I sat down with my harmonium. I saw his itinerary of talks and wondered, "Don't you get tired of that?" I was on the road, and I was getting a little bored, fatigued traveling. He said, "That's because you don't like your poetry." I said, "What do you know about poetry?" He said, "Why don't you do like the great poets do, like Milarepa? You're bored with reading the same poems over and over. Why don't you make poems up on the stage? Why do you need a piece of paper? Don't you trust your own mind?"

Actually, that was very good advice, the same advice given me by Kerouac many years before. It was right in the groove of everything I had been learning but coming from another direction entirely—the insight or mind-consciousness of a well-trained meditator and specialist, a kind of genius meditator.

Then I showed him mantras I had been chanting and playing and he put his paw, drunk, on the harmonium keys and said, "Remember, the silence is just as important as the sound."

We went out to supper and got more drunk, and he said, "Why are you hiding your face? I'd like to see your face. Why do you have that big beard?" I had a big '60s' beard, hung over into the '70s, and I said, "If you'll stop drinking, I'll shave my beard right this minute." I went into the drugstore, bought a razor and shaved my beard. And I came back and said, "Now you've got to stop drinking." And he said, "That's another matter. You didn't shave your beard completely." Because it was still in rough tufts.

We went off to his lecture and I remember he was sitting very sadly in a chair, talking to this group of San Francisco hippies, saying, "No more trips, please, no more trips, no more trips." Meaning whatever, acid, but also spiritual materialist trips, the accumulation of Blakian experiences for the purpose of impressing other people as credentials of one's own sanctity or accomplishment. It was probably the series of lectures called "Buddhadharma Without Credentials."

At this lecture I continued shaving and I came back out again, and he asked me to improvise. "This is Allen Ginsberg, the great poet. Now we are going to have him improvise." I couldn't think of anything: "Here we are in the middle of June/I just ate with you and I had a spoon/and we were talking about the moon." Actually, walking on the way over he'd said, "America is not ready for the full moon," meaning full doctrine, I think full dharma. And I said, "That shouldn't dismay the moon."

So I tried improvising but I didn't do very well, and he said, "You're too smart." But the next day I had a regular poetry reading at the Berkeley Community Theater as a benefit for Tarthang Tulku. So I resolved that I would go on stage without any paper at all, but I did bring the harmonium and improvised something like:

"How sweet to be born in America where we have like a devaloka where the god world is here and we have all the watermelons we want to eat and everybody else is starving around the world, but how sweet to be here in the heaven world which may last for a little bit of time but how sweet to be born." It was a bittersweet song, it's still at the height of the war. So it's "how sweet to be born in America where we're dropping bombs on somebody else but not on ourselves."

I've forgotten because it was improvised, but it actually did me a lot of good, his prompting, because from then on I was never scared to get up on stage even if I'd left my poetry back on the train or something. It was always a workable situation from then on.

A YEAR LATER I WAS INVITED TO BOULDER to do a poetry reading to raise money for the Rocky Mountain Dharma Center. Trungpa, Robert Bly, Gary Snyder—whom Trungpa had not met—and myself were all going to read at a big auditorium, the first big reading in Boulder for dharma.

So we were lined on stage and we had been joined by a sort of desert rat-Japanese-zen-lunatic-poet-meditator Nanao Sakaki, a very great character and good meditator and a really great Japanese poet, an old friend of Gary's and mine from the sixties in Kyoto. I was going to do some singing GATE GATE, and we each chanted our own version of Prajnaparamita: Gary, the regular Japanese "Kanji Zai Bo Satsu Gyogin Han Nya Ha Ra Mi Ta Ji. . ." and then Nanao a long KAAANNJJII using an extended breath, a really beautiful hollow voice, and Trungpa Rinpoche almost in pedestrian offhand Tibetan. I did a version that I had worked out from Suzuki Roshi's English telegraphese translation.

First Robert Bly read. Trungpa was drunk, as ever, but while Bly was reading, he did something very strange. He picked up the big gong and he put it over his head while Bly was reading. Bly couldn't see because we were all lined up parallel, so he didn't see what was going on there. The audience was tittering a little bit and I leaned over and said to Trungpa, "You shouldn't do that, they're making a benefit for you, they've come here to do you a favor, you shouldn't be carrying on like that." And he said, "If you think I'm doing this because I'm drunk, you're making a big mistake."

Then Gary Snyder read and while he was reading Trungpa Rinpoche took the gong and put it on my head. So I just sat there figuring well, he must know what he's doing, or if he doesn't, I don't, so I'm not going to get in the way. I'm not the host, I don't have to worry about it, though Gary was a friend of mine. After it was over then I read, and he didn't do anything while I read. I asked later why not and he said, "'Cause you don't know what you're doing."

A couple of weeks later I asked him why he did that and he said, "Well, Bly was presenting Robert Bly—a big ham, so to speak. Gary Snyder was presenting Gary Snyder as sort of the finished zen product. You know, neat and perfect and proper shoes and all of that." He said that the people in the audience were his students and he didn't want them to get the wrong idea of what was the ideal version of a poet. Later he wrote a spontaneous poem saying Robert Bly presented Robert Bly, Gary Snyder presented Gary Snyder, Ginsberg was Ginsberg, but only Trungpa was the original drunken poet.

So that was a kind of original take I had on poetry from him.

That year we gave a reading in New York, this time with Anne Waldman and Burroughs and Rinpoche and myself, and afterward I drove up with him to Karmê-Chöling, the retreat center in Vermont, then Tail of the Tiger. On the way back, I read him through Kerouac's *Mexico City Blues*, 'cause it's a 4-5 hour ride. And he kept laughing all the way at Kerouac's humor. I don't know if you're familiar with it, but it's a very good book of freestyle poetry and when we got to New York, he got out of the car and said, "It's a perfect manifestation of mind."

I was really amazed because Kerouac had been attacked for that book by Kenneth Rexroth—somewhat an accomplished scholar and Buddhist-oriented—as a book that "separates the men from the boys" and Kerouac was just "an amateur boy that didn't know what he was doing"—he was making a slapdash pastiche. All the San Francisco poets loved that book for its spontaneity and quick mind and quick notation of mind but it was widely attacked and considered like a jerk-off by the beatnik. Now here was a very accomplished lama saying "perfect manifestation of mind" and his understanding and appreciation was really quite amazing to me.

The next day he said he couldn't forget that voice, mine or Kerouac's or Anne's, or the style, and that it had changed his style of poetry, from more formal Tibetan five-seven-nine syllable verse form to more international freestyle spontaneous dictated English. He asked me to be his poetry teacher, and I asked him to be my meditation teacher and so we made a kind of exchange, of which I think I got the better in the bargain.

A year later, he invited me to attend and teach some poetry at his first Seminary, which is a 3-month retreat, and at that point I heard a detailed exposition of hinayana, mahayana and vajrayana styles and practices, a detailed map, not the actual practices, but the map with all the different stages of vajrayana yoga. And a little while thereafter began doing the foundation practices which are the prostration practices for the Kagyu lineage.

While I was sitting I had an idea for a poem but I didn't want to interrupt my sitting—we were doing *shamatha/vipashyana* on the breath—and I had this fantasy my breath was going out the window and over the mountain into Idaho and across the desert to San Francisco and then the zephyr was going under the Bay bridge, and then maybe a little tornado out in the Pacific and breeze in Guam and a typhoon in the China sea and an airplane flying through the clouds over Cambodia Angor Wat all the way through to papers scattered by the wind by the Wailing Wall and the Sunday Times lifting and settling in the breeze at Trafalgar Square or Picadilly, and then a breeze across the Atlantic across Labrador a cold wind and finally at the end, the breath coming back around the world to where we were in Teton Village in Wyoming, the last line being "a calm breath, a slow breath breathes outward from the nostril."

Mind Breaths was the title of the poem, and I said, is it legitimate to write poetry about meditation? He said, well, most poetry about meditation is shit because people are just repeating their neuroses in a sense, or writing out their complications rather than some objective description of the mind. So this is alright because it actually describes the process of meditation as related activities of scanning the mind in a sense. Related activities of observing mind and observing breath, observing space and observing the mind.

As I was still in those days dungareed and black-shirted, he suggested also that I try a white shirt on, and I said why, and he said, well, see how people treat you, see if they treat you any differently. And I was not sure because I thought, well, it takes a lot of money to get shirts cleaned so he said, well, wash them yourself. So I went out to the Salvation Army and I bought about a dozen white shirts (for twenty-five cents each in those days in the early seventies in Boulder) and tried them on, and I found that people treated me slightly differently, more trusting.

So I began noticing the three-piece suit sartorial manners of his vajra guards, his dharmapalas, and I decided, well, I'll try some more elegant clothes and I went to the Salvation Army and bought all sorts of Brooks Brother suits and pretty soon was all dressed up like a professor. And people treated me nicely befitting my age.

IN '74 TRUNGPA INVITED MYSELF, Anne Waldman, Diane DiPrima, John Cage, Gregory Bateson, Ram Dass, and others to Boulder to try a summer school, like a big smorgasbord festival, everybody all mixed up, and instead of a hundred or two hundred people we had about twelve hundred people registering.

So there was this enormous dharma culture explosion that took place, and after the summer was over Trungpa sat at a round table with myself and Cage and Waldman and Diane DiPrima asking us to take responsibility and take part in founding a Poetics school. So we took that responsibility, particularly Anne Waldman, and that was a whole education in itself. Trungpa's conception was that there were many varieties of practices for a kind of international tantra or international mahayana that could be adapted to an American style of Buddhism based on the Tibetan insights. It would make use of the American genius for certain things, which he saw in poetry particularly, and to some extent in painting and music, to transform those or alchemize those, paint them gold. That was his particular genius as a teacher, and a teacher of teachers.

The next interesting encounter (I'm trying to remember the pith exchanges that we had) was in 1976 when Vajradhatu decided to buy Karma Dzong. He gathered the whole sangha together to give a big lecture about how we are now citizens of America, we're establishing Buddhism in America, and we have to have property, and we shouldn't be cultivating what he would like to call Ginsberg resentments.

I was up in the balcony. Ginsberg resentment, what is he talking about? I remember I resented it terribly. After it was all over, I went down 'cause I didn't really have any objection to his buying a building, I had property of my own already, and I said "Ginsberg resentment is Mukpo dumbness"—Mukpo his family name—and he said, "Oh, I thought dumbness was a sign of genius in your vocabulary," which was true. In the little vocabulary that Kerouac and I had we would talk about dumb Harpo Marx saints, and I realized at the moment that I was resentful, and I realized what a well of resentment I had within me. So he had pointed out that one very specific thing that I really had to work with.

In 1978, I had my picture on the front page of the magazine section of the Denver paper, and we ran into each other and he said, "Oh, I saw your picture in the paper, are you proud?" And I thought that was a baited question, but I didn't know quite how to answer, but one saving grace, I said, "Well, the word never entered my mind," and he said, "Well, you should be proud, you've worked very hard, you've worked for a long time, you've done something, you should take pride in it. Be doubtless, go ahead and do it, and not be hesitant about what you're doing as poet, or as teaching poetry or reciting poetry."

And that was a kind of funny pat on the back or encouragement to take myself seriously as poet, or take the poetry seriously if not myself, to take the function or role of poet—as he would define it in Shambhala Training—as a kind of warriorship where you do face the phenomenal world and make your proclamation into that space.

He had all sorts of ideas of poetics that interested me, partly in the Shambhala tradition, such as the notion of speech, or samboghakaya, uniting heaven and earth, as in the traditional Taoist view that the emperor unites heaven and earth. That is, speech unites the impalpable heaven—mind, thoughts—with the physiological body-breath. So the body provides the palpable breath, the mind provides the impalpable thoughts, and the speech unifies them.

His phrase would be, speech synchronizes—proper speech synchronizes body and mind. He saw poetry as proclamation from the seat, from your seat or from your zafu or from your throne or from your chair as teacher, or from your chair as meditator or your chair as a human being or a vajrayana student. Poetry as unhesitating and doubtless proclamation. Proclamation of what? Proclamation of the actual mind, manifesting your mind, writing the mind, which goes back to Kerouac but also goes back to Milarepa, goes back to his original instructions—don't you trust your own mind? Why do you need a piece of paper?

So writing could be seen as "writing your mind." In other words, you don't have to make anything up, you don't have to fabricate anything, you don't have to fix up something to say, which causes writer's block. All you have to do is tap into the immediate mind of the moment—what are you thinking about?—and just note it down, or observe your own mind, or observe what's vivid coming to mind.

Where do you start? Well, with the chaos of your mind. How do you do it? Just tap into it and write what's there in minute, particular detail. For the purpose of relieving your own paranoia and others', revealing yourself and communicating to others, which is a blessing for other people if you can communicate and relieve their sense of isolation, confusion, bewilderment, and suffering by offering your own mind as a sample of what's palpable, visible, and whatever little you've learned.

AFTER TRUNGPA RINPOCHE'S DEATH IN 1986, I guess it must have been 1989 or so, Philip Glass and I got together. Philip was a Buddhist from a long time back, with a good deal more experience than myself in a long steady relationship with a teacher. He'd been asked by his teacher Domo Geshe Rinpoche to go out and help his friend Gelek Rinpoche and do a benefit for Rinpoche's Jewel Heart Center.

And so I came out to Ann Arbor with Philip and we were greeted at the airport by Gelek Rinpoche who immediately struck me because he had the same, or similar voice as Trungpa, and it turned out that they were friends, which I hadn't known, and had actually begun learning English together and shared a room when they were young, when they first came out of India. So there was like a family relationship and apparently Trungpa Rinpoche, a Kagyu, had invited the old enemy lineage, the Gelugpa, to visit and teach at Naropa. I felt if Trungpa felt he was trustworthy then I could trust him.

I began a friendship with Gelek Rinpoche that also involved a series of conversations which slightly altered my attitudes and refined my understanding of where I was at and what to do. One of the first things I was interested in—by this time getting on in age, 65 at the time—was what do I do when it's time to kick the bucket? Where do I put my mind?

Gelek Rinpoche's first answer was, well, cultivate a sense of openness, perhaps some emptiness, recur to the meditation practice you're most familiar with, cultivate some sense of sympathy or compassion for all sentient beings, and perhaps your teacher's face.

So I thought that's pretty good, I've had lots of experience with *shamatha/vipashyana* over the years, but then I remembered that a drowning man still has eight minutes after he's stopped breathing. So I suddenly realized, wait a minute, what happens after I stop breathing? What do I do with my mind then? Because *shamatha* depends on the breath. So what do I do then?

I went back, and he laughed and said, "Well . . ." and I said, "What about emptiness?" And he said, "Well, if I were you I wouldn't put all my eggs in that one basket." So he suggested the teacher's face as one thing I could grasp onto, and compassion, whatever combination I could get, but the teacher's face seemed to be the most available. [Yelled from the audience: "In the muck and slime of this age I long to see your face."] Yes, I still desire to see your face, even in the muck and slime of these dark ages I still desire to see your face, so that seems to be both a last resort and at the same time a romantic first resort, for a last glimpse.

Another question rose: how long is the world going to be able to maintain itself in the present rate of decay, destruction and muck and slime of the dark ages? If civilization's not going to be around that long, certainly not my books or records, what's the use of poetry, what function has poetry got if the world is going to hell in a handbasket? And Rinpoche's answer was really great and clear: the relief of suffering, the relief of the mass of human suffering.

That instruction or direction is a very good compass for any vocation but it's particularly applicable to the rudderless poet who is shifting from preservation of his own ego or projection of immortality or the romance of being a poet, to an activity that functions well for other people. There is a bodhisattva aspect of poetry particularly when you combine it with the notion of poetry as proclamation. So proclamation original mind—proclamation of primordial mind, proclamation of your candid mind, proclamation of your own chaos, proclamation of your own uncertainty, proclamation of your own fragility, proclamation of your sensitivity, proclamation of your own cheerful neurosis, so to speak, a cheerful attitude toward your nature which fits in well with the meditation practice suggestion in regular sitting on the breath, to take a friendly attitude toward your thoughts rather than trying to push them away or "invite them in to tea," merely observe them with a friendly attitude, and that can be applied to poetics, taking a friendly attitude toward your thoughts and when you catch yourself thinking, if you have an interesting and vivid thought, notating it, particularly the sequence of thoughts that might lead other people to notice their own mind.

In other words, if you can show your mind it reminds people that they got a mind. If you can catch yourself thinking, it reminds people they can catch themselves thinking. If you have a vivid moment that's more open and compassionate, it reminds people that they have those vivid moments.

So by showing your mind as a mirror, you can make a mirror for other people to recognize their own minds and see familiarity and not feel that their minds are unworthy of affection or appreciation. Basically, Poetics is appreciation of consciousness, appreciation of our own consciousness.

ALLEN GINSBERG's current projects include **Cosmopolitan Greetings: Poems 1985-1992**; **Allen Ginsberg Holy Soul and Jelly Roll: Poems and Songs 1949-1993**, *a four CD box set; and* **Journals 1954-1958**. *This article is an edited version of a talk given by Ginsberg at an annual Jewel Heart Retreat, led by Gelek Rinpoche, in Middleville, Michigan, on August 8, 1993. The title of the talk was spontaneously suggested by Gelek Rinpoche and members of the audience.*

Reprinted from *Shambhala Sun*, 1345 Spruce Steet, Boulder, CO 80302-4886. Subscription: $20.00/year.

ANCHORED IN A DIFFERENT PLACE

HUMAN RIGHTS, DEMOCRACY, AND TRANSCENDENCE

by VACLAV HAVEL

from NEW AGE JOURNAL

I would like to turn my thoughts today[†] to the state of the world and the prospects that lie before it.

There are thinkers who claim that if the modern age began with the discovery of America, it also ended in America. This is said to have occurred in the year 1969, when America sent the first men to the moon. From this historical moment, they say, a new age in the life of humanity can be dated.

I think there are good reasons for suggesting that the modern age has ended. Today, many things indicate that we are going through a transitional period, when it seems that something is on the way out and something else is painfully being born. It is as if something were crumbling, decaying, and exhausting itself, while something else, still indistinct, were arising from the rubble.

[†] *The following remarks were presented by the author on July 4, 1994, at Independence Hall, on the occasion of his receiving the Philadelphia Liberty Medal. The award, established in 1988, honors an individual who "has demonstrated leadership and vision in the pursuit of liberty of conscience or freedom from oppression, ignorance, or deprivation."*

Periods of history when values undergo a fundamental shift are certainly not unprecedented. This happened in the Hellenistic period, when from the ruins of the classical world the Middle Ages were gradually born. It happened during the Renaissance, which opened the way to the modern era. The distinguishing features of such transitional periods are a mixing and blending of cultures, and a plurality or parallelism of intellectual and spiritual worlds. These are periods when all consistent value systems collapse, when cultures distant in time and space are discovered or rediscovered. New meaning is gradually born from the encounter, or the intersection, of many different elements.

Today, this state of mind or of the human world is called postmodernism. For me, a symbol of that state is a Bedouin mounted on a camel and clad in traditional robes under which he is wearing jeans, with a transistor radio in his hands and an ad for Coca-Cola on the camel's back. I am not ridiculing this, nor am I shedding an intellectual tear over the commercial expansion of the West that destroys alien cultures. I see it rather as a typical expression of this multicultural era, a signal that an amalgamation of cultures is taking place. I see it as proof that something is happening, something is being born, that we are in a phase when one age is succeeding another, when everything is possible. Yes, everything is possible because our civilization does not have its own unified style, its own spirit, its own aesthetic.

This is related to the crisis, or to the transformation, of science as the basis of the modern conception of the world.

The dizzying development of this science, with its unconditional faith in objective reality and its complete dependency on general and rationally knowable laws, led to the birth of modern technological civilization. It is the first civilization in the history of the human race that spans the entire globe and firmly binds together all human societies, submitting them to a common global destiny. It was this science that enabled man, for the first time, to see Earth from space with his own eyes, that is, to see it as another star in the sky.

At the same time, however, the relationship to the world that modern science fostered and shaped now appears to have exhausted its potential. It is increasingly clear, that strangely, the relationship is missing something. It fails to connect with the most intrinsic nature of reality, and with natural human experience. It is now more of a source of disintegration and doubt than a source of integration and meaning. It produces what amounts to a state of schizophrenia: Man as an observer is becoming completely alienated from himself as a being. Classical modern science described only the surface of things, a single dimension of reality. And the more dogmatically science treated it as the only dimension, as the very essence of reality, the more misleading it became. Today, for instance, we may know immeasurably more about the universe than our ancestors did, and yet it increasingly seems they knew something more essential about it than we do, something that escapes us. The same thing is true of nature and of ourselves. The more thoroughly all our organs and their functions, their internal structure and the biochemical reactions that take place within them, are described, the more we seem to fail to grasp the spirit, purpose, and meaning of the system that they create together and that we experience as our unique "self."

And thus today we find ourselves in a paradoxical situation. We enjoy all the achievements of modern civilization that have made our physical existence on this Earth easier in so many important ways. Yet we do not know exactly what to do with ourselves, where to turn. The world of our experiences seems chaotic, disconnected, confusing. There appear to be no integrating forces, no unified meaning, no true inner understanding of phenomena in our experience of the world. Experts can explain anything in the objective world to us, yet we understand our own lives less and less. In short, we live in the postmodern world, where everything is possible and almost nothing is certain.

This state of affairs has its social and political consequences. The single planetary civilization to which we all belong confronts us with global challenges. We stand helpless before them because our civilization has essentially globalized only the surface of our lives. But our inner self continues to have a life of its own. And the fewer answers the era of rational knowledge provides to the basic questions of human Being, the more deeply it would seem that people, behind its back as it were, cling to the ancient certainties of their tribe. Because of this, individual cultures, increasingly lumped together by contemporary civilization, are realizing with new urgency their own inner autonomy and the inner differences of others. Cultural conflicts are increasing and are understandably more dangerous today than at any other time in history. The end of the era of rationalism has been catastrophic: Armed with the same supermodern weapons, often from the same suppliers, and followed by television cameras, the members of various tribal cults are at war with one another. By day, we work with statistics; in the evening, we consult astrologers and frighten ourselves with thrillers about vampires. The abyss between the rational and the spiritual, the external and the internal, the objective and the subjective, the technical and the moral, the universal and the unique constantly grows deeper.

Politicians are rightly worried by the problem of finding the key to ensure the survival of a civilization that is global and at the same time clearly multicultural; how generally respected mechanisms of peaceful coexistence can be set up, and on what set of principles they are to be established.

These questions have been highlighted with particular urgency by the two most important political events in the second half of the twentieth century: the collapse of colonial hegemony and the fall of communism. The artificial world order of the past decades has collapsed, and a new, more just order has not yet emerged. The central political task of the final years of this century, then, is the creation of a new model of coexistence among the various cultures, peoples, races, and religious spheres within a single interconnected civilization. This task is all the more urgent because other threats to contemporary humanity brought about by one-dimensional development of civilization are growing more serious all the time.

Many believe this task can be accomplished through technical means. That is, they believe it can be accomplished through the invention of new organizational, political, and diplomatic instruments. Yes, it is clearly necessary to invent organizational structures appropriate to the present multicultural age. But such efforts are doomed to failure if they do not grow out of something deeper, out of generally held values.

This, too, is well known. And in searching for the most natural source for the creation of a new world order, we usually look to an area that is the traditional foundation of modern justice and a great achievement of the modern age: to a set of values that—among other things—were first declared in this building. I am referring to respect for the unique human being and his or her liberties and inalienable rights, and the principle that a ll power derives from the people. I am, in short, referring to the fundamental ideas of modern democracy.

What I am about to say may sound provocative, but I feel more and more strongly that even these ideas are not enough, that we must go further and deeper. The point is that the solution they offer is still, as it were, modern, derived from the climate of the Enlightenment and from a view of man and his relation to the world that has been characteristic of the Euro-American sphere for the last two centuries. Today, however, we are in a different place and facing a different situation, one to which classically modern solutions in themselves do not give a satisfactory response. After all, the very principle of inalienable human rights, conferred on man by the Creator, grew out of the typically modern notion that man—as a being capable of knowing nature and the world—was the pinnacle of creation and lord of the world. This modern anthropocentrism inevitably meant that He who allegedly endowed man with his inalienable rights began to disappear from the world: He was so far beyond the grasp of modern science that He was gradually pushed into a sphere of privacy of sorts, if not directly into a sphere of private fancy—that is, to a place where public obligations no longer apply. The existence of a higher authority than man himself simply began to get in the way of human aspirations.

The idea of human rights and freedoms must be an integral part of any meaningful world order. Yet I think it must be anchored in a different place, and in a different way, than has been the case so far. If it is to be more than just a slogan mocked by half the world, it cannot be expressed in the language of a departing era, and it must not be mere froth floating on the subsiding waters of faith in a purely scientific relationship to the world.

Paradoxically, inspiration for the renewal of this lost integrity can once again be found in science. In a science that is new—let us say postmodern—a science producing ideas that in a certain sense allow it to transcend its own limits. I will give two examples.

The first is the Anthropic Cosmological Principle. Its authors and adherents have pointed out that from the countless possible courses of its evolution, the universe took the only one that enabled life to emerge. This is not yet proof that the aim of the universe has always been that it should one day see itself through our eyes. But how else can this matter be explained?

I think the Anthropic Cosmological Principle brings us to an idea perhaps as old as humanity itself: that we are not at all just an accidental anomaly, the microscopic caprice of a tiny particle whirling in the endless depths of the universe. Instead, we are mysteriously connected to the entire universe, we are mirrored in it, just as the entire evolution of the universe is mirrored in us. Until recently it might have seemed that we were an unhappy bit of mildew on a heavenly body whirling in space among many that have no mildew on them at all. This was something that classical science could explain. Yet the moment it begins to appear that we are deeply connected to the entire universe, science reaches the outer limits of its powers. Because it is founded on the search for universal laws, it cannot deal with singularity, that is, with uniqueness. The universe is a unique event and a unique story, and so far we are the unique point of that story. But unique events and stories are the domain of poetry, not science. With the formulation of the Anthropic Cosmological Principle, science has found itself on the border between formula and story, between science and myth. In that, however, science has paradoxically returned, in a roundabout way, to man, and offers him—in new clothing—his lost integrity. It does so by anchoring him once more in the cosmos.

The second example is the Gaia Hypothesis. This theory brings together proof that the dense network of mutual interactions between the organic and inorganic portions of the Earth's surface form a single system, a kind of mega-organism, a living planet—Gaia—named after an ancient goddess who is recognizable as an archetype of the Earth Mother in perhaps all religions. According to the Gaia Hypothesis we are parts of a greater whole. Our destiny is not dependent merely on what we do for ourselves but also on what we do for Gaia as a whole. If we endanger her, she will dispense with us in the interests of a higher value—that is, life itself.

What makes the Anthropic Principle and the Gaia Hypothesis so inspiring? One simple thing: Both remind us, in modern language, of what we have long suspected, of what we have long projected into our forgotten myths and what perhaps has always lain dormant within us as archetypes. That is, the awareness that we are not here alone nor for ourselves alone, but that we are an integral part of higher, mysterious entities against whom it is not advisable to blaspheme. This forgotten awareness is encoded in all religions. All cultures anticipate it in various forms. It is one of the things that form the basis of man's understanding of himself, of his place in the world, and ultimately of the world as such.

A modern philosopher once said: "Only a God can save us now."

Yes, the only real hope of people today is probably a renewal of our certainty that we are rooted in the Earth and, at the same time, the cosmos. This awareness endows us with the capacity for self-transcendence. Politicians at international forums may reiterate a thousand times that the basis of the new world order must be universal respect for human rights, but it will mean nothing as long as this imperative does not derive from the respect of the miracle of Being, the miracle of the universe, the miracle of nature, the miracle of our own existence. Only someone who submits to the authority of the universal order and of creation, who values the right to be a part of it and a participant in it, can genuinely value himself and his neighbors, and thus honor their rights as well.

It logically follows that, in today's multicultural world, the truly reliable path to coexistence, to peaceful coexistence and creative cooperation, must start from what is at the root of all cultures and what lies infinitely deeper in human hearts and mind than political opinion, convictions, antipathies, or sympathies: It must be rooted in self-transcendence. Transcendence as a hand reached out to those close to us, to foreigners, to the human community, to all living creatures, to nature, to the universe; transcendence as a deeply and joyously experienced need to be in harmony even with what we ourselves are not, what we do not understand, what seems distant from us in time and space, but with which we are nevertheless mysteriously linked because, together with us, all this constitutes a single world. Transcendence as the only real alternative to extinction.

The Declaration of Independence, adopted two hundred and eighteen years ago in this building, states that the Creator gave man the right to liberty. It seems man can realize that liberty only if he does not forget the One who endowed him with it.

Playwright and former anticommunist dissident Vaclav Havel is President of the Czech Republic. His activities as a human rights activist inspired the "velvet revolution" in 1989 that returned his country to democracy.

Adapted by *New Age Journal*, 42 Pleasant Street, Watertown, MA; Subscriptions: $24/year. For subscriptions call, (815) 734-5808.

Ecopsychology and the
Anima Mundi

by Theodore Roszak

from ReVision

Was somebody asking to see the soul?
See your own shape and countenance,
persons, substances, beasts, the trees,
the running rivers, the rocks and sands.
Walt Whitman

The Angst of Urban Man

Since the days of Freud and the Behaviorists, the standard understanding of the human mind in western society has been wholly focussed upon urban angst and the mechanics of the reflex arc. So if, for example, one checks the *Diagnostic and Statistical Manual*, the American Psychiatric Association's canonical listing of mental illnesses, one finds no mention of the nonhuman world beyond a passing reference to Seasonal Major Depressive Episodes—feeling blue when the weather turns gray. Otherwise, while neuroses of marriage, family, school, and the workplace are all painstakingly listed, the nonhuman habitat out of which the psyche evolved and on which the quality of our lives depend simply does not exist as a factor in our understanding of "civilization and its discontents."

We have become used to the idea that parents and children, husbands and wives can exist in abusive relationships; but we make no allowance for the possibility that our species as a whole may exist in an abusive relationship to the natural habitat. Anxiety, depression, or phobia in this context remain as invisible as dysfunctional relationships in the home were before "family therapy" was invented some thirty years ago—the last major expansion of the analytical context in the therapeutic mainstream.

Perhaps this is not remarkable. Modern western psychotherapy is after all the creation of citified intellect; it is intended to be applied to an urban clientele. It is practiced in an office, in a building, in a city or suburb; the client drives to the office in the building on a freeway, parks in a parking lot, finishes the 50 minute hour, drives home or to work in another room in another building. Therapy stops at the city limits.

Now there are signs that our radically nonecological psychology is in a state of critical transformation. A new generation of psychotherapists is seeking ways for professional psychology to play a role in the environmental crisis of our time. This change is arising at the same time that at least a few environmentalists are displaying a healthy curiosity about their need to find a more sustainable psychology. There is concern about the amount of anger, negativity, and emotional burnout one finds in the movement.

"Ecopsychology" is the name most often used for this emerging dialogue between the psychological and the ecological; but several others have been suggested: psycho- ecology, eco-therapy, global therapy, green therapy, Earth-centered therapy, re-earthing, nature-based psychotherapy, shamanic counseling . . . But by whatever name, the underlying assumption is the same: ecology needs psychology, psychology needs ecology. The context for defining sanity in our time has reached planetary magnitude.

I have referred to ecopsychology as "new"—but in fact, its sources are old enough to be called aboriginal. Once upon a time all psychology was "ecopsychology." No special word was needed. The oldest healers of the world—the people our society was once pleased to call "witch doctors"—knew no other way to heal than to work within the context of a sacred ecology. There was nothing sentimental about this; nothing "mystical" as we might understand these words. It was homely common sense that human beings must live in a state of vital reciprocity with the flora and fauna, the rivers and hills, the sky and soil on which they depend for physical sustenance and spiritual instruction.

We recognize our lingering connection with that earlier stage of psychotherapeutic practice whenever we refer to psychiatrists as "shrinks." We do so flippantly, implying that a certain residue of mumbo-jumbo still clings to our supposedly enlightened science of the mind. But by the same token might there not be something of value to be found in the supposedly superstitious practice of witchdoctoring?

Is there a "stone age psychiatry" that can be mined for similarly heuristic insights?

THE HEATHEN IN HIS BLINDNESS

Some will see an immediate obstacle to such a dialogue between the ancient and the modern. It has to do with the contrasting worldviews that divide us from the original headshrinkers. Indigenous peoples are "heathens"—or more politely "animists." They saw the world alive, filled with presences and intentions. This pagan sensibility has been deeply censored in all of us by both Judeo-Christian doctrine and scientific objectivity. In our culture, addressing the nonhuman world, listening for its voice as if it felt, heard, spoke would seem the very essence of madness to most modern people. Conventional sanity itself would seem to cut us off from using stone-age psychiatry as a resource for reinterpreting sanity.

Let me offer you a vivid example of the cultural disjuncture that parts us from the animist worldview. Here are the words of a popular Anglican hymn of the early nineteenth century.

In vain with lavish kindness
The gifts of God are strown
The heathen in his blindness
Bows down to wood and stone.

The hymn was written by Reginald Heber, an Anglican missionary who, before his death in 1826, went on to become the Bishop of Calcutta. Heber was born in 1783. Just one year later, another clergyman, Edmund Cartwright, would invent the power loom, the technological basis of the industrial revolution. By the time Heber had become Bishop of Calcutta, we have our first reports of smoke and soot sighted in the skies above Manchester. The environmental crisis had begun.

Only in our time are we beginning to recognize this deep psychic connection between western society's long-standing crusade against the "idolatry" of pagan peoples and the creation of the "dark Satanic mills."

Yet our very ability to raise that connection out of the depths of the psyche demonstrates that consciousness has its history and that it responds to needs we may not even be able to name. Within that history, both religion and science are subject to that sort of major transformation we have come to call a shift of paradigms. In the mainstream Christian churches, for example, there is an active discussion of planetary stewardship and creation spirituality that seeks to undo the long-standing prejudice against "pagan" culture and its insights. A new Earth and Spirit movement is exploring the possibility of a religiously based "biophilia."

Meanwhile, at least along the fringes of modern science, we have an emerging new cosmology grounded in an ever-deepening vision of ordered complexity on the Earth and in the universe at large. Scientists may remain reluctant to spell out the full philosophical relevance of this new worldview, but the implications of the new cosmology are becoming unmistakably clear: life and mind are coming to be seen as an integral part of an evolving universe, orders of complexity that are deeply rooted in all that came before. One cosmologist puts it this way: "We belong to this universe, we are the child of this universe, we are made out of stardust." Another, a bit more facetiously, but not inaccurately, tells us that: "hydrogen (the premier element) is an odorless, colorless gas that, given enough time, turns into people."

In earlier generations, what we see as a matter of evolving chemical relationships was understood to be a matter of soul. Soul was understood to be the link between person and cosmos. Soul was, indeed, understood to be universal and pervasive—hence the designation "animistic," "ensouled." The common philosophical name for this teaching was the *anima mundi*. Moderns—especially scientists—have trouble with concepts like this. They associate it with seemingly fantastic notions about nature deities—wood sprites and elves.

But now listen closely: here is exactly the same primordial insight that produced the idea of the *anima mundi*, but this time it is dressed in the rhetoric of contemporary science.

The Earth holds together, its tissues cohere, and it has the look of a structure that really would make comprehensible sense if we only knew enough about it. From a little way off, photographed from, say, a satellite, it seems to be a kind of organism. Moreover, looked at over geologic time, it is plainly in the process of developing like an immense embryo. It is, for all its stupendous size and the numberless units and infinite variety of its life forms, coherent. Every tissue is dependent for its existence on other tissues. It is a creature, or it you want a more conventional, but less interesting term, it is a system.

These are the words of the biologist Lewis Thomas, writing in *The New England Journal of Medicine* in 1978. What Thomas is calling "system" is precisely what was once called "soul": a vital organizing pattern that enables things—a human being, a tree, a flea, a living planet—to know what it is doing.

Rhetoric changes, metaphor changes, but myths like the *anima mundi* never die. They have the immortality of the phoenix. Reduced to ashes, they undergo miraculous transformations, returning to life with their essence intact. They might be described as a sort of ethereal gene passed from mind to mind across the centuries, mingling along the way, as all genetic traits do, with other cultural strains and intellectual mutations. Some myths have sufficient vitality to transcend the boundaries of history and ethnicity, finally to be absorbed into a permanent pool of images and teachings that become the common property of the human family. These are perhaps what Jung called "archetypes," the ageless furniture of the collective unconscious.

A Brief History of the *Anima Mundi*

In the case of the *anima mundi*, we are dealing with one of the oldest experiences of mankind, the spontaneous sense of dread and wonder primitive humans once felt in the presence of the Earth's majestic power. When they were no more than the first few representatives of a timid, scurrying new species in the world, these early humans must have greeted the immense creativity of nature with an awe that has since been lost to all but the poetic minority among us in the modern world. The Earth does go so powerfully and competently about her work, bringing forth the crops, ushering in the seasons, nurturing the many species that find their home in her vast body. She can of course also be a menacing giant; that too is remembered in myth and folklore. Many of the oldest rituals are acts of propitiation offered to a sometimes fierce and punishing divinity, an Earth who can be an angry mother as well as a bountiful one.

One of the oldest, and best-known depictions we have of the Mother Goddess is a lumpy little carving nicknamed by anthropologists the Venus of Willensdorf. A blatantly sexual image, all breasts and buttocks, she was intended to embody female divinity as our hunting and gathering ancestors understood it. It is difficult to imagine that so primeval an image could outlast the culture of the hunting camp and the agrarian village, but so she did. Mother Earth is as universal a symbol as our race possesses, at home even in those societies that have moved on to more civilized ways.

But at that point in her long history, as she leaves the land to enter the city, a significant change takes place. Her further adventures proceed along two contrasting, often conflicting routes, one religious, the other philosophical and eventually scientific. This bifurcation mirrors a deep psychological split that segregates emotion from intellect. And, as we will see, this dichotomy also corresponds to the masculine and feminine stereotypes that divide so many cultures. Along these lines, the transformations of the mother goddess underlie many tangled issues of sexual politics that have had to wait until our own time to be brought to the surface for discussion.

As late as the age of Plato and Aristotle, when Athens was the cosmopolitan hub of the ancient world, the Great Mother was still being worshipped in the groves and forests of Greece; but by then, her rites had become a religion of the oppressed, and principally of women, the notorious Bacchae who sought frenzied union with the mother deity through sacrificial ceremonies that were rumored to be obscene and bloody. Later still in the Roman-Hellenistic period, cults of Isis and *Magna Mater* flourished in the great cities. The urbanized versions of age-old agricultural rituals offered by the cults may have been tamer, but their promise was the same: the expiation of sin, the renewal of life, the merciful love of the divine mother. Once again the main adherents of these cults were women who apparently found little gratification in the official, male-dominated pantheon of the civil religion. The worship of the mystery cults was more emotional and personal; there they could be in the presence of a divine woman who knew a mortal woman's needs.

All the while, subtler, or at least more circumspect minds—and by and large they were *men's* minds—were seeking a tidier, more sophisticated conception of the Earth Mother than such ecstatic mysteries rites provided. In the minds of these male philosophers the image and the ecstasy of the ancient fertility goddess were dissolving more and more into metaphysical abstractions. She was becoming the *anima mundi*, the World Soul who was understood to be the governing intelligence of the physical universe. We first meet her in this new identity in the works of Plato and his followers.

Platonic cosmology inhabits the lofty realm of the incorporeal forms. It was inconceivable to Plato that the forms, in their pristine transcendence, could have any connection with the impermanent material world. How then do they take effect in nature? It was by way of answering this question that Plato conceived of the *anima mundi*. It or rather "she" (the *anima* is always female) serves as the intermediary between the changeless being of the forms and the grubby turbulence of this lower world. *Anima mundi* is mentality embedded in physicality, that which bestows rational shape upon what would otherwise be chaos. In Plato's view, she was the cosmic housekeeper performing a woman's traditional chores cleaning, straightening up, arranging on the largest scale.

One must look closely to find any recognizable trace of the voluptuous old Earth Mother in Plato's urbane metaphysical theories. In language and spirit, Plato takes us a long way from the sensuous, often savage rites with which the Great Goddess was still being honored by the bacchantes of his own day. With Plato we have the beginning of that sort of highly cerebral fastidiousness that characterizes modern science. Plato was loath to associate his philosophical abstractions with anything as grossly erotic as the Mother Earth.

Modern science has gone even further in disembodying the idea of the *anima mundi*. Science prefers a more controlled kind of empiricism, pretending that it works exclusively from physical facts and objective measurements. Nevertheless, it has borrowed heavily from the *anima mundi*. Without it, science itself may have never come to be. Why is there any point at all in trying to make sense of the world? Because we assume there is sense there to be found, an order that responds to the inquiring habits of the human mind. Our questions will be answered if they are properly formulated. It is the *anima mundi* that lays the foundations of all theory, teaching us that nature is a cosmos, an ordered whole. Behind its turbulent surface, it possesses a constant and intelligible structure.

During the medieval period, the *anima mundi* was often forced to travel incognita through Christian Europe. She carried rather too much heretical luggage with her to be wholly respectable: too many echoes of the old pagan deities, too many hints of animism. In the official view of the Church, nature was desacralized territory, created by God but apart from and wholly other than God. The *anima mundi* threatened to impart some aura of divinity to that profane and fallen realm. Some have seen in mainstream Christianity's entrenched hostility to nature worship one of the deep roots of our environmental crisis. Orthodox Christianity proscribed teachings that compromised the uniqueness and transcendence of God; nevertheless, we can still find traces of the *anima mundi* among medieval philosophers, especially those who filtered their Christianity through Plato or Plotinus. Some Christian Platonists cautiously allowed her the status of a lesser deity; she was God's handmaiden in the running of the universe. Others assimilated her to the study of astrology, a subject not altogether banned by the Church of the middle ages. The *anima mundi* was frequently entrusted with mediating the influence of the stars in human affairs.

While medieval theologians respected the *anima mundi* as a metaphysical principle, cults of Hecate and the Earth Mother, sometimes assimilated to the Virgin Mary, continued to flourish in the countryside and in the remote villages, and once again primarily among women. In these surviving traces of the pagan mysteries, we can see the earliest adumbrations of European witchcraft, later to become a prime target for religious persecution.

But it was the alchemists, working along the shadowy fringes of medieval culture, who made the most consequential use of the *anima mundi*. For the alchemists, the *anima mundi* became the reigning mistress of all natural forces. While all alchemists shared the goal of penetrating her secrets so that they might share her powers, they differed markedly about how this might best be done.

One school, the spiritual alchemists, believed a harmonious communion with the *anima mundi* might only be achieved by prayerful purification of the soul. Their practice of the Great Work may have been a quasi-Christian, quasi-gnostic form of nature mysticism in which, it is worth noting, femininity played a significant if secondary role. In their quest for the mysterious philosopher's stone, those who regarded themselves as "high alchemists" frequently employed a female assistant, the *soror mystica* (the mystic sister) kept close at hand to remind them of "the eternal feminine."

But there was a second kind of alchemy, vulgar alchemy, from which we inherit the stereotype of the scruffy sorcerer in his dank and smoke-filled workshop, surrounded by bizarre apparatus, brewing up evil-smelling concoctions in bubbling vats and convoluted retorts, seeking the secrets of the material world in mixtures of mercury and mare's dung. Their ways with the *anima mundi* were very different. Their hope was that by occult means, they might harness the forces of the universe. High and vulgar alchemy represent two divergent approaches to the natural world, one based on respectful communion, the other on brute force.

Of these two, it was vulgar alchemy that was destined to inherit the future, though in a highly unpredictable way. As comically antiquated as these alchemical "puffers" may seem to us now, in a crucial sense their activities foreshadow the coming scientific era. When people identify alchemy as a kind of primitive forerunner of chemistry, it is vulgar alchemy they have in mind. When it comes to underlying intentions, they are not far off the mark in seeing a connection between the two.

By the later middle ages, this profane species of alchemy had spun off into a school of "natural magic," which sought and often claimed to have acquired miraculous powers. Natural magic survived among learned men until the age of Newton. Natural magic was always careful to distinguish itself from demonic magic, which was prepared to traffic with devils and other unclean spirits. Demonic magic was the magic of Doctor Faustus, a dangerous and forbidden pursuit. In contrast, natural magic worked more respectfully with the *anima mundi*, whose power was understood to be derived from God.

This association of the *anima mundi* with alchemy and magic is a significant departure in western history. Here we have pursuits aimed at mastering or at least effectively manipulating natural forces. The enterprise is pursued with conviction because it is based on the assumption that there is a responsive mind on the "other side" of nature whose sympathy we can win and whose secrets we can probe.

Notice the difference: for Plato, the *anima mundi* was an object of contemplation, there to be studied and described; but as the alchemists saw it, she is capable of being used either gently by persuasion or forcibly. In either case, these are ways to tap her power. This represents an entirely new relationship between man and nature. It is not Plato's passive meditation, nor is it the supplication of folk religion. It is a willful act based upon the assumption of human superiority over all natural things. Today we would refer to that knowledge as "know-how," the basis of technology.

The sixteenth and seventeenth centuries are the watershed in the long life-story of the *anima mundi*. Educated minds of that era still took her existence seriously; in the many microcosmic diagrams that were drawn in that period, she is always prominently stationed just below

God, just above the Earth, a regal and imposing presence in the cosmos. Prominent scientists still featured her in their theories. William Gilbert based his research into magnetism on the assumption that the lodestone was a piece of the *anima mundi* exerting her occult attraction on the metals of the Earth. Gilbert was indeed among the most organic and anthropomorphic of the early scientists. He speaks defensively of the Earth against all who would dismiss her as lowly and brutish. For him, she is "the mother of us all"; her magnetic field is referred to as a "mind"; its attractive power is a form of "coition." Similarly, as late as the end of the eighteenth century, the pioneering geologist James Hutton was prepared to speak of the Earth as an organism possessing a metabolism.

But by that time, metaphysical notions like the *anima mundi* were growing quaint; except among the Romantic poets, the metaphors and symbols that sustained the Great Goddess were wearing thin. A new metaphor was displacing her, that of the machine; and a new symbolism mathematics had become the principal language of science.

For the next two centuries, the *anima mundi* would go into deep eclipse in our culture. When she appeared once again, it would be in a very different guise as a hypothesis developed out of abstruse studies in gas chromatography in a distinctly high tech setting. The language that ushered her back into the world would be that of modern chemistry and would involve many refined calculations; but she would retain one of her traditional names: Gaia.

THE GAIA HYPOTHESIS

In the mid-sixties, the chemist James Lovelock found himself part of a team at the Jet Propulsion Laboratory whose assignment was to search for life on Mars. The Lab was committed to carrying out this project by way of robotic landing-craft—the expensive, military-industrial way to go. Lovelock was certain that this was not necessary. Life could be detected remotely and far more cheaply by long-range scrutiny of the planetary atmosphere, whether on Mars or on any other world.

This thesis was connected with Lovelock's earlier invention of a technique called electron capture detection, which was able to identify faint traces of specified chemical substances. Lovelock's contention (as he developed his theory in partnership with the microbiologist Lynn Margulis) was that living things, once they appeared on our planet, took charge of the global environment in a creative way. They became full-fledged partners in the shaping of the Earth, its rocks and water and soil. The goal of life is global homeostasis. This transforms the planet into what might be viewed as a single self-regulating ecology. This in essence is the hypothesis that Lovelock and his close collaborator Margulis were to call "Gaia." Here is how Margulis summarizes the hypothesis:

> Gaia, the superorganismic system of all life on earth, hypothetically maintains the composition of the air and the temperature of the planet's surface, regulating conditions for the continuance of life. . . . On earth the environment has been made and monitored by life as much as life has been made and influenced by the environment.

Lovelock was struck by the fact that the biomass, in its long-term self-regulation, exhibits "the behavior of a single organism, even a living creature." Thus he called the hypothesis "Gaia," borrowing the name of the ancient Greek Earth mother. The name at once touched the idea with magic; it took on an astonishing popularity that was far beyond anything Lovelock and Margulis intended. The *anima mundi* was being reborn.

Gaia has proved to be especially attractive to the Deep Ecologists.

Deep Ecology, the mystical wing of the environmental movement, seeks to replace our anthropocentric worldview with a biocentric ethic based upon the sort of animistic communion with nature that can (with enough poetic license) be read into the Gaia hypothesis. Some ecofeminists have gone even farther. For them, Gaia represents scientific validation for a semi-legendary "goddess culture" where, once upon a time, men and women lived in respectful partnership and the more ecologically sensitive qualities were paramount.

The Gaia Hypothesis has become deeply embedded in ecological thought over the past twenty years. But as ambitious and as controversial as the hypothesis is, it is actually not big enough to do justice to the place of life and mind in the universe. We are coming to see that what Gaia represents is but one system among countless systems, some of them dating back to the origin of the universe. Matter itself is now seen as an ancient system, a tightly coordinated pattern of particles and energies that evolved out of the earliest transformations of the cosmos. Life on Earth, the most recent and complex of all systems to emerge from this grand hierarchical progression, is therefore very old, very deeply rooted.

As nature around us unfolds to reveal level upon level of structured intricacy, we are observing the steady elaboration of an ecological universe in which life and mind are rooted all the way back to the initial conditions that followed the Big Bang. We now know that the very stuff of which we are made—the heavy elements like carbon—was forged in the fiery core of ancient stars. It is no longer a matter of scientific necessity for us to regard ourselves as "strangers and afraid in a world we never made."

In a very real sense, the ecologist's web of life now spreads out to embrace the most remote galaxies. The new cosmology is well on its way to becoming our cooler, more detached and analytical version of the animistic world that our ancestors once honored in myth and ritual. We are learning that the womb of the Goddess may be as vast as the universe. And in that sense, we are healing the long-standing breach between Above and Below, between the gods of the sky and the goddess of the Earth. As scientific mind comes home to life on Earth, we may be watching a grand and fateful unity coming into existence.

THE ECOLOGICAL UNCONSCIOUS

This is where the new study of ecopsychology begins: at that intersection of Gaia and psyche I have called the "ecological unconscious." Ecopsychology takes with the utmost, literal seriousness the basic ecological teaching that we reside within a planetary web of life; but it includes the psyche within that web, insisting that the psyche is as much a child of the Earth's evolutionary labor as any limb or organ.

Like all forms of psychology, ecopsychology concerns itself with the depths of the personality. Unlike other mainstream schools of psychology which limit themselves to the intrapsychic mechanisms or to a narrow social range that may not look beyond the family, ecopsychology proceeds from the assumption that at its deepest level the psyche is sympathetically bonded to the Earth which mothered us into existence. That bond must be taken into account—and can be taken into account as we would all the other relations that lay claim to our emotional energy. Ecopsychology clings to a desperate article of faith: that all of us, even those who live in the industrial heartland can, with enough help, still hear some murmur of the Earth's insistent voice through a wall of reinforced concrete about fifty miles thick.

Ecopsychology suggests that we can read our transactions with the natural environment—the way we use or abuse the planet—as projections of unconscious needs and desires, in much the same way we can read dreams and hallucinations to learn about our deep motivations, fears, hatreds. Our wishful, willful imprint upon the natural environment reveals our collective state of soul—and does so more tellingly than the dreams we wake from and shake off, knowing them to be unreal. Far more consequential are the dreams which we take with us out into the world and set about making "real"—in steel and concrete, in flesh and blood, out of the substance of the planet.

Precisely because we have acquired the power to work our will upon the environment, the planet has become like that blank screen of the unconscious on which we project our fantasies. Toxic wastes, the depletion of resources, the annihilation of our fellow species: all these speak to us, if we would hear, of our soul's condition.

The person and the planet. Here is a connection—a political connection—which is a distinctly contemporary discovery, one that could only come to light after our economic institutions had reached a certain critical size and complexity, a certain dizzy level of dynamism and unfeeling efficiency. Only now do we see that the scale of things can be an independent problem of our social life, a factor that may distort even the best intentions of policy. It has taken our unique modern experience with public and private bureaucracies, the mass market, state and corporate industrialism to teach us this lesson.

We have learned that human beings can create systems that do not understand human beings and will not serve their needs. And at exactly the same time, we have learned how easily these industrial systems can shred the environmental fabric on which all life depends, perhaps even without our realizing what irreparable harm we do.

At this point, if I were to put the matter as succinctly as possible, I would have to weaken in the direction of poetic license, suggesting a model of the Earth as a sentient being, capable in her own mysterious way of intelligent adaptation and skillful maneuver for the sake of defending her life-giving mission in the universe. If you wish, take that model to be no more than a metaphor, or a convenient hypothesis—as many Gaian ecologists prefer. For my own part, I will confess that the image goes deeper than poetry or theoretical convenience, reaching into an intersection of the mind that blends science and myth, fact and feeling, objective accuracy and subjective conviction.

Suppose, then, that we and the Earth who mothered us out of her inert substance are indeed bound together in a single organic pattern within which it has been our special human role to be the planet's risky experiment in self-conscious intelligence.

Suppose the main purpose of that experiment has now been achieved: the creation of an interdependent global society that promises physical security for all and a world-cultural synthesis.

Finally, suppose—as is all too apparent—that the planet's prime need is now to restrain our technological and organizational violence so that all her endangered children might live.

What then does the Earth do?

She begins to speak to something in us—to our sense of moral identity. She digs deep into our unexplored nature to draw forth a passion for therapeutic self-knowledge and personal recognition that has lain slumbering in us like an unfertilized seed. And so, quite suddenly, in the very heartland of urban-industrial society, a generation appears that instinctively yearns for a quality of life wholly incompatible with the giganticism of our economic and technological structures. And the cry of personal pain which that generation utters in its need for healing is the planet's own cry for rescue, her protest against the bigness of things becoming one with our own. So we begin to look for alternatives to that person-and-planet-crushing colossalism. We search for ways to disintegrate the bigness—to disintegrate it creatively into humanly scaled, organically balanced communities and systems that free us from the deadly industrial compulsions of the past.

After our long, strenuous industrial adventure, we are being summoned back along new paths to a vital reciprocity with the Earth who mothered us into our strange human vocation. But she summons us now, not by way of an external image or graphic symbol, but by way of the deep self, out of the underworld of the troubled psyche.

And her name this time is our name—yours, mine, his, hers, all our names, and for each of us the one name we have freely chosen for ourselves.

Listen closely and you will hear. . .
Her Voice, Your Voice, Our Voice.

THEODORE ROSZAK is Professor of History and Director of the Ecopsychology Institute at California State University, Hayward. He is the author of **The Voice of the Earth***. His most recent books are* **Ecopsychology: Restoring the Earth, Healing the Mind***, edited with Mary Gomes and Allen Kanner, and the novel* **The Memoirs of Elizabeth Frankenstein***, which he describes as a study in sexual politics and the fate of the Earth. The Ecopsychology Institute publishes the* **Ecopsychology Newsletter***, available for a $10 subscription payable to the Institute from The Ecopsychology Newsletter, Box 7487, Berkeley, CA 94707.*

This is a slightly revised version of an article that originally appeared in *ReVision*, 1319 18th Street NW, Washington, DC 20036. Subscription: $24/year.

DEEP POLITICS AND GRACE

A POSTMODERNIST VIEWPOINT

by MATTHEW FOX

from CREATION SPIRITUALITY

The fifteenth century is when the modern era of politics began—with the invention of the printing press and the introduction of Machiavelli's *The Prince*. Up to this time, the theory of politics from the Middle Ages and from Aristotle was that a politician was a person of virtue who led people virtuously. But Machiavelli secularized politics. This was one of the beginning moments of the secularization of society which the modern era has fully carried out. Instead of talking about virtues of justice, for example, Machiavelli said that rules of politics should be whatever is appropriate to the situation and leads to success. He said that growth and expansion is more important than justice and constitutes the law of life. He came up with the image of what we call today the modern state.

The movement from modern to postmodern is the movement from honoring an ego or political "star" to people empowering themselves. From ego-centric (which is always anthropocentric) to omnicentric. It is the movement from "politics as usual" to *deep politics*. It is the resurrection of community passion, including moral outrage at the Babylon of modern politics around the world. Deep politics is also the passion of what we really do believe in. It moves politics from game playing to the lower chakras where pain and sorrow and survival dwell. Moving politics from secularization (anthropocentric) to sacralization (holding all sacred) is the work of postmodern politics. We humans are the only species that can choose to cut ourselves off from the sacred: we have done it in politics; we've done it in science; we've done it in education; and we've done it in religion, and in art. This is why we elders of our society are building prisons for our young people instead of giving them spiritual opportunities. The modern world has been very hostile to the experience of the sacred. Even the churches and synagogues have run from it and have tried to sell us religion instead of awakening our spiritual empowerment. So this phrase *deep politics* is a turning point in four hundred years of modern politics in society and church.

What totally differentiates post-modern politics from modern is grace. It isn't nihilistic. It isn't pessimistic—it's graceful. This is the religious dilemma of the West: the dualisms between Nature and Grace. When you separate the two you have an energy crisis. We have to get our grace from the original fire, the original fireball and all the fires that have been born since then. We have to draw on this well of grace that is present in the Universe. A great wound exists in our consciousness because of this dualism. When religion separates Nature from grace, it becomes afraid of nature. Nature becomes the enemy, and by Nature I mean everything from our psyches to our sexuality to our passion for justice to our relationship to all the other beings of nature. This creates a subject/object relationship with Nature. When you are afraid of Nature, you fall into a coercive mode in order to control her. Because, the fact is, Nature is bigger than all of us.

Look at earthquakes and volcanic eruptions, for example: they are reminders that we are guests here—we are not in control. That is what all of modern politics of church and state is about—control. We have to learn to respect the fact of our fragility on this planet. Fundamentalism and religious and political fascism occur as power mechanisms to control Nature, to hold her in. This is why religious fascism and political fascism are linking up together so well in our time.

Ecological devastation occurs because if Nature is not sacred in itself, then humans can do to it whatever they want. And we will, if we are afraid of it. We will wipe out the so-called savage, the wilderness, the wildness wherever we can. But then, all of a sudden, we will begin to feel our cosmic loneliness—which is what we are beginning to feel at this moment in history.

When we cut ourselves off from Nature awe is lost. And we have to make titillating awe and sensational awe. Then comes our fascination

70

with violence and our fixation on the privacy of those in the public forum, because we are not in touch with the real awe of our relationship with the cosmos, with cosmic history, with our bodies. Anthropocentric awe, which is pseudo-awe, replaces natural awe. Then drugs and addiction, including addiction to sports and shopping and every other kind of addiction, takes over our civilization because we are made for awe.

We need a politics that tells the truth, that names this cosmic moment for us, that leads us from a modern to a postmodern paradigm, that brings back what is missing from all politics—soul. This is precisely what was cut out, lobotomized in the modern era when Descartes located the soul in the pineal gland. Not in our gut where we feel outrage; not in our heart where we feel love; not in our lower chakras where we feel a connection to all the energies of the Universe, all the music and vibration that every being in the Universe makes—no! Descartes shot our soul right up into our heads; academia studies from there and is built from there. Our whole system, our professions, our work worlds, our worship are mostly from right there—in our heads. Our heart and body, our soul are missing.

In addition, when religion separates grace from Nature, grace becomes more and more scarce. It's as if a leakage of grace is going on all over the place! Then an ideology develops that there is only so much grace to go around—there is "trickle-down" grace! And guess who controls it? The clerical establishment: only the few, the governing elite, the ordained ones control this rare trickle down grace. The rest of us are expected to get on our knees in acts of submission in order to be "dispensed to" (that is actually the phrase used—"dispensing grace"). The priesthood ought to be a midwifing to the grace process: it is not about giving grace out; it is about helping it along, eliciting it from, helping grace to flow. It is to help heal the blockages—the sins of the spirit—that block-up grace. Church is by no means the only dispenser of grace— Nature is a dispenser of grace also and always has been. Meister Eckhart in the fourteenth century healed the whole Western religious dilemma when he said: "Nature is grace!" Learning to trust your dreams and your experiences and the wisdom of your ancestors and your people are all needed today because that is part of the move from modern to postmodern, from knowledge to wisdom.

The return to a sense of community where people hold all things as sacred is an affirmation about the grace within human nature itself. We are meant to grace one another: to be sources of grace and healers of grace. So grace is an abundance; it is not a scarcity. And that is why nihilism and pessimism are not the proper modes for our time. But creativity is, and this comes through grace. Grace comes through our art: the art of our living, the art of our language, the art of our relationships, the art of our forgiving. This is how and why we can be graceful. Forgiveness is so essential to politics and is the foundation of deep, postmodern politics. If we can't let go and forgive and move on, our passages for grace will always be blocked: we will still be replaying the old dilemmas and the old struggles (the destructive games of *realpolitick*). Grace is a state of being thankful and blessed because of who we are: not political partisans, narrowly visioned, but citizens of the Universe whose political cause is the fellowship of all beings. Only with this graced and awesome vision can we redeem the politics of the parties and birth the deep politics that will welcome us into the next millennium.

MATTHEW FOX is an international lecturer and author. His latest book is **The Reinvention of Work: A New Vision of Livelihood for Our Times**.

Reprinted from *Creation Spirituality*, PO Box 19216, Oakland, CA 94619. Subscription: $24/year.

LIBERATING SEXUALITY

TANTRA TALK

an interview with MIRANDA SHAW

from TRICYCLE

Miranda Shaw has a Ph.D. in Buddhist Studies from Harvard University, is the recipient of a Fulbright Fellowship, and is currently Assistant Professor of Buddhist Studies in the Department of Religion at the University of Richmond. Her book *Passionate Enlightenment: Women in Tantric Buddhism* (Princeton University Press) clarifies the importance of women in the tradition of tantric teachings and practices. Tantric Buddhism is a nonmonastic, noncelibate strand of Indian, Himalayan, and Tibetan Buddhist practice that seeks to weave every aspect of daily life, intimacy, and passion into the path of liberation. Historians have long viewed the role of women in tantric practices as marginal and subordinate at best and degraded and exploited at worst. Shaw argues to the contrary. In addition to interviews and fieldwork conducted in India and Nepal over a two-year period, Shaw recovered forty previously unknown works by women of the Pala period (eighth through twelfth centuries C.E.) and has used them to reinterpret the history of tantric Buddhism during its first four centuries. Shaw claims that the tantric theory of this period promoted an ideal of cooperative, mutually liberating relationships between women and men while encouraging a sense of reliance on women as a source of spiritual insight and power.

Tricycle: *Are there certain overarching principles that one finds in the literature on tantric sexuality?*

Shaw: Yes. The Tantras, or sacred tantric texts, make it clear that the purpose of the relationship is for the mutual enlightenment of both persons involved. It cannot be for the ego-gratification of one person. This purpose must be clear to both and agreed upon absolutely and explicitly by both. Another principle that could prevent the kind of exploitation that has occurred in the West is that the woman always takes the initiative in the Tantras. Always.

Tricycle: *Can the man ask and the woman say yes?*

Shaw: That would be a breach of form, because the initiative is in the woman's hands. But if he does approach her, which is unusual, he must use an elaborate decorum that is set out in the tantric texts. He must be extremely respectful and use secret nonverbal gestures to communicate with her. He also looks for certain signs to determine whether she is a tantric practitioner, and he shows her that he is a worthy tantric companion by using these gestures and by rendering the forms of homage that are required of him. These forms of homage are laid out in the *Yogini Tantras*, what the Tibetans call the "Mother Tantra" texts. He has to prostrate to her, circumambulate her, and use a form of etiquette called "behavior of the left," in which he stays on her left side when they walk together, takes the first step with his left foot, and makes offerings to her with his left hand. When they eat together he should always serve her first. These behaviors demonstrate that he does not regard this relationship as one of ego-fulfillment or self-service. He is showing that he is civilized enough and refined enough to become her spiritual companion and that he understands that this relationship will serve her.

Tricycle: *And this is between student and teacher?*

Shaw: No, this is between man and woman, whether the woman is the teacher or the man is the teacher or, more often, neither is the teacher of the other. The stories that come down to us include various types of cases. In tantric sexuality, the relationship is focused upon his offerings to her even though both partners are seeking to achieve certain yogic transformations. It is believed that they will bring their psychic states into resonance with one another and slowly lift each other, increasing and intensifying the energy that each has available for traversing the tantric path. So it is not the case that one person is gaining something psychically while the other person is being left behind. The partners must enter this realm, this experience of transcendental bliss, together.

Tricycle: *How do they recognize each other?*

Shaw: First, they are looking for a tantric practitioner who understands the underlying principles of the relationship. A person who is new to the study and practice of Buddhism is not a potential tantric partner. One of the key qualifications is that both must have taken tantric vows, the vows that accompany Anuttara-yoga initiation. The vow, or *samaya*, is a commitment to the worldview in which these principles are operative. The keeping of such vows will confirm the ability to keep a commitment, to maintain a relationship of profound, ultimate significance and import to both people and to surround it with the necessary integrity and secrecy.

Tricycle: *Does that imply monogamy?*

Shaw: It means impeccable integrity in their dealings with each other. For example, one partner could not be secretive about a relationship with someone else. One of the reasons for this—actually different from what we might expect—is that the partners are literally sharing their karma, their psychic resonance. They are communing on the most intimate level possible, mixing their spiritual destinies. That is one of the reasons it is called *Karma Mudra* practice: you are imprinting on one another's karma. That is why you must choose a partner so carefully. If another person becomes involved, then his or her karma is brought into the equation, so it has to be with the knowledge and consent of the other person. The other person must at least be able to choose whether to continue or not, whether they want to interact with this quality of energy.

Tricycle: Can you say more about the formalities?

Shaw: The criteria for choosing a tantric partner are more stringent than those for selecting a mate or sexual partner. The principles that surround a tantric relationship are more thoroughgoing, because you are entrusting your spiritual growth to a relationship in which both partners will be undergoing profound yogic transformations. It is explicitly stated in the tantric texts that the woman has her own set of transformations that reflect the subtle anatomy of her psychic body, or yogic body, or what is called the vajra body. The man is instructed in how to make the series of offerings that relate to her increasingly subtle and interiorized experiences. As he approaches her, he makes offerings that please the senses, including kind, gentle words. It is said that he should not criticize the woman or speak harshly. He should be very agreeable, very pleasant, and make offerings to the buddha in her. She should also recognize the male buddha, the enlightened essence, in him.

Tricycle: *Does she make any offerings?*

Shaw: She makes no form of obeisance. This is to insure that the balance of power in no way tips toward him. After he makes the outer offerings to the senses as he approaches her, the next level of offering is sexual pleasure. The tantric texts are very specific about this. He must be a person who is knowledgeable and skilled in that area. The texts describe this with great delicacy and beauty. He must be erotically skilled, an erotic virtuoso as well as a yogic virtuoso.

Tricycle: *For the benefit of sexual pleasure?*

Shaw: The point of giving her sexual pleasure is to awaken the bliss that she will then combine with meditation on emptiness in order to attain enlightenment. The instructions are extremely clear on that. Both partners must remind each other as the pleasure builds not to descend into ordinary passion or lose their mindfulness, because it is very easy to do that. So they may say mantras, or scratch or tap one another with their fingernails lightly to remind one another to maintain wakefulness. One of the reasons his virtuosity is so important is that as they begin to meditate on emptiness, the physical interaction must be very subtle and delicate in order not to distract her from her meditation on emptiness. At this point they both apply their understanding of emptiness to the experiences that they are undergoing. They start to deconstruct the bliss, the relationship, and the object and source of the pleasure as empty.

Tricycle: *How would this apply to charges of sexual abuse against teachers involved with their students?*

Shaw: I think it is very important that people become knowledgeable about tantric relationships and tantric intimacy. Once they become knowledgeable about it they will have something against which to measure any experience, any relationship they enter. At any stage they can evaluate, is this proceeding for mutual benefit? Is this proceeding for the sake of the enlightenment of both persons involved and for the sake of the enlightenment of all sentient beings? People can also apply this knowledge to the actions of Buddhist teachers. For example, one may hear about a teacher who verbally manipulated or emotionally coerced a woman to have sexual relations with him, was dishonest in his dealings with her, and displayed no yogic mastery in their relationship. This behavior can easily be seen to bear no resemblance to tantric practice.

Tricycle: *What if two people who have not had any tantric initiations, which must be given by a lama or a teacher, want to practice tantric exercises anyway?*

Shaw: This kind of information can be put to use by people who are not interested in gaining enlightenment but are interested in taking some of these methods from the East in order to enhance their sex life. Motivation is the dividing line between tantric practice and its more secular adaptations. I have a feeling that the people you might be describing would want to become a little knowledgeable about tantra to add new dimensions to their sex life.

Tricycle: *So is this practice only available to lay Buddhists?*

Shaw: It is available to those who have not taken monastic ordination. In the Nyingma school of Tibetan Buddhism, for example, there are two routes one can take: one is *thab-lam*, the perfection stage practice with a yogic partner, and the other is *dro-lam*, the perfection stage practice without a partner for fully ordained monastics who do not want to give up their ordination or who are not ready to do this kind of practice. In many cases, in Tibet, the people who do not do tantric practice with a partner refrain because they feel they are not yet advanced enough. It is not that they believe that the monastic path is inherently superior.

Tricycle: *Why do you think these practices have been so misinterpreted in the West?*

Shaw: We in the West are at a very early stage of assimilation of Buddhism. We are very much where seventh-century Tibet was when the Buddhist texts started streaming over from India. In India, these texts and teachings emerged slowly over hundreds of years, but when Indian Buddhism went to Tibet, all of the texts came together on the back of a yak, so they say. There was a lot of discussion, and confusion, because so many texts came all at once. Now in the West we also have received a wide variety of teachings, and we have to sift through them. There are so many Buddhist texts that it takes time for the ones that are pertinent to any given issue to be translated.

Tricycle: *Do you find that any of these texts were suppressed because they were translated by men?*

Shaw: In Tibet, for example, the tantric texts that I am talking about were expurgated in their canonical versions. In the earlier versions we find all the references to women and interactions between men and women intact. I find that in later canonical versions such references began to be expurgated because the translators increasingly were monks, so they had a vested interest in removing the references to women, the purity and glories of female bodies, and the grandeur of sexuality and sensuality in the religious context. Also in China these texts were expurgated

77

and references to women were changed to references to men. I find that as these texts are translated into English, male translators typically render generic, ambiguous, and plural constructions into masculine terms and pronouns, and in the Sanskrit original where gender is specifically marked, in many cases I have found that what ends up in our English translations as a male reference was originally a female reference.

Tricycle: *So this is a profound breakthrough. You are offering an English-speaking reader much more than just a "translation."*

Shaw: It is a paradigm shift because I have been working with different hermeneutical principles, a different approach to translation and interpretation. The philosophy that has held sway is that all religious texts are written by men, about men, and for men. I did not share that presupposition, particularly when I was looking at tantric texts that are clearly talking about something that is practiced by both men and women. I did not therefore assume that the texts contained only male experiences, insights, and points of view, and that revolutionized the way that I read the texts. Even though I had been trained for many years in the androcentric method of reading, I had a series of breakthroughs as I realized that the texts were talking about women, women's experiences, embodiments, and sexuality from a female point of view, and religious practice from a female perspective.

Tricycle: *Where will this new information take us?*

Shaw: Academically it is going to open up a new field of research. Much more attention will be turned toward the origins of tantric Buddhism, the female founders of the movement, and the treatment of gender in tantric texts. I have worked with a certain number of texts, but a great deal of work remains to be done. Now that this door is open I am assuming a lot of researchers will take up this area of study.

Tricycle: *How might this affect Buddhist practice in the West?*

Shaw: People will no longer be able to use ignorance of the tantric teachings as an excuse for sloppy relationships and interactions. They can't just say, Well, if it is a Buddhist teacher and it is sex, it must be tantra. I've had conversations with some teachers who have been accused of engaging in exploitative sexuality, and found in many cases that early in our conversation they might be cutesy and throw the word *tantra* about in a very offhand but suggestive way, hoping that I would let the topic drop and let that explain whatever it was that they had done. But as I started to ask them about specific texts and teachings and they realized that I was knowledgeable about the sources, they dropped all pretense of practicing tantra and immediately would confess that of course they had no knowledge of tantra and were not practicing Buddhist tantra. Teachers like these will no longer be shielded by the label of tantra, because we will know what this label means.

Tricycle: *There will be a standard.*

Shaw: Yes. Particularly because the classical tantric works that I have looked at—the *Cakrasamvara*, the *Hevajra*, and to a lesser extent the *Guhysamaja*, are the major Tantras that are used in Tibet. I also consulted the *Candamaharoshana*, which was one of the major texts in India and is presently one of the major Tantras used in Nepal. So I have consulted the major sources. I have not gone to minor, obscure sources.

Tricycle: *Does your work have new implications for feminism within Buddhism?*

Shaw: One of the things people can gain from my work is the realization that the problems we are facing are not new. We are not uniquely facing the challenge of creating a relationship, of pursuing enlightenment in the context of an intimate relationship. We are not the first ones to discover that men and women need to enter into right relationship with one another in order to gain enlightenment. It is not really viable for everyone to separate themselves out and isolate themselves in a monastery. That can create very problematic relationships between the feminine and the masculine. Avoidance itself can become an obstacle to enlightenment. We in the West are not the first to discover this, nor are we uniquely equipped to face this challenge. Many people claim that American women are bringing a new feminist perspective to Buddhism. I disagree with that. We may have done some Buddhist practice, obtained a college education, and have a feminist perspective, but this does not mean that we have a more privileged perspective on femaleness than the many women who practiced before us. Those women practiced for many years; many of them were highly educated, and in addition to that, many of them were enlightened. They knew a great deal. We can learn from them. It is not just that we have something to teach Buddhism. Buddhism has a lot to teach us. It is somewhat contemptuous toward the Buddhist women of the past to suggest that we automatically know more than they. If they were enlightened, then they knew things that we are still trying to discover.

Tricycle: *But we sense that the daily context for them was one of sexist restraints.*

Shaw: In the literature I have studied there were many women who were not dominated by men and who manifested complete freedom in their lifestyles. They were not dependent on men for their self-esteem or growth or for spiritual teaching. The women taught each other, and they taught men. They rebuked men, openly condescended toward men, and in no way conceded any superiority or preeminence to men. They were indomitable women.

Tricycle: *Why do you think that got lost?*

Shaw: It did not get lost. That has survived as a strand of the living tradition in Tibet and Nepal. The reason that in the West we have not recognized that aspect of the tradition is that the first thing we encountered was the most visible and impressive representatives of that culture, which are the monastic universities. These universities have existed in a relationship of competition with the yogic, non-celibate strand. Slowly these elements are becoming more visible to us. There were many, many enlightened women and female teachers in Tibet at the time of the Chinese takeover. Some of the people living today know their names and have their texts. They are often handwritten manuscripts that are kept by their students. I have confirmed the existence of some of their works, but their guardians would not show them to me, in part because the manuscripts contain the precious records of the visions and enlightenment of these women. Many of the women were self-styled, unconventional yoginis. Some of them went naked, some wore rags, some lived by the side of the road. Many of them traveled on perpetual pilgrimage. There was one woman in Tibet named A-tag Lhamo, which means Divine Tiger Woman. She united with many men. When she died, her father, who was a lama, said that every man who had united with her, who had sexual union with her, would never have a lower rebirth after that. They would either be reborn in a heaven realm or a pure land, because of the power of the blessing of uniting with her. That is just one example. Someone should collect these stories. Many are written in texts that are difficult to read. You have to have expertise in the language and you have to pry them away from their students. You have to prove yourself to be worthy to read them because it takes more than a scholar to translate a text which is talking about highly rarefied spiritual experiences. That is why their guardians rightfully will not entrust the texts to just anyone.

Tricycle: *What did you have to do to gain access to the primary materials for your book?*

Shaw: I had to gain the cooperation and help of a large number of yoginis and yogis. They were very conscious that by teaching me they were playing a role in the transmission of these teachings to the West. Therefore, one of the things that they were very concerned about, I could tell, was my motivation. They would question me at some length about what I was doing and why I was doing it, and they would question me about my dreams. In some cases they would not teach me until they had received a sign from the dakinis. That sign would usually be something in the sky, because the dakinis are sky dancers. Dakinis are both women and female spirits of exalted spiritual attainment and freedom. The teachers would look at the sky for unusual cloud formations or a rainbow or something out of the ordinary. When they received that confirmation, they would work with me while continuing to watch for signs. They felt that it was significant that I was a woman. These teachings have been guarded by female spirits through the centuries, and the teachers felt it was natural that the dakinis would choose to reveal the teachings to a woman at this time. So they felt that I had been sent or chosen by the dakinis to translate these teachings in the West. They believed that these teachings could not be revealed without the cooperation and blessings of the dakinis. That is not to say that there is anything special about the transmitter, the method that was chosen to transmit them. What is special is the transmission.

Reprinted from *Tricycle*, TRI Box 3000, Denville, NJ 07834, 1-800-950-7008. Subscription: $20/yearly.

THE CARAVAN OF SUMMER

by PETER LAMBORN WILSON

a paper read at the annual meeting of

THE MUHYIDDIN IBN 'ARABI SOCIETY

Something of the real difference between pilgrim and tourist can be detected by comparing their effects on the places they visit. Changes in a place—a city, a shrine, a forest—may be subtle, but at least they can be observed. The state of the *soul* may be a matter of conjecture, but perhaps we can say something about the state of the *social*.

Pilgrimage sites like Mecca may serve as great bazaars for trade and they may even serve as centers of production (like the silk industry of Benares)—but their primary "product" is *baraka* or *mana*. These words (one Arabic, one Polynesian) are usually translated as "blessing," but they also carry a freight of other meanings.

The wandering dervish who sleeps at a shrine in order to dream of a dead saint (one of the "People of the Tombs") seeks initiation or advancement on the spiritual path; a mother who brings a sick child to Lourdes seeks healing; a childless woman in Morocco hopes the *Marabout* will make her fertile if she ties a rag to the old tree growing out of the grave; the traveler to Mecca yearns for the very center of the Faith, and as the caravans come within sight of the Holy City the *hajji* calls out, *"Labaika Allahumma!"*—"I am *here*, O Lord!"

All these motives are summed up by the word *baraka*, which sometimes seems to be a palpable substance, measurable in terms of increased charisma or "luck." The shrine *produces* baraka. And the pilgrim takes it away. But blessing is a product of the Imagination—and thus no matter how many pilgrims take it away, there's always more.

In fact, the more they *take*, the more blessing the shrine can produce (because a popular shrine *grows* with every answered prayer.) To say that baraka is "imaginal" is not to call it "unreal." It's real enough to those who feel it. But spiritual goods do not follow the rules of supply and demand like material goods. The more demand for spiritual goods, the more supply. The production of baraka is *infinite*.

By contrast, the tourist desires not baraka but *cultural difference*. The tourist *consumes* difference. But the production of cultural difference is not infinite. It is not "merely" imaginal. It is rooted in languages, landscape, architecture, custom, taste, smell. It is very physical. The more it is used up or taken away, the less remains. The social can produce just so much "meaning," so much difference. Once it's gone, it's gone.

THE MODEST GOAL OF THIS ESSAY is to address the *individual traveler* who has decided to resist tourism. Even though we may find it impossible in the end to "purify" ourselves and our travel from every last taint and trace of tourism, we still feel that improvement may be possible.

Not only do we disdain tourism for its vulgarity and its injustice, and therefore wish to avoid any contamination (conscious or unconscious) by its viral virulency—we also wish to understand travel as an act of *reciprocity* rather than alienation. In other words, we don't wish merely to avoid the negativities of tourism, but even more to achieve *positive travel,* which we envision as a productive and mutually enhancing relation between self and other, guest and host—a form of *cross-cultural synergy* in which the whole exceeds the sum of parts.

We'd like to know if travel can be carried out according to a secret economy of baraka, whereby not only the shrine but also the pilgrims themselves have "blessings" to bestow.

Before the Age of the Commodity, we know, there was an Age of the Gift, of reciprocity, of giving and receiving. We learned this from the tales of certain travelers, who found remnants of the world of the Gift among certain tribes, in the form of potlach or ritual exchange, and recorded their observations of such strange practices.

Not long ago there still existed a custom among South Sea islanders of traveling vast distances by outrigger canoe, without compass or sextant, in order to exchange valuable and useless presents (ceremonial art-objects rich in *mana)* from island to island in a complex pattern of overlapping reciprocities.

We suspect that even though travel in the modern world seems to have been taken over by the Commodity—even though the networks of convivial reciprocity *seem* to have vanished from the map—even though tourism *seems* to have triumphed—even so—we continue to suspect that other pathways still persist, other tracks, unofficial, not noted on the map, perhaps even "secret"—pathways still linked to the possibility of an economy of the Gift, smugglers' routes for free spirits, known only to the geomantic guerrillas of the art of travel.

As a matter of fact, we don't just "suspect" it. We *know* it. We know there exists an art of travel.

PERHAPS THE GREATEST AND SUBTLEST practitioners of the art of travel were the Sufis, the mystics of Islam. Before the age of passports, immunizations, airlines and other impediments to free travel, the Sufis wandered footloose in a world where borders tended to be more permeable than nowadays, thanks to the transnationalism of Islam and the cultural unity of *Dar al-Islam,* the Islamic world.

The great medieval Moslem travelers, like Ibn Battuta and Naser Khusraw, have left accounts of vast journeys—Persia to Egypt, or even Morocco to China—which never set foot outside a landscape of deserts, camels, caravanserais, bazaars, and piety. *Someone* always spoke Arabic, however badly, and Islamic culture permeated the remotest backwaters, however superficially. Reading the tales of Sinbad the sailor (from the *1001 Nights)* gives us the impression of a world where even the terra incognita was still—despite all marvels and oddities—somehow familiar, somehow *Islamic.* Within this unity, which was not yet a uniformity, the Sufis formed a special class of travelers. Not warriors, not merchants, and not quite ordinary pilgrims either, the dervishes represent a *spiritualization of pure nomadism.*

According to the Koran, God's Wide Earth and everything in it are "sacred," not only as divine creations, but also because the material world is full of "waymarks," or signs of divine reality. Moreover, Islam itself is born between two journeys, Mohammad's *hijra* or "flight" from Mecca to Medina, and his *hajj,* or return voyage. The hajj is the movement toward the origin and center for every Moslem even today, and the annual Pilgrimage has played a vital role, not just in the religious unity of Islam, but also in its cultural unity.

Mohammad himself exemplifies every kind of travel in Islam: his youth with the Meccan caravans of Summer and Winter, as a merchant; his campaigns as a warrior; his triumph as a humble pilgrim. Although an urban leader, he is also the prophet of the Bedouin and himself a kind of nomad, a "sojourner"—an "orphan." From this perspective travel can almost be seen as a *sacrament*. Every religion sanctifies travel to some degree, but Islam is virtually unimaginable without it.

The Prophet said, "Seek knowledge, even as far as China." From the beginning, Islam lifts travel above all "mundane" utilitarianism and gives it an epistemological or even gnostic dimension. "The jewel that never leaves the mine is never polished," says the Sufi poet Saadi. To "educate" is to "lead outside," to give the pupil a perspective beyond parochiality and mere subjectivity.

Some Sufis may have done all their traveling in the Imaginal World of archetypal dreams and visions, but vast numbers of them took the Prophet's exhortations quite literally. Even today dervishes wander over the entire Islamic world—but as late as the 19th century they wandered in veritable hordes, hundreds or even thousands at a time, and covered vast distances. All in search of knowledge.

UNOFFICIALLY, THERE EXISTED TWO BASIC TYPES of wandering Sufi: the "gentleman-scholar" type, and the mendicant dervish. The former category includes Ibn Battuta (who collected Sufi initiations the way some occidental gentlemen once collected Masonic degrees), and—on a much more serious level—the "Greatest Shaykh" Ibn Arabi, who meandered slowly through the 13th century from his native Spain, across North Africa, through Egypt to Mecca, and finally to Damascus.

Ibn Arabi actually left accounts of his search for saints and adventures on the road, which could be pieced together from his voluminous writings to form a kind of *rihla* or "travel text" (a recognized genre of Islamic literature) or autobiography. Ordinary scholars traveled in search of rare texts on theology or jurisprudence, but Ibn Arabi sought only the highest secrets of esotericism and the loftiest "openings" into the world of divine illumination; for him every "journey to the outer horizons" was also a "journey to the inner horizons" of spiritual psychology and gnosis.

On the visions he experienced in Mecca alone, he wrote a 12-volume work (*The Meccan Revelations*), and he has also left us precious sketches of hundreds of his contemporaries, from the greatest philosophers of the age to humble dervishes and "madmen," anonymous women saints and "Hidden Masters." Ibn Arabi enjoyed a special relation with Khezr, the immortal and unknown prophet, the "Green Man," who sometimes appears to wandering Sufis in distress, to rescue them from the desert, or to initiate them. Khezr, in a sense, can be called the patron saint of the traveling dervishes—and the prototype. (He first appears in the Koran as a mysterious wanderer and companion of Moses in the desert.)

Christianity once included a few orders of wandering mendicants (in fact, St. Francis organized one after meeting with dervishes in the Holy Land, who may have bestowed upon him a "cloak of initiation"—the famous patchwork robe he was wearing when he returned to Italy—but Islam spawned dozens, perhaps hundreds of such orders.

As Sufism crystallized from the loose spontaneity of early days to an institution with rules and grades, "travel for knowledge" was also regularized and organized. Elaborate handbooks of duties for dervishes were produced which included methods for turning travel into a very specific form of meditation. The whole Sufi "path" itself was symbolized in terms of *intentional travel*.

In some cases itineraries were fixed (e.g., the Hajj); others involved waiting for "signs" to appear, coincidences, intuitions, "adventures" such as those which inspired the travels of the Arthurian knights. Some orders limited the time spent in any one place to 40 days; others made a rule of never sleeping twice in the same place. The strict orders, such as the Naqshbandis, turned travel into a kind of full-time choreography, in which every movement was pre-ordained and designed to *enhance consciousness*.

By contrast, the more heterodox orders (such as the Qalandars) adopted a "rule" of total spontaneity and abandon—"permanent unemployment" as one of them called it—an insouciance of bohemian proportions—a "dropping-out" at once both scandalous and completely traditional. Colorfully dressed, carrying their begging bowls, axes, and standards, addicted to music and dance, carefree and cheerful (sometimes to the point of "blameworthiness"!), orders such as the Nematollahis of 19th century Persia grew to proportions that alarmed both sultans and theologians—many dervishes were executed for "heresy." Today the true Qalandars survive mostly in India, where their lapses from orthodoxy include a fondness for hemp and a sincere hatred of work. Some are charlatans, some are simple bums, but a surprising number of them seem to be people of *attainment* . . . how can I put it? . . . people of self-realization, marked by a distinct aura of grace, or baraka.

ALL THE DIFFERENT TYPES OF SUFI TRAVEL we've described are united by certain shared vital structural forces. One such force might be called a "magical" worldview, a sense of life that rejects the "merely" random for a reality of signs and wonders, of meaningful coincidences and "unveilings." As anyone who's ever tried it will testify, intentional travel *immediately* opens one up to this "magical" influence.

A psychologist might explain this phenomenon (either with awe or with reductionist disdain) as "subjective"; while the pious believer would take it quite literally. From the Sufi point of view neither interpretation rules out the other, nor suffices in itself, to explain away the marvels of the Path. In Sufism, the "objective" and the "subjective" are not considered opposites, but complements. From the point of view of the two-dimensional thinker (whether scientific or religious) such paradoxology smacks of the forbidden.

Another force underlying all forms of intentional travel can be described by the Arabic word *adab*. On one level adab simply means "good manners," and in the case of travel, these manners are based on the ancient customs of desert nomads, for whom both wandering and hospitality are sacred acts. In this sense, the dervish shares both the privileges and the responsibilities of the *guest*.

Bedouin hospitality is a clear survival of the primordial economy of the Gift—a relation of reciprocity. The wanderer must be taken in (the dervish must be fed)—but thereby the wanderer assumes a role prescribed by ancient custom—and must give back something to the host. For the Bedouin, this relation is almost a form of clientage—the breaking of bread and sharing of salt constitutes a sort of kinship. Gratitude is not a sufficient response to such generosity. The traveler must consent to a temporary adoption—anything less would offend against adab.

Islamic society retains at least a sentimental attachment to these rules, and thus creates a special niche for the dervish, that of the full-time guest. The dervish returns the gifts of society with the gift of baraka. In ordinary pilgrimage, the traveler receives baraka *from* a place, but the dervish reverses the flow and brings baraka *to* a place. The Sufi may think of himself (or herself) as a permanent pilgrim—but to the ordinary stay-at-home people of the mundane world, the Sufi is a kind of perambulatory shrine.

Now tourism in its very structure breaks the reciprocity of host and guest. In English, a "host" may have either guests—or parasites. The tourist is a parasite—for no amount of money can pay for hospitality. The

87

true traveler is a *guest* and thus serves a very real function, even today, in societies where the ideals of hospitality have not yet faded from the "collective mentality." To be a host, in such societies, is a *meritorious act.* Therefore, to be a guest is also to *give merit.*

The modern traveler who grasps the simple spirit of this relation will be forgiven many lapses in the intricate ritual of adab (how many cups of coffee? Where to put one's feet? How to be entertaining? How to show gratitude? etc.) peculiar to a specific culture. And if one bothers to master a few of the traditional forms of adab, and to deploy them with heartfelt sincerity, then both guest and host will gain more than they put into the relation—and this *more* is the unmistakable sign of the presence of the Gift.

Another level of meaning of the word adab connects it with *culture* (since culture can be seen as the sum of all manners and customs); in modern usage the Department of "Arts and Letters" at a university would be called *Adabiyyat.* To have adab in this sense is to be "polished" (like that well-traveled gem)—but this has nothing necessarily to do with "fine arts" or literacy or being a city-slicker, or even being "cultured." It is a matter of the "heart."

"Adab" is sometimes given as a one-word definition of Sufism. But insincere manners (*ta'arof* in Persian) and insincere culture alike are shunned by the Sufi—"There is no *ta'arof* in *Tassawuf* [Sufism]," as the dervishes say; "*Darvishi*" is an adjectival synonym for informality, the laid-back quality of the people of the Heart—and for *spontaneous adab,* so to speak. The true guest and host never make an obvious effort to fulfill the "rules" of reciprocity—they may follow the ritual scrupulously, or they may bend the forms creatively, but in either case, they will give their actions a depth of sincerity that manifests as natural grace. Adab is a kind of *love.*

A COMPLEMENT OF THIS "TECHNIQUE" (OR "ZEN") of human relations can be found in the Sufi manner of relating to the world in general. The "mundane" world—of social deceit and negativity, of usurious emotions, inauthentic consciousness (*"mauvaise conscience"*), boorishness, ill-will, inattention, blind reaction, false spectacle, empty discourse, etc. etc.— all this no longer holds any interest for the traveling dervish. But those who say that the dervish has abandoned "this world"—"God's Wide Earth"—would be mistaken.

The dervish is not a Gnostic Dualist who hates the *biosphere* (which certainly includes the imagination and the emotions, as well as "matter" itself.) The early Moslem ascetics certainly closed themselves off from everything. When Rabiah, the woman saint of Basra, was urged to come out of her house and "witness the wonders of God's creation," she replied, "Come *into* the house and see them," i.e., come into the heart of contemplation of the oneness which is above the manyness of reality. "*Contraction*" and "*Expansion*" are both Sufi terms for spiritual states. Rabiah was manifesting Contraction: a kind of sacred melancholia which has been metaphorized as the "Caravan of Winter," of return to Mecca (the center, the heart), of interiority, and of ascesis or self-denial. She was not a world-hating Dualist, nor even a moralistic flesh-hating puritan. She was simply manifesting a certain specific kind of grace.

The wandering dervish, however, manifests a state more typical of Islam in its most exuberant energies. He indeed seeks Expansion, spiritual joy based on the sheer multiplicity of the divine generosity in material creation. (Ibn Arabi has an amusing "proof" that *this* world is the *best* world—for, if it were *not*, then God would be ungenerous—which is absurd. Q.E.D.) In order to appreciate the multiple waymarks of the Wide Earth precisely as the unfolding of this generosity, the Sufi cultivates what might be called the *theophanic gaze*:—the opening of the "Eye of the Heart" to the experience of certain places, objects, people, events as *locations of the "shining-through"* of divine Light.

The dervish travels, so to speak, both in the material world, and in the "World of Imagination" simultaneously. But for the eye of the heart, these worlds interpenetrate at certain points. One might say that they mutually reveal or "unveil" each other. Ultimately, they are "one"—and only our state of tranced inattention, our mundane consciousness, prevents us from experiencing this "deep" identity at every moment. The purpose of intentional travel, with its "adventures" and its uprooting of habits, is to shake loose the dervish from all the trance-effects of ordinariness. Travel, in other words, is meant to induce a certain state of consciousness or "spiritual state"—that of Expansion.

For the wanderer, each person one meets might act as an "angel," each shrine one visits may unlock some initiatic dream, each experience of Nature may vibrate with the presence of some "spirit of place." Indeed, even the mundane and ordinary may suddenly be seen as numinous (as in the great travel haiku of the Japanese Zen poet Basho)—a face in the crowd at a railway station, crows on telephone wires, sunlight in a puddle. . . .Obviously one doesn't *need* to travel to experience this state. But travel can be used—that is, an art of travel can be acquired—to maximize the chances for attaining such a state. It is a *moving meditation*, like the Taoist martial arts.

The *Caravan of Summer* moved outward, out of Mecca, to the rich trading lands of Syria and Yemen. Likewise, the dervish is "moving out" (it's always "moving day"), heading forth, taking off, on "perpetual holiday" as one poet expressed it, with an open Heart, and attentive eye (and other senses), and a yearning for Meaning, a thirst for knowledge. One must remain *alert*, since anything might suddenly unveil itself as a *sign*. This sounds like a kind of "paranoia"—although "metanoia" might be a better term—and indeed one finds "madmen" amongst the dervishes, "attracted ones," overpowered by divine influxions, lost in the Light. In the Orient the insane are often cared for and admired as helpless saints, because "mental illness" may sometimes appear as a symptom of too much holiness rather than too little "reason." Hemp's popularity amongst the dervishes can be attributed to its power to induce a kind of intuitive attentiveness which constitutes a controllable insanity—herbal metanoia. But travel in itself can intoxicate the heart with the beauty of theophanic presence. It's a question of *practice*—the polishing of the jewel—removal of moss from the rolling stone.

IN THE OLD DAYS (WHICH ARE STILL GOING ON in some remote parts of the East), Islam thought of itself as a whole world, a wide world, a space with great latitude within which Islam embraced the whole of society and nature. This latitude appeared on the social level as *tolerance*. There was room enough, even for such marginal groups as mad wandering dervishes. Sufism itself—or at least its austere orthodox and "sober" aspect—occupied a central position in the cultural discourse. "Everyone" understood intentional travel by analogy with the Hajj—everyone *understood* the dervishes, even if they disapproved.

Nowadays however, Islam views itself as a partial world, surrounded by unbelief and hostility, and suffering internal ruptures of every sort. Since the 19th century Islam has lost its global consciousness and sense of its own wideness and completeness. No longer therefore, can Islam easily find a place for every marginalized individual and group within a pattern of tolerance and social order. The dervishes now appear as an *intolerable difference* in society. Every Moslem must now be the same, united against all outsiders, and struck from the same prototype. Of course, Moslems have always "imitated" the Prophet and viewed his image as the norm—and this has acted as a powerful unifying force for style and substance within Dar al-Islam. But "nowadays" the puritans and re-formers have forgotten that this "imitation" was not directed only at an early-medieval Meccan merchant named Mohammad, but also at the *insan al-kamil* (the "Perfect Man" or "Universal Human"), an ideal of *inclusion* rather than *exclusion,* an ideal of *integral culture,* not an attitude of purity in peril, not xenophobia disguised as piety, not totalitarianism, not reaction.

The dervish is persecuted nowadays in most of the Islamic world. Puritanism always embraces the most atrocious aspects of modernism in its crusade to strip the Faith of "medieval accretions" such as popular Sufism. And surely the way of the wandering dervish cannot thrive in a world of airplanes and oil-wells, of nationalist/chauvinist hostilities (and thus of impenetrable *borders*), and of a puritanism which suspects all difference as a threat.

This puritanism has triumphed not only in the East, but rather clos-er to home as well. It is seen in the "time discipline" of modern too-Late-Capitalism, and in the porous rigidity of consumerist hyper-conformity, as well as in the bigoted reaction and sex-hysteria of the "Christian Right." Where in all this can we find room for the poetic (and parasitic!) life of *Aimless Wandering*—the life of Chuang Tzu (who coined this slogan) and his Taoist progeny—the life of Saint Francis and his shoeless devotees—the life of (for example) Nur Ali Shah Isfahani, a 19th century Sufi poet who was executed in Iran for the awful heresy of mean-dering-dervishism?

HERE IS THE flip SIDE OF THE "PROBLEM OF TOURISM": the problem of the *disappearance of "aimless wandering."* Possibly the two are directly relat-ed, so that the more tourism becomes possible, the more dervishism becomes impossible. In fact, we might well ask if this little essay on the delightful life of the dervish possesses the least bit of relevance for the contemporary world. Can this knowledge help us to *overcome* tourism, even within our own consciousness and life? Or is it merely an exercise in nostalgia for lost possibilities—a futile indulgence in romanticism?

Well, yes and no. Sure, I confess I'm hopelessly romantic about the *form* of the dervish life, to the extent that for a while I turned my back on the mundane world and followed it myself. Because of course, it hasn't really disappeared. Decadent, yes—but not gone forever. What little I know about travel I learned in those few years—I owe a debt to "medi-eval accretions" I can never pay—and I'll never regret my "escapism" for a single moment. *But*—I don't consider the *form* of dervishism to be the answer to the "problem of tourism." The *form* has lost most of is efficacy. There's no point in trying to "preserve" it (as if it were a pickle, or a lab specimen)—there's nothing quite so pathetic as mere "survival."

But: beneath the charming outer forms of dervishism lies the conceptual matrix, so to speak, which we've called *intentional travel*. On this point we should suffer no embarrassment about "nostalgia." We have asked ourselves whether or not we *desire* a means to discover the art of travel, whether we *want and will* to overcome "the inner tourist," the false consciousness which screens us from the experience of the Wide World's waymarks. The way of the dervish (or of the Taoist, the Franciscan, etc.) interests us—finally—only to the extent that it can provide us with a key—not *the* key, perhaps—but . . . a key. And of course—it does.

*PETER LAMBORN WILSON is the author **Sacred Drift** and several books and studies exploring the role of hersey and mysticism in Islam. Wilson spent 10 years wandering in the Middle East. He now wanders the streets of New York City.*

The Muhyiddin Ibn 'Arabi Society publishes an annual journal as well as monographs on the teachings of Ibn 'Arabi (thirteenth century). Annual dues are $50. For more information, contact the Society at P.O. Box 425988, San Francisco, CA 94142-5988. Phone (415) 653-2201.

PITY AND TERROR IN WACO

by JAMES S. GORDON

from COMMON BOUNDARY

The end of each century has been a time when many hope for profound change. The approach of the third millennium, the year 2001, is producing far more intense unease and passionate longings. Astrologers say the Piscean is yielding to the Aquarian Age; the Mayan and Hopi calendars are coming to an end. The planet continues to be fractured by ideology and torn apart by nationalistic violence and sectarianism. AIDS attacks our vulnerable collective biology, and environmental degradation threatens the air we breathe and the ground we stand on. Many of us feel the axis shifting in our bones.

In this climate of fearfulness and expectation, we may yearn for a change that will sweep away the old, purify the contaminated, and prepare the way for the new. Some—like David Koresh, the Branch Davidian leader who perished in fire with his followers one year ago—believe they have special knowledge of this change. It is clear to them what is happening and why, how the old will be obliterated and the new born. A few proclaim the message; many others are drawn to these "prophets" and their articulation of collective, if inchoate, longings.

For some leaders and followers, the New Testament's Book of Revelations supplies both map and script for the coming calamitous times. It is proclaimed there that a battle between good and evil is imminent;

worldwide destruction will be the prelude to the 1,000-year reign of Christ, the Son of the House of David; out of this global destruction and under the rule of the returned Christ, renewal will come through a transformed "saving remnant."

As a young man David Koresh became convinced that he was the Christ who would rule and redeem. The Branch Davidians, who looked to him as a leader and savior, came to believe that they were the saving remnant. In the coming years, it is likely that more self-proclaimed sons of this house will appear and that many more will lend their lives to world-saving missions. It is entirely possible, too, that other messiahs will threaten to use force to convert or destroy unbelievers or to precipitate the apocalypse for which they long.

In the aftermath of the Branch Davidians' fiery end, everyone had an opinion about what happened and why. Ninety-three percent of those polled by *USA Today* said that Koresh was "responsible for the outcome," and 73 percent agreed that the FBI acted properly in trying to flush the group out with tear gas. Meanwhile, some politicians accepted and others evaded responsibility, and all called for investigations.

A year later, the Bureau of Alcohol, Tobacco, and firearms (ATF) has been condemned for the planning and execution of its original raid, the FBI has been largely exonerated for the assault that precipitated the deaths of 81 Branch Davidians, and, most recently, 11 Davidians have been acquitted of conspiring to murder the four ATF agents who died in the raid. Almost no one, however, seems to care who the Davidians were, what motivated them, or how the tragedy came about.

This lack of interest is terribly short-sighted. In some ways it may be as responsible for the tragedy as Koresh himself. Our ignorance, which was directly responsible for our government's assaults, also obscures the causes that produced Koresh and the Davidians. If we don't understand their motives and our own reactions to them, more people—members of as-yet-anonymous apocalyptic groups that will inevitably make themselves known—may die. Equally important, we will continue our failure to understand the tragedy as a symptom of the far larger historical and social diseases that need addressing.

We must begin by revising the emotionally convenient but inaccurate belief that these people are different from us. They are not. The men and women who joined this group and other "new religions"—Jim Jones's People's Temple, Sun Myung Moon's Unification Church, the International Society for Krishna Consciousness, or Bhagwan Shree Rajneesh's commune—are not brainless or brainwashed. If they are "faceless," as one *Washington Post* article asserted, it is only because we haven't taken the trouble to look closely at them.

In fact, they are ordinary people who have been troubled and hurt by the world. They are looking for a better, more loving way to live; they are seeking a sureness amid the world's uncertainty. They are searching for a way to do God's will—and for someone to tell them what that is. Certainly, some of them have serious psychiatric disorders; the vast majority, however, do not. (Some of my colleagues, including Mark Galanter, a New York University psychiatrist, have studied this carefully.) In groups like the Davidians they find a powerfully convincing leader, a loving spiritual family, and a supportive community in which each aspect of life is sanctified by its meaning and importance to a world-saving mission.

Nor is it useful to dismiss the leaders of these groups as insane or psychopathic. Demonizing and pathologizing them tends to put them beyond comprehension. And when push comes to shove, as it did in Waco, it makes us despair of useful communication with them. They are as comprehensible as any human beings and, indeed, share some common characteristics. Their individual histories—Jim Jones, Bhagwan Shree Rajneesh, and Swami Prabhupada, founder of the International Society for Krishna Consciousness, come to mind—often reveal a sense of specialness alongside feelings of separateness and alienation, attractiveness coupled with unhappiness and anger. As children, they often exercised a striking influence over their peers. As adolescents, they may have challenged the accepted order of church and family. Later, in a time of crisis, they probably had one or more powerful, boundary-shattering, mystical experiences. The conviction that these experiences yielded special power and knowledge justifies their call to disciples.

Those leaders who become fanatical are likely to have taken their experience too literally. What happened to them is not simply similar to what Christ and Krishna experienced; each believes he *is* the new Christ or Krishna. This misplaced concreteness—to borrow 19th-century critic John Ruskin's phrase—and overblown pride are pistons in an engine that demands obedience and obliterates irony and paradox. Ultimately, it may seem to require annihilation of those who challenge the leaders or the self-induced destruction of the group that can no longer sustain their grandiosity against disbelief and opposition.

Close observation reveals that the relationship between these leaders and their followers is a dance as well as a dictatorship. Although some may be deceived on entering—the Unification Church was famous for seductions—group members are not restrained against their will. Those who stay (only a small fraction of those who sample the group's experience) do so because the belief system is persuasive and membership seems rewarding.

As time goes on, however, followers may deny what they don't want to see. Little by little, they rationalize actions that before joining would have been unacceptable; they follow orders that once would have seemed absurd. In the context of others' unquestioning assent, they come to believe that their leader behaves in a particular way because he knows better than they do. They begin not to trust or rely on their own judgments. Each contradiction is seen as a koan to be pondered; every insult is a pain that may yield gain. The followers become ridiculous in their mindless obedience. The leader in turn encourages and profits from this unquestioning adulation. He becomes inflated with his own importance and cynical about those who lend it to him.

This process is a gradual one, often invisible to those in the group who do not want to believe it is happening. The paranoia of the last days is usually only a faint note in the first chords of the leader's song and the group's chorus. Jim Jones, who killed children and African Americans, originally was a champion of their human and civil rights. Bhagwan Shree Rajneesh, who established a community of near-total control in Oregon, attracted his followers because he was seen as the ultimate anarchic rebel.

Little by little, as the leader's power grows greater and the followers' adherence stronger, his unresolved conflicts come to be writ large in the group's style and structure. His need to be special and singular is echoed in their belief that they have a corner on the truth. His—unacknowledged—cruelty to them may reappear as their cruelty to one another and the adults' abuse of their children. His drive to preserve his own power becomes their arrogance and contempt for outsiders. As time passes, his sense of specialness and exclusivity comes to pervade the group. Finally, his and their survival comes to depend on differentiation and isolation from "evil" outsiders, who must be either saved or destroyed.

This kind of analysis, so valuable in understanding and predicting a group's behavior, was apparently absent from the deliberations of the ATF and the Justice Department. They seemed—to put it charitably—totally, if not deliberately, ignorant of apocalyptic groups. In their ignorance, they believed that threats and intimidation from an obviously superior force would produce disorganization and capitulation. While a few members did defect under this pressure, ATF's tactics created more rather than less cohesion within the Davidians. They ratified Koresh's predictions and confirmed his followers' conviction that the outside world was bent on their destruction. When such a group's ideology is apocalyptic, when calamity seems to herald the beginning of the desired end, persecution may be welcomed, even precipitated, and destruction embraced.

In an apocalyptic context, guns—*legal or illegal*—are tinder for the fires. In Waco, guns were symbols of defiance. They aroused the fears and hostility of the surrounding community and were an aggressive challenge to law enforcement. They precipitated the ATF raid and killed government officers as well as Davidians. They provoked Oregonians when Rajneesh's well-armed followers threatened to defend their ranch to the death; in Philadelphia, they precipitated the police bombing of the MOVE headquarters; and they were the instruments that kept mothers and children in the line to the Kool-Aid vat in Jonestown.

Departmental investigations and Congressional committees have tried to find out what went wrong in Waco. Although such inquiries are appropriate, they miss the point. It is not enough to affix blame or to sharpen procedures. We need to resist matching the incomprehension, intransigence, and arrogance of these groups with our own. We need to begin by making a commitment to eliminating access to the instruments of destruction—all guns and explosives—that make them a danger to others and themselves. Without arms, it is unlikely that a religious schism can be inflated to apocalyptic warfare. Most important of all, we need also to understand the world that produced the Davidians, to see that they were responding to conditions of danger, alienation, and meaninglessness in which we all live. Their desperate need for spiritual rebirth is more symptomatic than psychopathological. Their violent response is only a token of the larger violence that pervades our society.

When one of these groups—agitated by prophecy, constrained by authoritarianism, and maddened by frustrations—seems dangerous, we should act with intelligence and respect as well as firmness. We should foster communication and understanding between those within and those outside, not isolate those who challenge us. We know that friends, parents, children, lawyers, therapists, and theologians can test the opinions and question the beliefs of group members; tug at the conscience and pride of leaders; and offer everyone alternative sources of emotional support—in other words, a way out.

In Waco, the emphasis was on isolation, not contact. The FBI experts were either students of the "criminal mind" or veterans of hostage negotiations. They saw Koresh as a con man, a fanatic captor of unwilling victims. Guided by these perceptions, they advised that Koresh and his followers could only be apprehended by using overwhelming force. The strategy called for rendering the Davidians powerless, not encouraging them to use their own power to find a mutually satisfactory solution.

In Oregon, authorities resisted calls for an assault on Rajneesh's community and an on-site arrest of the group's leader. Instead, they treated Rajneesh and his group with respect and negotiated. Bloodshed was averted. In Waco, the ATF behaved as if the Davidians were incapable of intelligent or even self-interested action, and stormed their home. Months later the FBI tried to smoke them out. The result was a deadly inferno.

In ancient Greece, tragedy evoked pity and terror and ultimately produced catharsis; it offered an opportunity for individual healing and collective self-knowledge. Perhaps the flames of Waco, the unnecessary deaths of children and adults, and the arrogance and fear of David Koresh and his followers—as well as our own—will guide us to some greater wisdom.

JAMES S. GORDON, M.D., is director of the Center for Mind-Body Medicine in Washington, D.C., and a clinical professor of psychiatry at Georgetown Medical School. The author of **The Golden Guru: The Strange Journey of Bhagwan Shree Rajneesh**, *he has spent 20 years studying new religious groups and their leaders.*

Reprinted from *Common Boundary*, PO Box 445, Mt. Morris, IL 61054, 1-800-548-8737. Subscription: $22/year.

DOES A GLOBAL VILLAGE
WARRANT A GLOBAL ETHIC?

AN ANALYSIS OF *A GLOBAL ETHIIC*, THE
DECLARATION OF THE 1993 PARLIAMENT
OF WORLD RELIGIONS

by JUNE O'CONNOR

from RELIGION

The "global village" metaphor for life in this century is now commonplace. The "global village" has become a way of capturing in the shorthand of poetry the impact of modern telecommunications and travel, the reality of economic interdependencies, and the frequency of cultural and political interactions throughout the world. These facts of contemporary life have moved a notable number of religious leaders and scholars to articulate a "global ethic." Their document, entitled The Parliament of the World's Religions *Declaration Toward a Global Ethic*, has been posited as one of the enduring contributions of the 1993 Parliament of the World's Religions, at which nearly 7,000 persons gathered in Chicago, August 28-September 5, 1993.[†]

Does our global village warrant a global ethic? Assuming the word "ethic" to connote a commonly shared and fundamental value perspective rather than a detailed statement of vision, decision, and action, is such a perspective realistic to our highly conflictual and diverse world? We may indeed live in a global village, but evidence abounds that we have a difficult to impossible time living there together. Those difficulties reside in the fact that we see the very same realities in very different ways; we feel markedly differently about the very same facts and values; and we act on behalf of notably different convictions, commitments, and aspirations. Is it realistic to assert, as the drafters and supporters of this document assert, that a fundamentally shared moral attitude or value perspective already exists in the ancient religious, ethical, and spiritual traditions of the world? What is this ethic and is it worthy of our receptivity and creative engagement or is the more appropriate response, rather, creative resistance by way of critique? Furthermore, is it appropriate for the phrase "global ethic" to become as acceptable in our discourse as the phrase "global village" has become? Or will it—should it?—remain the hope of a few?

I wish to address these questions in two parts: first, by offering a summary of the declaration; and secondly, by examining the document in terms of its authorship and history, its promising and problematic features.

DECLARATION TOWARD A GLOBAL ETHIC: A SUMMARY

THE DECLARATION TOWARD A GLOBAL ETHIC takes it as a given that our world is in crisis economically, ecologically, and politically, that hundreds of millions of human beings suffer from unemployment, poverty, hunger, and the destruction of their families. Lives are burdened by social, racial, ethnic, sexual, and intergenerational conflicts and our planet's ecosystem is severely threatened. The document notes that leaders and members of religious traditions often exacerbate the world's distress, inciting aggression, fanaticism, hatred, and xenophobia that result in violent and bloody conflicts that are encouraged as justifiable. To their description of the facts, the authors respond, "We are filled with disgust." They continue,

> We condemn these blights and declare that they need not be. An **ethic** already exists within the religious teachings of the world which can counter the global distress. Of course this ethic provides no direct solution for all the immense problems of the world, but it does supply the moral foundation for a better individual and global order: a **vision** which can lead women and men away from despair, and society away from chaos (pp. 17-18).

> Given their religious and spiritual heritages, these authors sense "a special responsibility for the welfare of all humanity and care for the planet Earth. We do not consider ourselves better than other women and men," they continue, "but we trust that the ancient wisdom of our religions can point the way for the future" (p. 19).

100

By a global ethic we do not mean a global ideology or a single unified religion beyond all existing religions, and certainly not the domination of one religion over all others. By a global ethic we mean **a fundamental consensus on binding values, irrevocable standards, and personal attitudes** (p. 21).

Without a fundamental consensus, they expect chaos or dictatorship to threaten every community and individuals to despair (p. 21).

What the 1948 United Nations' Universal Declaration of Human Rights formally proclaimed on the level of rights is here affirmed and deepened from the perspective of an ethic: "...the intrinsic dignity of the human person, the inalienable freedom and equality in principle of all humans, and the necessary solidarity and interdependence of all humans with each other" (p. 20).

This means that every human being without distinction of age, sex, race, skin colour, physical or mental ability, language, religion, political view, or national or social origin possesses an inalienable and untouchable dignity. And everyone, the individual as well as the state, is therefore obliged to honour this dignity and protect it (p. 23).

Convinced that laws, prescriptions, and contractual agreements alone are insufficient to create a better global order, the drafters and supporters of this document emphasize the importance of moral insight and readiness to act justly as they spotlight the importance of personal consciousness, responsibility, and duty..

Placing the accent on the similarities rather than the differences among the world's religions, the document articulates five directives identified as unconditional ethical norms. These norms are offered not as "bonds and chains, but [as] helps and supports" (p. 23) for people looking for direction, orientation, and meaning. These directives are claimed to be discoverable in many religious and ethical traditions and are regarded as pertinent not only to individuals, but also to families, nations, races, and religions. The fundamental directive is this: **what you do not wish done to yourself, do not do to others**; or, **what you wish done to yourself, do to others**.

Four additional directives structure the bulk of the document's discussion. The second, **you shall not kill** or **have respect for life**, is described here as pertaining to both the human and non-human world, relevant to the ways we relate to animals and plants, the earth, air, water, and soil, as well as to one another as humans. Themes of dependence, interdependence, and harmony are lifted up as more adequate categories for understanding human relationships to non-humans than categories of dominance and domination.

Tolerance, respect, and appreciation for others are invoked as features of this global ethic. Even as these voices claim, however, that noone has the right to torture or kill, discriminate, 'cleanse,' exile, or liquidate persons or groups who are regarded as different or foreign, and even as "persons who hold political power must...commit themselves to the most non-violent, peaceful solutions possible" (p. 25), "they should work for this within an international order of peace which itself has need of protection and defence against perpetrators of violence." Thus, the document contains a both/and position vis-a-vis violence and nonviolence. While clearly preferring and prescribing nonviolent resolution of conflict, they judge that the order of peace itself needs protection and defense in the face of violence, and thus imply the legitimacy of violence in some circumstances. They underscore the importance of creating a **culture** of non-violence through education in home and school. Young people must learn that "violence may not be a means of settling differences with others" (p. 26).

A third directive, **you shall not steal** or **deal honestly and fairly** (p. 27), spotlights a vision of the common good and the necessity of a commitment to a just economic order. Distinctions must be made in first World and Third World alike between necessary and limitless consumption, between socially beneficial and non-beneficial uses of property, between justified and unjustified uses of natural resources, and between a profit-only and a socially beneficial and ecologically oriented market economy (p. 28).

Moderation and modesty with respect to money, prestige, and consumption must replace the greed that diminishes human life: "In greed humans lose their `souls', their freedom, their composure, their inner peace, and thus that which makes them human" (p. 29). The nurturing of a spirit of compassion with those who suffer and the cultivation of mutual respect must replace "thinking only of unlimited power and unavoidable competitive struggles" (p. 29).

The fourth ancient religious and spiritual directive, **you shall not lie** or **speak and act truthfully**, is offered to all, but especially applied to politicians, business people, and the mass media, for whom lies, propaganda, and misinformation are too often employed to achieve limited goals. This maxim applies also to scientists and other researchers for whom vested economic interests can function to further research that violates fundamental ethical values. This directive pertains as well to representatives of religions who dismiss other religions as of little value, who stir up hatred and enmity of those who believe differently from themselves, who nourish fanaticism and intolerance rather than respect and understanding ("they deserve the condemnation of humankind and the loss of their adherents" [p. 31]). This directive, we are told, reminds us that "No woman or man, no institution, no state or church or religious community has the right to speak lies to other humans" (p. 30).

IN ITS EFFORT TO CLARIFY THINKING and encourage moral sensibility, the document sustains its attention to distinctions. It urges readers not to confuse "freedom with arbitrariness or pluralism with indifference to truth"; to cultivate "truthfulness in all our relationships instead of dishonesty, dissembling, and opportunism"; to seek and to serve "truth and incorruptible sincerity" with constancy and trustworthiness instead of fostering "ideological or partisan half-truths" out of "opportunistic accommodation to life" (p. 32).

The fifth directive, **you shall not commit sexual immorality** or **respect and love one another**, is presented as condemning "sexual exploitation and sexual discrimination as one of the worst forms of human degradation" (p. 33). Sexuality should be characterized by love, partnership, and care for one another's happiness. Voluntary sexual renunciation is an ideal in some religious traditions where it, too, is regarded as "an expression of identity and meaningful fulfilment" (p. 33). Sexuality is to be taught to children as a creative and affirmative—not a negative, destructive, or exploitative—force. Wherever domination and exploitation are preached or tolerated (even in the name of religious conviction), whenever prostitution is fostered or children misused, human beings have the duty to resist and refuse.

This global ethic insists that mutual respect, partnership, and understanding must displace patriarchal domination and degradation, for these latter are expressions of violence that engender counter-violence. Mutual concern, tolerance, readiness for reconciliation, and love must displace possessive lust and sexual misuse. Concluding with a section entitled "A Transformation of Consciousness," the authors highlight the importance of personal responsibility and appropriation of the attitudes and directives discussed. They view it to be the special task of religions to keep this sense of responsibility alive, to deepen it, and to sustain it from generation to generation. Feeling that they have been realistic in what constitutes this consensus, the authors also recognize work to be done.

First, they grant that it will be difficult to attain universal consensus beyond general norms, specifically on many disputed questions in the specific areas of bioethics, sexual ethics, economic and political ethics. Yet they urge that solutions be sought, for they are convinced that solutions in keeping with the fundamental principles developed in this statement are attainable. Second, the authors encourage those in the professions (physicians, journalists, scientists, business people, politicians) to develop updated codes of ethics that provide specific guidelines for the "vexing questions" of their particular professions. Third, the drafters of this document urge the diverse communities of faith to formulate specific ethical statements pertaining to their traditions regarding the meaning of life and death, suffering and forgiveness, sacrifice and renunciation, compassion and joy. These more specific statements will "deepen, and make more specific, the already discernible global ethic" (p. 36). Their concluding lines are these:

> Therefore, we commit ourselves to a common global ethic, to better mutual understanding, as well as to socially-beneficial, peace-fostering, and Earth-friendly ways of life.
>
> **We invite all men and women, whether religious or not, to do the same** (p.36).

More than one hundred and fifty religious leaders from various religions (Bahai, Brahma Kumaris, Buddhism, Christianity, Native Religions, Hinduism, Jainism, Judaism, Islam, Neo-Pagans, Sikhs, Taoists, Theosophists, and Zoroastrians) and inter-religious organizations signed the document.

Assessment of the declaration requires recognition of its authorship and history, problems and promise.

AUTHORSHIP AND HISTORY, PROBLEMS AND PROMISE

HANS KUNG, DIRECTOR OF THE INSTITUTE for Ecumenical Research at the University of Tubingen, Germany, and author of *Global Responsibility: In Search of a New World Ethic*,[1] drafted the declaration at the request of

Parliament leaders. His account of the history of the document informs us that more than one hundred and fifty consultants from diverse religious traditions and perspectives had been consulted by July, 1993, when the final draft was submitted by Kung, and then finalized and approved by the Parliament's Board of Trustees.[2]

An undergirding assumption of the document is that this global ethic is implicit in the ancient religious and ethical traditions of humankind and that the declaration has made this ethic explicit. Kung himself holds that this statement of consensus toward a global ethic is a "new discovery," not a "new invention,"[3] a description, not a creation. Since the declaration contains neither footnotes nor quotations from source materials, it will be the work of scholars and other inquirers to document whether its claims are accurate vis-a-vis specific traditions, highlighting ways in which individual traditions correspond to the global ethic or not. Kung perceives this statement as a "minimal ethic," based on common denominators among the world religions rather than a "maximal ethic" embedded in the foundational sources of the traditions themselves. A mere nine pages of typescript, the declaration is not intended to serve as a substitute for the Jewish Torah, the Christian Sermon on the Mount, the Muslim Qur'an, the Hindu Bhagavadgita, the Discourses of the Buddha, or the Sayings of Confucius.[4] Thus, it will be useful for scholars also to identify ways in which given traditions have distinctive and unique contributions to make to a discussion on global ethics over and above this minimal, consensual statement.

I hope this document will receive widespread attention and examination because I see it as carrying the capacity to stimulate attention, discussion, and extended research on religio-ethical issues. The declaration will serve us well if it generates curiosity about the religious and ethical traditions of the world which are asserted as the document's sources. Given the absence of citations, the document by its very nature invites independent investigation of source material and will, hopefully, motivate readers to enter the religious literatures of the world and to think comparatively and critically about these materials. The promise and some of the problems of the declaration, in my view, can be discussed in terms of the following features of the document: the distinction between the legal and the moral, the spirit of self-critical questioning, and the authors' commitment to consensus.

THE LEGAL AND THE MORAL: AN IMPORTANT DISTINCTION

AS A SCHOLAR AND TEACHER WORKING in the field of comparative religious ethics, I applaud the effort to focus global attention on the ethical dimension and to highlight the important distinction between the ethical and the political-legal arenas of life. As a teacher and scholar, I see this distinction to be of critical importance and as a citizen I see it to be in need of regular attention and reminder. To acknowledge the difference between the ethical and the social-civil-legal orders, in a statement of this sort, carries the potential of being very useful in a variety of educational forums.

People who are not in touch with the moral and ethical heritages of human life and those who ignore, dismiss, or repudiate those heritages tend to rely on individual rights, contractual agreements, political arrangements, and cultural conventions for a sense of what is good. Yet history documents an enduring tension between the ethical and the legal, a tension that makes visible a difference between them. Resistance movements of diverse sorts (democratic, socialist, anarchic), civil rights and other human rights movements, ethnic pride movements, and women's liberation movements, for example, illustrate in multiple and various ways a single point: social and civil laws and cultural customs can be morally unjustifiable, ethically intolerable.

Laws designed by human beings that support apartheid, arrest without recourse, slavery, extermination, racism, sexism, classism, and other forms of discrimination are called before the moral court of justice, fairness, and decency in these movements for change. The moral visions animating these movements (and often accounting for differences within them) provide perspectives from which the political, legal, and social spheres are assessed and addressed. Indeed, this is one of the fundamental ways in which religions function, as meaning-laden and value-laden horizons by which persons are positioned to evaluate cultural mores, the social ethos, and widely-acknowledged or self-proclaimed authorities.

The *Declaration Toward a Global Ethic* displays this role of religion by endorsing selected features of the ancient religious, ethical, and spiritual traditions as valuable and renewable resources in our time. Whether or not one *believes* in a given tradition or traditions is peripheral to the fact that these heritages stand as broad, cultural resources for information, reflection, deliberation, decision, and action. Religions are not limited to the domain of believers, members, or participants, but can

106

rightly be construed, in the words of David Tracy, as "classics" to be tapped, "as public, utopian symbols worthy of serious reflection, dialogue and argument by all inquirers."[5]

This document is thus as much an invitation as it is a declaration. As such it invites all readers to focus on the ethical features of life, on fundamental attitudes, values, and aspirations, and to do so in terms of the challenging dilemmas and crises of contemporary life. Part of that task is to think critically about oneself and one's loyalties.

SELF-CRITICAL QUESTIONING: A FEATURE OF THE ETHICAL LIFE

ALTHOUGH THE DECLARATION REFLECTS TRUST, confidence, and hope that the ancient religious and ethical traditions of the world have something important to say and something valuable to offer a world in distress today, its religious roots and religious loyalties do not make it blind to the evils condoned by religions, do not render it deaf to legitimate and appropriate self-critical reflection. The document blatantly admits that hatred, envy, jealousy, and violence exist not only between and among individuals and groups, classes, races, and nations, but also within, between, and among religions.[6] Its words gain credibility, in my judgment, by virtue of its opening these lines of analysis. Yet more needs to be said about this matter of criticism, if not within the document, then by those of us who interpret and assess it. Although the document critiques representatives of religions "who preach fanaticism and intolerance instead of respect and understanding" (p. 30), it says nothing about mutual criticism as a legitimate feature of religious interactions and scholarly judgments on religions.

Granted, respect is a critically important scholarly attitude and advisable assumption in the quest for understanding, yet the document serves us poorly if it intends or permits the impression that with respect to religion, criticism of the other, that is, critique of one another, is disallowed. Criticism of religions must be as appropriate in principle as is the criticism of philosophies, sciences, technologies, economic theories and systems, therapies, and artistic expressions.

The point to be defended is that critical disagreement and judgment be based on factual accuracy, disciplined study, and explicit criteria for judgment rather than on prejudices, hidden assumptions, or self-aggrandizing goals. Some criteria for mutual critique are suggested in the following claim: "When [religions] stir up prejudice, hatred, and enmity towards those of different belief, or even incite or legitimate religious wars, they deserve the condemnation of humankind and the loss of their adherents" (p. 31). While this statement, like many statements in the declaration, invites more nuanced discussion, it does suggest that "mutual respect" need not obviate critical judgment of religions, whether one's own or another's. Although self-critical reflection is encouraged, critique of the other and of one another is admittedly a minimal concern in this document, for the declaration is driven by a desire to articulate consensus. This is both good and bad.

THE DRIVE FOR CONSENSUS

THE COMMITMENT TO CONSENSUS that shaped this document arose from the ecumenical roots and interests of the leaders of the Parliament of the World's Religions who commissioned it. The Parliament was formed

• To promote understanding and cooperation among religious communities and institutions.

• To encourage the spirit of harmony and to celebrate, with openness and mutual respect, the rich diversity of religions.

• To assess and to renew the role of the religions of the world in relation to personal spiritual growth and to the critical issues and challenges facing the global community.[7]

Thus, its self-determined charge was to welcome and to celebrate diversity, but to do so within an overarching framework of unity. Common human concerns and sufferings, common planetary interests, and common hopes for the future are identified as the ties that bind together peoples of varying cultural heritages and religious loyalties. Voicing these concerns in terms of a global ethic then became the work of the declaration's authors and consultants. On the one hand, they wished to rally the various religious communities of the world to acknowledge these points of commonality and to garner their energies as a global force for good. On the other hand, they recognized the necessity of proscribing discussion of many controversial ethical and institutional issues that remain unresolved within religious communities themselves. It is deliberate, for example, that there is no mention of abortion, euthanasia, divorce and remarriage, or the ordination of women. The statement also avoids mention of characteristic beliefs, symbols, and ceremonial practices, where differences among the traditions loom large.

The accent on similarity is likely to trouble scholars and teachers of the world's religions. For professors rightly resist easy generalizations from students who exude enthusiastic claims that "all the religions are really saying the same thing, deep down" or that "the world's religions are simply different paths to the same reality." On the contrary, scholars and teachers invite students to enter the complexity of the religions, to explore the contradictions of the religions, and to study the cultural and historical specificity of religions. They tend to discourage the discovery of similarity as too easy for the new student, as premature in effort, and thus as superficial and inaccurate in conclusion.

The Parliament document's commitment to consensus is bound to generate discomfort on other grounds as well. Whose consensus? Out of what context—and in whose interests—are the "fundamental" ethical directives and attitudes judged to be both central and cross-cultural? And to what ends is the claim made that these directives, attitudes, and norms come from "the great ancient religious and ethical traditions of humankind" (p. 25, see also pp. 19, 23, 27, 30, 32)? Given the contemporary awareness that knowledge claims are tied to power as well as to the quest for factual accuracy and valued insight, the self-critical imperative discussed above must be applied not only to human beings as moral or to religious persons as religious, but also to the drafters and signers of this document.

Given the great historical influence and cross-cultural presence of the Christian tradition, given its expansionist role in the world, and given its complicity with the educated elites who introduced or cooperated with colonialism in the past and who benefit from neocolonialism today, it should not be surprising that some invited signatories received or approached Hans Kung's draft of the *Declaration Toward a Global Ethic* with frowned wonder and some measure of reluctance. These facts, together with the one-week time frame for on-site revisions—together with the decision by the Parliament leadership to make the signing of the Declaration not only a parliament event, but also a media event,—hint at some of the pressures that faced the signatories and those who chose not to sign. Some potential signatories, for example, faulted the declaration for being too "western," for not mentioning "God," for being equivocal on the issue of non-violence, and for refraining from confronting disputed, concrete, ethical questions.

Farid Esack, Professor at Selly Oak College in Birmingham, United Kingdom, an Islamic scholar-activist with expertise in South African affairs, for example, wrote an open letter to Parliament participants that expressed discontent with the declaration. Dated September 2, 1993, the letter is entitled "Open Letter to the Trustees and Fellow Members of the Assembly at the World Parliament of Religions." His criticisms are directed to both process and content.

First, Esack questioned the process by which Parliament Assembly members were chosen, and, secondly, he questioned the process by which the document on a global ethic was written. Having had no information on either question at the point he was invited to sign, Esack was distanced by the fact that the Assembly members who were asked to sign the document were not necessarily among the consultants who contributed to the draft. Third, he rejected what he interpreted in the document to be a "blanket rejection of the option of self-defence which all oppressed peoples of the world have." And fourth, he was vigorously opposed to any hint of a position "that all change must take place in individuals first," arguing that individual and socio-economic structures must be transformed simultaneously. "The logic of `privatized reformation' as a condition of socio-political change," he explained, "had been used for too long by the Apartheid regime for me to now assent to it in Chicago." Although he was not opposed in principle to the project of formulating a global ethic, Esack's letter of protest pressed for "a more representative way of consultation and drafting," even if that meant delaying the process of formulation.

Scholar Paul Knitter's assessment of the declaration has focused on the function of language. Influenced by the work of Michel Foucault, Knitter raised the question in a recent forum that since language functions to secure power, authors and readers alike need to be on alert about ways in which moral discourse becomes "managerial discourse," that is to say, discourse that manages what will be discussed, how it will be discussed, and to what ends. In managerial discourse whatever does not fit given determinations is vulnerable to being judged disruptive, closed-minded, driven by self-interest, and the like.[8] This warning is less a critique of the authors' intentionality than a description of the ways in which language operates. Since neither the document nor Kung's commentary offers attention to the relation between power and knowledge, to the ways in which words function to shape agendas, determine allowable categories, and to include and exclude conversation partners, this will be a particularly important theme to listen for in whatever debate the document generates. Adherents of some of the "new religions," for example, to the extent that they see themselves as "new," may critique the document for favoring the "ancient" religious, ethical, and spiritual traditions of humankind. To the extent that they see their roots in these ancient traditions, however, this may not be a troubling issue. Wicca and Neo-pagan religions (three of whose representatives signed the document), for example, categorized as "new religions" in sociological and demographic descriptions, are commonly defended by adherents to be contemporary expressions of the ancient religions of the goddess. Thus, adherents of these "new religions" may recognize themselves in the "ancient traditions" cited in the declaration.

The questions raised at the outset of this essay invite response from a wide variety of voices. Is a fundamental value perspective realistic to our highly conflictual and diverse world? Shall we give it our support our our resistance? Will it resonate broadly with readers throughout the world or will it remain the hope of a few? Garnering answers to these questions will be both fascinating and important, for these findings will enable us to see more clearly a number of important features of the declaration: 1) to what extent this document is agreed to be a discovery and to what extent a construction; 2) to what extent it is regarded as a valuable and useful initiative and to what extent a homogenizing exercise that dilutes valuable ethical diversity; and 3) to what extent it functions as an expression of power-over by ecumenical religious elites and/or an empowering instrument that assists people throughout the globe to name evil and to mobilize effectively on behalf of the good (personally, communally, and ecologically considered).

The declaration invites work. Although this "Global Ethic" is presented as an ethic of responsibility with strong emphases on attitudes and dispositions, norms and principles, it is clearly a twentieth-century and not an a-historical, document. It speaks of two world wars and the end of a cold war, it alludes to the realities of fascism and nazism, to the challenges leveled against communism and colonialism, and to the rise of the modern nation-state. It affirms the 1948 United Nations Universal Declaration of Human Rights as it acknowledges the global proportions of drug trafficking and organized crime. It recognizes the contemporary facts of dictatorships, political torture and mutilation, and the taking and killing of hostages. It is realistic about the dialectic of violence and counter-violence in the face of dramatic inequities regarding the distribution of the earth's resources. It notes the debt crisis of the Third World, the destructiveness of patriarchy, and the horrors of sexual abuse. Every one of these allusions calls for attention, investigation, analysis, and recommendations for dramatic change. The declaration toward a global ethic thus identifies an ethical agenda as we face the future even as it declares an ethical consensus rooted in the past.

Cross-cultural discussion of this document will inform and sensitize us to the primary ethical categories in which, through which, and with which peoples around the world think and imagine. Norms, principles, and axioms have been useful in the west in the quest for clarity and conciseness, and these categories are plentiful in this declaration. It is important to note, however, that while norms and principles summarize the cognitive content of moral discourse, other genres, such as proverbs, songs and stories, dances, conversations, and ceremonial events are, for most people, the more powerful carriers of moral meaning. For these genres, unlike the abstractions of axioms, directives, and principles evoke not only the cognitive, but also the affective and imaginative depths of moral sensibility and desire. By becoming familiar with the distinctive proverbs and principles, songs and stories, precepts and ceremonies of the various traditions, people will be positioned also to discover for themselves the commonalities the document points to and the differences the document ignores.

Does a global village warrant a global ethic? My answer is this: a global village warrants global attention to the ethical frameworks, orientations, and attitudes that shape our perceptions and generate our actions. It is entirely likely that the *Declaration Toward a Global Ethic* will function to inform, inspire, disappoint, and perhaps even infuriate. No matter. If, by spotlighting the ethical dimensions of life on this globe at this time in history, the document generates curiosity about ethics together with a heightened sensitivity to and engagement in ethical inquiry, reflection, and action, it will have fostered a critically important social process.

NOTES

† See *A Global Ethic: The Declaration of the Parliament of the World's Religions* with commentaries by Hans Kung and Karl-Josef Kuschel (New York: Continuum, 1993). All textual citations to the declaration come from this edition. The declaration itself is found on pages 17-36 in this edition; this is preceded by a three page introduction and followed by a three page list of signatories.

1. New York: Crossroad, 1991.

2. See Kung's commentary on the declaration, entitled "The History, Significance and Method of the Declaration Toward a Global Ethic," pp. 43-76, in *A Global Ethic,* cited in note 1.

3. Ibid., p. 71.

4. Ibid.,, p. 73.

5. David Tracy, "Theology, Critical Social Theory, and the Public Realm," in Don S. Browning and Francis Schussler fiorenza, eds., *Habermas, Modernity, and Public Theology* (New York: Crossroad, 1992), p. 25.

6. These topics were given sustained attention in an excellent Parliament Symposium on "Religion and Violence." Four sessions, entitled "Jealousy, Envy and Hate Among the World's Religions," fostered discussion of these themes in terms of Hinduism, Buddhism, Judaism, Christianity, and Islam.

7. These three items are listed among six that comprise the Mission Statement of the Council for a Parliament of the World's Religions. See the *1993 Parliament of the World's Religions* program book, p. 2.

8. "Pitfalls and Promises for A Global Ethics" (p. 4), a paper presented at the American Academy of Religion Annual Meeting in Washington, D.C., November 22, 1993.

JUNE O'CONNOR is professor and chair of the Department of Religious Studies at the University of California, Riverside, USA. She has published numerous articles in academic journals and is author of **The Moral Vision of Dorothy Day: A Feminist Perspective***. Dr. O'Connor attended the 1993 Parliament of the World's Religions as an academic observer and delegate.*

Reprinted from *Religion*. Harcourt Brace and Company, Foots Cray, High Street, Sidcup, Kent DA14 5HP, U.K. Subscription: $60/year.

BOSNIA

SOME RELIGIOUS DIMENSIONS OF GENOCIDE

by MICHAEL A. SELLS

from RELIGIOUS STUDIES NEWS

April 1994 in Bosnia marked the second anniversary of what we have come to know as "ethnic cleansing." Aspects of the Bosnia tragedy such as the seige of Sarajevo have captured world attention. Widely misunderstood, however, is the true extent of the "ethnic cleansing" and its fundamentally religious character.

All major Bosnian populations (Serb, Muslim, and Croat) trace their descent from the same south Slavic tribes, and (despite protestations of nationalists) all speak the same language. The term "ethnic" in "ethnic cleansing" actually refers to religious affiliation. The testimony in the UN War Crimes Commission reports suggests that what is called "cleansing" is actually genocide; that is (according to *Webster's Ninth*) "the deliberate and systematic destruction of a racial, political, or cultural group."While it is true that there have been abuses on all sides (as in most conflicts), the vast majority of victims have been unarmed Bosnian Muslim civilians. An estimated 200,000 Bosnian Muslims have been killed (out of a pre-war Bosnian total population of some 4 million).[1]

The "ethnic cleansing" consists of: 1) Attacks on lightly defended settlements by heavily armed forces; 2) Savage shelling of settlements that resist; 3) Daily mass-killings, torture, and deliberate starvation; 4) Systematic use of rape; 5) Deliberate annihilation of cultural heritage (mosques, libraries, schools, museums, cemeteries, manuscript collections);[2] 6) An economy of pillage with regular "caravans" of Muslim loot taken across the Drina river into Serbia proper; 7) Final, ritualized dehumanization in which survivors are stripped of every personal possession.

The treatment of Bosnian Muslims as an ethnic group is usually traced to the 1971 Yugoslav constitutional establishment of Bosnian Muslims as a Yugoslav "nationality." Both the notion of religion as "ethnicity" and the notion of "cleansing" have far deeper roots, however, in the religious ideology of slavic nationalists, Christoslavism, which maintains that Slavs are, by nature, Christian. Any deviation from Christianity, therefore, is race-betrayal. We cannot hope to understand this genocide in Europe on the 50th anniversary of the Holocaust unless we understand this religious ideology.

THE KOSOVO MYTH: SLAVIC MUSLIMS PORTRAYED AS CHRIST-KILLERS IN THE MOUNTAIN WREATH

IN 1389, THE SERB PRINCE LAZAR was defeated and killed in a battle against Ottoman Turkish Sultan Murad on the plain of Kosovo. While historians dispute the significance of the battle, in Serbian mythology it entailed the loss of Serb independence, a loss that was represented in cosmic terms. Lazar is portrayed as a Christ figure. He has a Last Supper with his nobles, one of whom, Vuk Brankovic, is a traitor and gives the battle plans to the Turks. During the battle, the Christ-Prince Lazar is slain and with him dies the Serb nation, to rise again only with the resurrection of Lazar. Turks are thus equated with Christ-Killers and Vuk Brankovic, the "Turk within," becomes a symbol (and ancestral curse) of all slavic Muslims.

Thus the same manipulation of the "Christ-Killer" charge used in persecutions of Jews from the time of the First Crusade in 1096 also formed a rationale for the persecution of slavic Muslims. The classic illustration of this rationale is *The Mountain Wreath,* written by Prince-Bishop Petar II, known by the pen-name of Njegos, which portrays the 18th century Montenegrin extermination of slavic Muslims (*Istraga Poturica*).

The drama opens with Bishop Danilo, the play's protagonist, brooding on the evil of Islam, the tragedy of Kosovo, and the treason of Vuk Brankovic. Danilo's warriors suggest celebrating the holy day (Pentecost) by "cleansing" (*cistimo*) the land of non-Christians (v. 95). The chorus chants: "the high mountains reek with the stench of non-Christians [v. 284]." One of Danilo's men proclaims that struggle won't come to an end until "we or the Turks [slavic Muslims] are exterminated." The reference to the slavic Muslims as "Turks" crystallizes the view that by converting to Islam the Muslims have changed their racial identity and have become the Turks who killed the Christ-Prince Lazar.

Recently, the killing in Bosnia has been misrepresented as a "blood-feud." In *The Mountain Wreath*, however, the genocide is explicitly placed *outside* the category of the blood-feud. In tribal Montenegro and Serbia, a blood-feud, however ruthless and fatal, could be reconciled; it was not interminable. The godfather (Kuma) ceremony was used to reconcile clans who had fallen into blood-feud. In *The Mountain Wreath*, when the Muslims suggest a Kuma reconciliation, Danilo's men object that the Kuma ceremony requires baptism. The Muslims offer an ecumenical analogy, suggesting that the Muslim hair-cutting ceremony is a parallel in their tradition to baptism. Danilo's men respond with a stream of scatological insults of Islam, its prophet, and Muslims. With each set of insults, the chorus chants *Tako, Vec Nikako* (this way; there is no other) to indicate the "act" that must be taken. The play ends with the triumphant extermination of slavic Muslims as a formal initiation of Serb nationhood.

By moving the conflict from the realm of blood feud into a cosmic duality of good and evil, Njegos placed slavic Muslims in a permanent state of otherness. The sympathetic qualities of the Muslims are the last temptation of Danilo. However sympathetic in person, Muslims are Christ-killers, "blasphemers," "spitters on the cross." After slaughtering the Muslims—man, woman, and child—the Serb warriors take communion without the confession that was mandatory after blood-vengeance.

In 1989, about a million Serb pilgrims streamed into Kosovo for the Passion Play commemoration of the 600th anniversary of the battle of Kosovo.[3] On this occasion, Serb President Slobodan Milosevic announced his change from communist apparachnik to champion of the Serbdom. And those who directed the Passion Play, who acted in it, and who sat in the first rows in 1989, were those carrying out the most unspeakable depravities against Bosnian civilians only three years later.[4]

Just as Good Friday remembrances of the passion of Christ were used by anti-Semites to instigate attacks on Jews, so the Kosovo Passion Play (which puts the slavic Muslims in the position of "Christ-killers") became the occasion for persecution. *The Mountain Wreath* is memorized and quoted by radical Serb nationalists today. In Bosnia, nationalist Serb "ethnic cleansers" wear patches depicting the battle of Kosovo. Milovan Djilas, one of *The Mountain Wreath*'s admirers, argued that the historical extermination of Montenegrin Muslims was a "process" rather than a single "event," and that Bishop Petar shaped it into a single act for literary and ideological purposes.[5] While there is doubt whether the "extermination of the Slavic Muslims" (*Istraga Poturica*) occurred as a single event in the late 18th century, the eight U.S. War Crimes Reports to the UN War Crimes Commission and the two Helsinki Watch Reports (see. n. 2) suggest that it occurred in 1992-93.

CHRISTOSLAVISM IN THE WORK OF IVO ANDRIC

"RACE-BETRAYAL" IS A MAJOR THEME of *The Mountain Wreath* and the strand of Serbian literature it represents. By converting to Islam, Njegos insisted, slavic Muslims became "Turks."The novelist Ivo Andric presents race-conversion in clear ideological terms. He begins by grounding it the work of Bishop Petar:

Njegos, who can always be counted on for the truest expression of the people's mode of thinking and apprehending, portrays in his terse and plastic manner the process of conversion thus: "The lions [i.e. those who remained Christian according to Andric's footnote] turned into tillers of the soil, / the cowardly and covetous turned into Turks." [6]

If this is the message of "the people," Bosnian Muslims are by definition not part of the people.Andric gives a historical rationale for such exclusion. For Andric, the ancient Bosnian Church, persecuted as heretic by both Catholic and Orthodox forces, was a sign of a "young slavic race" still torn between "Heathen concepts with dualistic coloring and unclear Christian dogmas."[7] Most Bosnians believe that the members of the Bosnian Church, called Bogomils or Patarins, were the ancestors of the Bosnian Muslims. Andric portrays Bosnian Muslims not only as cowardly and covetous and the "heathen element of a young race," but finally as the corrupted "Orient" that cut off the slavic race from the "civilizing currents" of the West.[8]

Andric's most famous novel centers on the bridge on the Drina River commissioned by Mehmet Pasha Sukolovic (a Serb who had been taken to Istanbul and become a Pasha). To appease fairies (*vila*) holding up the bridge's construction, the builders must wall up two Christian infants within it. Two holes that appear in the bridge are interpreted as the place where the infants mothers would come to suckle their infants. The story crystallizes the view that an essentially Christic race of Slavs is walled up within the encrustation of an alien religion. It also represents an obsession with the Ottoman practice of selecting Serb boys (such as Sukolovic) to be sent to Istanbul and brought up Muslim; such people, however successful, remain perpetual exiles to themselves, cut off from the Christian essence of their slavic souls. Andric is a hero to both Serb and Croat nationalists who have been "cleansing" Muslims from Bosnia.[9]

This brief reading of Njegos and Andric cannot do justice to the range of their work nor is it meant to explain the genocide in Bosnia. It is meant only to illustrate that religion (despite frequent denials) is indeed a powerful and operative element in the tragedy.

RESPONSES TO RELIGIOUS CLEANSING IN BOSNIA

LAST WINTER, RUSSIAN NEO-NAZI Vladimir Zhirinovsky visited the highest ranking surviving SS officer in Germany, and then went to Serb occupied Bosnia where he was given an adoring welcome by Bosnian Serb ethnonationalists.[10] While it would be wrong to equate genocide in Bosnia with the Holocaust, it is equally wrong to ignore the moral implications of genocide in Europe, against a non-Christian population. Some governmental and church leaders in the region and in the international community have failed to respond to the Bosnians' calls for assistance. More disturbing has been the active support by Serbian religious leaders of those Serbian military and governmental officials responsible for designing and implementing the policy of "ethnic cleansing."

For example, Metropolitan Nikolaj, the highest ranking Serb Church official in Bosnia, stood between General Ratko Mladic and Bosnian Serb President Radovan Karadzic—architects of the "ethnic cleansing"—and spoke of Bosnian Serbs' struggle as following the "hard road of Christ."

Serbian priests have blessed militias on their return from kill-and-plunder expeditions and have waved incense over a boxing match put on by the warlord (a criminal known as "Arkan") associated with the worst atrocities against Muslims. Ethnonationalists celebrated the feast of St. Sava, founder of the Serbian Church, by burning down the 300-year-old mosque at Trebinje and massacring the towns Muslims. The mayor of Zvornik (a previously Muslim majority city) celebrated the completion of "ethnic cleansing" and the town's new status as one hundred percent Muslim-free by erecting a new Church to St. Stepan and kissing a crucifix.[11] Serbian Church leaders in America have vilified Muslims and have refused to condemn the systematic ethnic cleansing of the Bosnian Serb government.[12]

The Serbian Church earlier had paved the way for the Greater Serbia and the annihilation of Bosnian-Herzegovina in the fall and winter of 1988-89;the Church organized a procession of the relics of Prince Lazar throughout lands claimed as Serbian, particularly in Bosnia. The Church also organized disinterments of relics of Serb victims from WW2 in ceremonies surrounded by nationalist ideology. The result of these two activities was a symbolic linking of the relics of Lazar killed by the Turks (figured as Christ-Killers in Kosovo Mythology) and the relics of WW2 victims. The enormous emotional charge generated through this matrix of religious symbols and rituals played a key role in radicalizing the Serbian population in Bosnia-Herzegovina along ethnoreligious lines.

Immediately after the Sarajevo Market Massacre, The National Council of Churches, which has been reticent in speaking out on Bosnia, wrote President Clinton praising "restraint" in the use of force.[13] For two years, a civilian Muslim populace was "cleansed," with a kill rate (number of people killed per day as percentage of total population) that may equal that of WW II Nazi occupation in Bosnia. The killing was carried out with a UN arms embargo against the victims and little effort to disarm the aggressors in front of the largest military alliance in the history of humankind. The UN showed restraint by refusing to enforce some thirty resolutions forbidding shelling of civilians, abuse in detention camps, interference with food convoys, and attacks on "safe havens."A language of complicity was developed, with half-truths (at best) such as "age-old ethnic antagonisms," "civil war," and "blame on all sides" used to justify restraint in the face of genocide and interpreted (correctly) by the aggressors as a green light for more ethnic cleansing. After the Sarajevo Market Massacre, the United States and the UN ran out of restraint and enforced a resolution. The shelling of Sarajevo stopped.

Despite the generous actions of individual Christians, charges of inaction have been leveled at organized Church bodies.[14] Given the religious aspect of the conflict and the history of genocide in Europe, many will be listening to the Churches' response to issues still posed by "ethnic cleansing" in Bosnia. Will religious leaders indirectly endorse ethnic cleansing by supporting a peace settlement that rewards it? Will they argue that the perpetrators be held accountable? Will they act to ensure that the victims (many of whom are now being held in inhuman conditions in European refugee camps) be treated with humanity? Will they continue to acquiesce in the use of Jesus' name to authorize this activity?

As scholars of religion, we are frequently concerned with how religions bind together communities, offer a framework for moral decisions, relate ethos and world view, and guide inquiry into fundamental questions of human existence. Yet religions can also be used to authorize the most inhuman behavior. The acceptance of the term "ethnic cleansing" is a sign of the widespread desire to deny this latter aspect of religion. In a post cold-war world of increasing religious militancies, an examination of the relation of religion and genocide, uncomfortable a topic as it may be, may be one of our more pressing priorities.

POSTSCRIPT

SINCE THIS ESSAY APPEARED IN *Religious Studies News*, major new programs of "ethnic cleansing" have been launched by the Bosnian Serb leadership in an effort to complete the expulsion of all non-Serbs from the 70% of Bosnia now controlled by the Bosnian Serb army. The "cleansings" are directed from Bijeljina, the stronghold of Serbian nationalism, which is under the power of Vojkan Djurkovic the head of the Bosnian Serb Republic's "Population Exchange Commission." The major NATO powers ignored an extraordinary plea by the International Red Cross to stop the "ethnic cleansing." At the same time, Bishop Pavle, the leader of the Serbian Orthodox Church, announced full support of the Bosnian Serb Government, denounced the "51-49" peace-plan of the Contact Group, and remained silent on the "cleansings."

The expulsions follow a clear pattern. Women, children, and old people are told to leave, under threat of death, and given only a few minutes to prepare. They are stripped of all currency, jewelry, and other valuables. Their homes are either given away or looted, first by militiamen, later by local Serb villagers who strip it down to the carcass, taking floor tiles, plumbing, and other items. Refugees suspected of trying to hide valuables are beaten. Rape is commonplace. Refugees are then marched across the front lines into the refugee-swollen Bosnian city of Tuzla. Young men are sent to slave-labor camps to which the Red Cross has, ominously, been refused admittance.

The expulsions have three aims: 1) to secure a religious and ethnically pure Serb state; 2) to gain major fortunes for the leaders; and 3) to force a reaction by the Bosnians in Tuzla against the Serb population. This last point is critical for understanding the ideology of religious genocide. As Djurkovic told one Muslim refugee, when he took away many of the young Muslim men to forced-labor camps: "Expel 150 Serbian families from Tuzla and take their homes, just as we expelled you, and then you will get back your husbands, brothers, and sons."[15] The goal is not only to make the "Serbian Republic" ethnically and religious pure, but also to compel any Serbs remaining in Bosnia-Herzegovina to leave, by whatever means necessary.

It has been suggested that the earlier version of this article might contribute to a "demonization of Serbs."[16] I would suggest the opposite. As long as we fail to place responsibility on the particular Serb and Serbian Church leaders and regimes responsible for the ethnic cleansing and the ideology that fosters it, all Serbs, rather than Serb nationalists, will receive a generic blame. In fact, no group has been more courageous and more devastatingly accurate in its detailing of the criminality of Serbian governments than non-nationalist Serb dissidents in Belgrade, who have all too often been ignored by the West.[17] In Bosnia, Serb dissidents have been killed, tortured, threatened, and raped for refusing to attack their Muslim or Croat neighbors, or for hiding non-Serb civilians in their homes.[18]

The theme of "ethnic cleansing" within Njegos's work is a sensitive subject. The writings of Njegos helped crystallize Serbian aspirations. It would be anachronistic to accuse him of sponsoring the genocide of 1992-94, but that tragedy is too deeply grounded in the Kosovo mythology of *The Mountain Wreath* to allow us to read Njegos without thinking of it. As with treatments of the Jews in some New Testament texts, the divinely-ordered genocide in the books of Joshua and Kings, and the Qur'anic allusions to the killing of the men of the last Jewish tribe in Medina, *The Mountain Wreath* is one of those texts that help found a tradition, but which also demand from scholars in religious studies some sustained inquiry, and which demand from religious leaders both courage and clarity in refusing to allow such texts to be used to justify genocide.

Finally, the focus on Serbian mythology is not meant to exonerate other religious leaders of their responsibilities. The horrendous suffering in Bosnia has led to the radicalization of some Bosnian Islamic leaders.

The visit by Pope John-Paul II to Croatia brings out a tragic irony. In 1982 the Serbian Church urged the Catholic Church to begin a serious discussion of WW2 genocide, but there was little response. Recently, John-Paul II praised Cardinal Stepinac, the leader of Croatia's Catholics during WW2, whose silence in the face of the Nazi and Ustashe atrocities has led to enduring bitterness in Serbia.[19] Ironically, the Serbian Church leaders are now repeating the silence of Cardinal Stepinac: general words in praise of peace, but refusal to condemn, in specific terms, the "ethnic cleansing" that has been systematically carried out by Serbian militias, in the name of Serbs, Serb culture, and Serb religion.

A press release of the World Council of Churches, dated September 22, 1994 challenges the Serbian Orthodox Church to as a peacemaker. Despite the failures of institutionalized religious hiearachies, there are courageous people in Sarajevo working to bridge religious differences and encouraging the non-sectarian teaching of comparative religions.[20] The post-cold war has seen a movement of religions toward polarization, militancy, and fundamentalism, and a dangerous chasm between religious leaderships and intellectuals. To recognize the depths of the problem at this time may help us recognize the importance of such efforts to overcome it. The outcome of the struggle to resist religious polarization in Sarajevo, in the heart of the maelstrom, will have consequences far beyond Bosnia-Herzegovina.

As of this writing, October 21, 1994, the "Serbian Republic" (Republika Srpska) that controls 70% of Bosnia is close to its goal of 100% racial and religious purity. The last few remaining Muslims, Gypsies, Croats and other non-Serbs are being killed or driven out.[21]

NOTES

1. Gutman, who won the 1993 Pulitzer Prize for his reports on Bosnia, estimates 200,000—250,000 dead by June of 1993. See Roy Gutman, *A Witness to Genocide* (New York: Macmillan, 1993). The number 200,000 is also used, as a general estimate, by Frank McCloskey of Indiana and John Olver of Massachussetts, two leading congressional experts on the Bosnian tragedy.

2. Helsinki Watch, *War Crimes in Bosnia-Herzegovina*, vol. 1, 1992 and vol. 2, 1993, personal interviews with survivors, and the 8 U.S. State Department War Crimes Commission Reports found in the *U.S. Department of State Dispatch* 3 (1992) 39; 3.44; 3. 46; 3.52; 4 (1993) 6; 4. 15; 4.16; 4.30. Serbs have suffered as well, many of them killed for refusing to engage in atrocities

or for trying to save their Muslim neighbors. For a superb recent book on contemporary Bosnia, see Rabia Ali and Lawrence Lifschultz, eds., *Why Bosnia? Writings on the Balkan War* (The Pamphleteer's Press, 1993). For a lucid account of the "ethnic cleansing" policies of both the Serbian Republic [of Bosnia] and the Croatian Defense Force (HVO), see Ed Vulliamy, *Seasons in Hell: Understanding Bosnia's War* (New York: St. Martin's Press, 1994).

3. In Sarajevo, the Bosnian Serb army destroyed the Oriental Institute, the largest repository of Jewish and Islamic manuscripts in SE Europe, the National Library, and the Territorial Museum. A few objects, such as the Sarajevo Haggadah (brought to Sarajevo by Sefardic Jews expelled from Spain) were saved in a multireligious salvage operation during a firestorm of shelling. The Colored Mosque of Foca and the Ferhadiyya Mosque of Banja Luka—two masterworks of European architecture—were annihilated. The mayors of Foca and Zvornik (formerly Muslim majority, now "Muslim-free") deny that there ever was a mosque in either. See Andras Riedlmayer, *Bosnia's Cultural Heritage and Its Destruction*, a slide-lecture first given at the Middle East Studies Association annual conference, Research Triangle Park, North Carolina, 1994; VHS video version, 1994, Community of Bosnia Foundation, Haverford College, Haverford, PA 19041.

4. Cf. Thomas Emmert, *Serbian Golgotha: Kosovo, 1389* (New York: East European Monographs, 1990).

5. Noel Malcom, Bosnia: A Short History (London: MacMillan, 1994), pp. 213 ff. See also the account of this day, June 28, 1989, St. Vitus' Day, in the Belgrade journal of democratic Serb dissidents,*Vreme* 145 (July 4, 1994).

6. See Misha Glenny, *The Fall of Yugoslavia* (London: Penguin, 1992), p. 39.

7. P. Njegos, *The Mountain Wreath*, translated and edited by Vasa Mihailovich (Irvine, Ca: 1986); M. Djilas, *Njegos* (New York, 1966).

8. Ivo Andric, *The Development of Spiritual Life in Bosnia under the Influence of Turkish Rule*, translated by Z. Juricic and J. Loud (Duke University Press, 1990), p. 20.

9. Ibid., p. 12.

10. Ibid., p. 16ff. For a careful historical study, see John Fine, *The Bosnian Church* (Boulder, 1975).

11. Ivo Andric, *The Bridge on the Drina*, translated by L. Edwards (New York, 1959). Andric's omniscient narrator mimics the supposedly "Muslim" thoughts of Turks. Even lower than Turks are gypsies, who specialize in torturing Christians at the behest of Turkish overlords, but who cannot even carry out their bestiality in a trustworthy way. When ordered to throw Serb martyr's bodies to the dogs, they sell them to the Christians for burial instead. The evil of the gypsies, in this novel written in 1942, is not individual

(they are not named), but in their race.

12. For the revival and nationalistic politicization of the works of Andric and Njegos, see Sabrina Petra Ramet, *Balkan Babel: Politics, Culture, and Religion in Yugoslavia* (Boulder and Oxford: Westview Press, 1992), pp. 28-29; and Misha Glenny, *The Fall of Yugoslavia* (New York: Penguin, 1992), p. 22.

13. Zhirinovsky was celebrated in Bijeljina, the hot-bed of Serbian nationalism within Bosnia.

14. N. Darnton, *The New York Times*, April 19, 1993.

15. For a brief account of the "cleansing" of Trebinje, see the *Sixth U.S. State Department Report to the United Nations War Crimes Commission* under the date January, 1993.

16. Roger Cohen, "In a Town 'Cleansed' of Muslims Serb Church Will Crown the Deed," *NYT*, 7 March 1994. As one of Serbian-American heritage, with Bosnian Serb relatives who are now refugees, I note this defiling of Serbian traditions with particular sadness.

17. Metropolitan Christopher, *The Historical Background of the Contemporary Situation of the Orthodox Church in Yugoslavia*, Lecture by Metropolitan Christopher, Catechetical Conference, Detroit, 1992 (Belleville, Mi: Firebird Video, VHS). Metropolitan Kovacevich (on Larry King Live, March, 1994).

18. *Boston Globe*, Feb. 12, 1994.

19. Cf. Adrian Hastings, "The Church Has Failed Bosnia," *Ottawa Citizen*, 10 July 1993.

20. Lujljeta Goranci, Associated Press, "1,300 weeping Muslims forced from homes in Serb-held Bosnia," *The Philadelphia Inquirer*, September 19, 1994. Detailed accounts of other expulsions throughout the month of September can be found in the Serb dissident journal *Vreme* (September issues) and in *The New York Times*, beginning on August 30, 1994 and appearing regularly throughout the month of September.

21. See the letter by Paul Mojzes, *Religious Studies News* 9 (September, 1994) 3.

22. The journal *Vreme*, which comes out weekly, has offered comprehensive analyses of the structure of "ethnic cleansing " and cultural genocide in Banja Luka, the atrocities against Muslims in Zvornik, the relationship of various militia to the Yugoslavic army and police, the network of bank-fraud, money laundering, arms and fuel smuggling, black marketeering, and pillage that makes religious genocide a large-scale, international, criminal enterprise. See VREME NEWS DIGEST AGENCY, Beograd, Misarska 12-14, E-mail distribution: p00981@psilink.com.

23. As documented in the eight U.S. War Crimes reports. Similar courage has been shown by Croats and Muslims who have protected innocent neighbors of other religions, against the pressure of religious nationalists.

See Michael A. Sells "Resisting 'Ethnic Cleansing': Quiet Heroism in Bosnia-Herzegovina," *Newsletter of the Community of Bosnia Foundation* 1.3 (November, 1994).

24. A number of reports have examined the controversial statements of the Bosnian Culture Minister, Enes Karic, and pressures by some Islamic nationalists against Serbs in Bosnia-Herzegovina. What is remarkable is how strongly many Bosnians oppose religious nationalism. In World War 2, the U.S. government placed Japanese-Americans in deternment camps; nothing of similar scope has happened in Bosnia despite the carnage Bosnians have suffered on their own soil for two years. Another controversy concerns Alija Izetbegovic, the President of Bosnia-Herzegovina. Izetbegovic was the author, in 1970 of a document entitled The Islamic Declaration which addresses Muslims around the world and describes, in abstract terms, an Islamic State.Izetbegovic's attitudes seem to have changed in later writings and his defenders claim that the discussion of the Islamic State was never meant to apply to Bosnia. Still, it was naive at best to think that the Serb population, with wounded memories of life under the Ottomans, would be convinced that Izetbegovic was now in favor of a multi-cultural state.Some Muslim nationalists republished the work in Sarajevo in 1990, further inflaming the controversy.

For the English version of the Islamic Declaration, see Alija Izetbegovic, The Islamic Declaration, *South Slav Journal*, 6 (Spring, 1983) 1: 56:89. For a philosophical arguement for Islam as an alternative to communism and consumerism, see 'Alija Izetbegovic, *Islam between East and West* (Indianapolis: American Trust Publications, 1984, second edition, 1989).

25. While Cardinal Stepinac made some "petitions" to the Ustashe chief, Ante Pavelic, he did not condemn in consistent and specific terms the forced conversions and atrocities being committed in the name of Catholicism, nor did Pope Pius XII take a specific, public stand against them. See Lazo M. Kostich: *Holocaust in the Independent State of Croatia* (Chicago: Liberty Press, 1981).

26. Among those involved in this effort is Marko Orsolic, director of the International Center for Promoting of Interreligious Dialogue, Justice, and Peace of Sarajevo.

27. See Jasmina Kuzmanovic, Associated Press: "Centuries of sharing are ending. For non-Serbs, there may be no return: Terror, expulsions seal Serbs' control of much of Bosnia," *The Philadelphia Inquirer*, October 5, 1994. Numbers dehumanize. It is imperative to remember individuals humans. During one "expulsion" of Bosnian Muslims, Fahira Selimovic, a young Muslim woman, was seen by a Republika Srpska soldier talking to an official of the United Nations High Commission on Refugees. UNHCR Refugee work-

ers report that she was taken out of line and led away to a building where sounds of a beating could be heard. There is no word of her fate. This article is dedicated to Fahira Selimovic.

MICHAEL A. SELLS is associate professor of Islam and comparative religions at Haverford College. He is the author of **Mystical Languages of Unsaying** *and* **Desert Tracings***.*

Reprinted from *Religious Studies News*, c/o Scholars Press, PO Box 15399, Atlanta, GA 30333-0399, (404) 727-2345. Subscription: $20/year.

RETURN OF THE SACRED

by JERRY MANDER

from RESURGENCE

To the extent that we have been brainwashed
to believe in technological utopias, we have been correspondingly brainwashed to believe that alternative philosophies, represented by the many
thousands of indigenous societies on the planet that survived successful-
ly for millennia, are somehow inferior to the "higher" visions that we
and our machines have to offer. In fact, it may be the central unifying
premise of Western technological society that it improves on everything
that came before it. We seem to believe that there is actually virtue in
overpowering nature and native peoples; that all the invasion of the natural world and its conversion to commodities, and the invasion of every
corner of the globe to seek more and more resources is all in service to a
higher cause: to relieve human beings from toil, to provide us with comfort, leisure and security, and that our technological genius would be the
path to that outcome.

The problem that native peoples face has been directly related to
these assumptions. It is directly related to the needs of Western society
to find resources to feed its incessant growth. Indian people continue to
live where most of the remaining resources are located. The natives must
be got out of the way, in service to this "higher cause."

The process has been going on for a long while. But it greatly accelerated 500 years ago with the "discovery" by Europeans of the new resource bonanza called the New World. The only difficulty even then was that Indians were already there.

Today this invasion of native lands continues in other New Worlds, as our society seeks gold, coal, oil, uranium and other metals, animals, fish, timber, and land. As we survey the world—whether it is the Canadian Arctic, the Malaysian jungles, the high plateaus of Tibet and Ladakh, the Brazilian rainforest, or the tiny islands of the central Pacific—the same interaction is taking place for the same reasons, involving the same institutions. It's no longer the Hudson's Bay Company perhaps; now it's the World Bank, the transnational corporations, and the monolithic world-view that this is all a good idea.

All of this is made possible by one fundamental rationalization, that our society represents the ultimate expression of evolution, its final flowering. It is this attitude, and the corresponding belief that native societies represent an earlier, lower form on the evolutionary ladder, upon which we occupy the highest place, that seems to unify all modern political perspectives: Right, Left, Capitalist, and Marxist.

Lately we have begun to hear resistance from such activists, groups as bioregionalists, Greens, and deep ecologists who have at least questioned these assumptions. But most people in Western society remain convinced of the central point of our own superiority. That makes it okay to humiliate—to find insignificant and thus subject to sacrifice— any way of life that stands in the way of the kind of progress that we invented, scarcely a few centuries ago. Having assumed superiority, it becomes more than acceptable for us to bulldoze nature and native societies. To do so actually becomes desirable and inevitable.

But the assertion that technological society is something higher than what came before is surely wrong. Given its catastrophic effects on the Earth, it is in fact already clear that the Western pathway has failed. The problem, however, is that we continue to lurch forward, expanding our reach and becoming still more arrogant and dangerous.

Most liberal-minded people, even when expressing sympathy for native people, tend to speak of the problem as something in the distant past. "Too bad," they will say, "but there is nothing now to be done about it."

Indian issues are *not* of the distant past. There are still millions of native people around the planet who live in a relatively traditional man-

RETURN OF THE SACRED

ner, while suffering from the expansionism of our society. In case after case, whether in Alaska, or Guatemala, or Bolivia or the jungles of Peru, or among the ancient cultures of the Maori and Aborigine, traditional leaders are saying they see our pathway as heading toward death and destruction. All they want is to be left alone and to have confirmation of their control of the lands they live on.

For 500 years they have been saying this, and for all that time we have been ignoring it. They have been saying that something critical is missing in our approach to living on the Earth—in my view, that would be "the absence of the sacred"—but to have heeded what the Indians have said would have meant reconsidering our own pathway. This we have avoided, and instead chose to invade Indian lands, push them off, convert them, or kill them, as we continue to do today.

There is yet another dimension to this conflict between the native and the modern-technological view of how to be on the Earth: the two views are in diametric opposition. If our society accepted the existence of the native people of the Earth, their validity, their right to exist, their viability, then it would immediately open questions as to our right to live as we do. This is a very important point.

THERE ARE MANY DIFFERENCES BETWEEN the Western world-view and the native that, finally, must be viewed as *irreconcilable*. All compromise between the two becomes impossible. I will deal here with only three of these that I think are particularly important.

The first and most fundamental native concept is that *the planet is a living entity*. Throughout my travels among native populations of the world, the one thing that was universally true of all of them—whether they were American Indians, Eskimos, Aborigines, or the Sami of the Scandinavian north—is that they all share the basic viewpoint that the Earth is a living entity of which we are only one creature among others, and that the Earth is our mother. "Mother Earth." You hear that in all native languages.

A second fundamental concept is that *you cannot buy or sell or even own private land;* all land is a commons, shared by all people and all other creatures. A tribal nation may stake out territorial lines, of course, and assert its control of certain lands, but the idea of *selling* land, or digging into it to bring out minerals, is unthinkable to native people and utterly outrageous. This goes back thousands of years.

A third fundamental concept, perhaps not universal throughout the world, but nearly so among North American Indian people, is *democratic*

129

decision-making, that is, decision-making without hierarchy or top-down structures, combined with very *slow-moving* governmental processes. Of course this point itself goes against the prevailing Western view of the native as a despotic savage. The idea should have been put to rest decades ago with the work of Pierre Clastres and others, who explained to the uncomprehending Western mind that most native societies work without coercive authority of any kind. Even the concept of "chief" has been badly (and deliberately) misinterpreted to mean "ruler" or "king," a self-serving interpretation, when in fact a "chief" actually acts without direct power over his or her community, is frequently removed from office, and is viewed more as a kind of administrator rather than as having coercive authority. In fact, most tribes that I have worked with have dozens of chiefs simultaneously. They should more precisely be called "teachers." There are medicine chiefs, social chiefs, war chiefs, agricultural chiefs, and so on. All of them maintain leadership only by virtue of their wisdom, and all of them are subject to removal from office by the simple act of being ignored.

This confusion about what is a "chief" was a significant factor in the early history of European-Indian contact. When we arrived into the New World, we came ready to make deals, and seek the central authority with whom to do our business. We wanted land, we wanted minerals, we wanted access to the territories of the Indians. But in the 1600s, we couldn't find any Indian "ruler" who could authoritatively sign on the dotted line; we couldn't find anyone to make a deal with. Instead we ran into cultural strictures against selling or mining land. These two factors—the lack of central authority, and the resistance to selling tribal lands—frustrated the advancement of the invader societies, causing them eventually to just shoot their way in.

A fourth major concept is the idea that the spiritual aspects of life are utterly integrated with all others. It is impossible to separate a sense of the Earth as a living being from the manner of doing economics or politics. They are all enmeshed as part of the single spiritual whole.

The combination of these four characteristics made native societies very difficult to deal with, and also incomprehensible. It also made it difficult for the invader societies to appreciate the native societies as valid in their own right, so we killed them, as we continue to do today.

Now I want to go a bit more deeply into two of the four dimensions mentioned: the political and the economic.

LET'S LOOK FIRST AT INDIAN governmental systems.

Like most Americans I was raised with the idea that American constitutional democracy represented a new and unique political system, a utopian system that proved itself workable in actual practice. I held the usual American prejudices against other structures of government. It never passed through my mind that so-called primitive peoples might have something to offer in the way of democratic forms of government. Such a possibility was never mentioned in schools or in the media. Indian governments, when referred to at all, were described with terms like "anarchy" or "despotisms." They were viewed as representing an early stage of political development of which we are the advanced form.

Describing Indian governance systems so negatively was yet another way for us to justify our interventions in their societies; we offered *the gift of democracy*. More than hubris, it turns out that this is a direct distortion of the truth. Many native nations, especially those of the Americas, practiced a very high form of participatory democracy for thousands of years. Many continue to do so today. In fact, there is a growing body of evidence among scholars of history that the Great Binding Law of the Iroquois Confederacy may have been the primary model and inspiration for the U.S. Articles of Confederation, and for the Constitution itself. Such a possibility was not even mentioned as part of the celebration of the bicentennial of the constitution in 1987. You can surely understand why. What would it mean for the American psyche if it was discovered that our founding fathers, and mothers, were actually Indians?

According to oral histories, the Iroquois Confederacy was founded at least a century before the landing of Columbus. The work of Indian scholars, such as Donald Grinde, Jr. of the University of California, has confirmed that the federation of five and then later six Indian nations was formed to end a history of warfare among them. The nations worked out a very complex set of democratic arrangements which allowed each of their nations to remain largely autonomous. But it also set up quite a few centralized democratic bodies, with elected representatives, full and open public debate, the right of recall of representatives, consensus decision-making, several legislative houses in each nation and in the central government, and universal suffrage, something that was not achieved in the United States until four centuries later. Most of all, however, from the point of view of the American colonists of the thirteen states during the 1700s, the Iroquois offered a model of how to confederate separate states in a peaceful and democratic manner.

Recent scholarship by Dr. Grinde and numerous other Indian and non-Indian researchers has produced extensive reports from the 1700s of long meetings between Benjamin Franklin, John Adams, Thomas Jefferson and other of our famed founding fathers and the political chiefs of the Iroquois Confederacy. The Iroquois were invited to all meetings where the notions of separation from England and the means to establish non-monarchical governments were discussed.

It's important to keep in mind that at this time there was no working model of a democratic confederation anywhere in the experience of the colonists. Europe in those days was ruled entirely by monarchs, many of whom claimed Divine Right. There were some stirrings of democratic ferment in the writings of Montesquieu, Locke, and Hume. And there was the 2,000-year-old Greek model. But Greece was only a partial democracy, it was not a federation, and it existed in an utterly different geopolitical context. And, it included slavery. Meanwhile, living side by side with the European colonists in the New World, and in constant contact with them, was an Indian society that had already developed a successful democratic law that has proven viable for many centuries. That this would *not* have been a major factor in the colonists' awareness and thinking, would be preposterous.

The major urban settlements of the American colonies at that time were Albany, Philadelphia, Boston, and New York. Albany was the site of most of the important meetings about confederation. It had a population at that time of less than 3,000 people. In 1754, it had 200 houses. Philadelphia was the largest city in the colonies, with a population of 13,000.

These places were really tiny towns, with only mud roads, separated from each other by hundreds of miles of forest—several days' travel. Within those forests, of course, were Indians. In fact, the Indians were a far stronger society than the colonists at that time, having yielded only a small percentage of their coastal territory.

The colonists were vulnerable. It was exceedingly important to them to get along with the Indians, who were everywhere apparent. The Indians and colonists often had to discuss mutual arrangements: safe passage, commerce, land agreements (treaties) and military alliances. In fact, militarily, alliances with the Iroquois were a major factor in the wars with the French. If the Iroquois had not finally fought on the side of the English, Americans today would all be speaking French, and probably be part of Quebec.

According to reports that researchers have unearthed from the files of Madison and Franklin, many of the negotiations with the Indians were "in the Indian manner." They were part of the Indian confederacy council meetings, and followed Indian rules of discussion and procedure. So the colonists who negotiated with the Indians had great knowledge of their decision-making process. They also spent time together socially. Good relations with the Indian nations were as important to the colonists of that day as, say, good relations with France are now for England.

Given the intimacy of contact, and the lack of models of democratic confederation anywhere else in the world, and given the literally hundreds of stipulations of the Iroquois law that can now be found nearly verbatim in the U.S. Constitution—especially in the areas of rights reserved to states, as opposed to the federation, and the rights of democratic participation—it is ridiculous to believe that the U.S. Constitution was created out of thin air, without being influenced in a major way by the Indians. Would that they were given some credit.

LET ME NOW MENTION TWO STIPULATIONS of the Great Law of the Iroquois that I think have particular meaning today. Much of the original research of the Great Law was undertaken at the turn of the century by the celebrated Indian (Seneca) anthropologist and historian, Arthur C. Parker, who gathered the codes of the Great Law directly from oral histories of Iroquois elders of that time, and from wampum belts, which are themselves historical records. He translated what was an oral tradition into written form, an imperfect process perhaps, but one which retained the overall meaning of the main tenets and which remains the basis of Iroquois governing systems to this day.

The first is that among the instructions given to the elected council members as to how they are supposed to make their decisions, is the rule that every decision must benefit the seventh generation not yet born. The council members are not to act in terms of immediate self-interest. This standard, acting on behalf of seven generations in the future, is an outstanding protection standard for the planet, and for human welfare, and it is one that is diametrically opposed to the capitalist ideal, which uses every resource as quickly as possible on behalf of direct self-interest, and has no thought of a sustainable future.

The second important stipulation holds that the more significant the decision, the *slower* it should be made. Rules and procedures are spelled out to assure this slower process. Here's how Parker's translation of the law puts it: "When a great emergency is presented before the Iroquois Council, and the nature of the matter affects the entire body of the

Six Nations," then the central council is not permitted to act without first going back to the six national councils for full discussion and consensus decision on the local level.

This is exactly the opposite of how we do business today. In most Western societies—and technology is a big factor in this—the most apocalyptic decisions, especially military ones, are always made by governments quickly, often secretly, without consultation with the people. This speed and secrecy in our societies is justified precisely because of the importance of the matter, and by the need for rapid action. Often this reflects how technology has accelerated the pace of events, creating such possibilities as "launch on warning" for nuclear war.

In the United States, the president basically makes all war decisions by himself. We have recently seen U.S. presidents bomb or invade Vietnam, Cambodia, Laos, Grenada, Lebanon, Panama, and Nicaragua without seeking public approval. (In the case of Iraq, the public approval was a sham, given only after 450,000 troops were already in the area and a *fait accompli* had been achieved.)

I don't know of any society of Indians where a war chief could undertake military action without first holding long meetings with the tribe, taking days or even weeks. Even when a military response is approved, warrior recruitment is voluntary. If an insufficient number of warriors join the force, there is simply no army, or else the war chief goes out there himself. The Iroquois Confederacy institutionalized this cautious rule, requiring that the most significant decisions be made thoughtfully, and with everyone involved.

This is hardly an inferior form of governance.

In fact, the Iroquois Confederacy government is one that still operates today among the same six nations, located mostly in the northeastern United States, and has helped secure their role as one of the most powerful and viable of the still functioning Indian nations in the United States. They remain the most effective and fiercest advocates for native sovereignty rights, and the power of their law makes it possible.

IF ONE FRAUDULENT JUSTIFICATION FOR WESTERN aggression upon native lands has been that *we* bring the gift of democracy, an equally fraudulent justification is that we bring "freedom from toil." Our mythology has it that native peoples have always lived in conditions of awful poverty and oppression, caught in mere "subsistence economics," a term that by its mere utterance brings forth waves of pity and images of squalor. We are here to save these people from that, and it's our technology that will do it.

Leaving aside for now that our dear technology, especially such disasters as "the green revolution," has achieved the opposite of what it set out to do—causing further separation of people from their lands, our premises about the viability of native economies are very wrong.

Most Westerners tend to be shocked when they learn that the majority of native people on the Earth do not wish to climb onto the Western economic machine. They say, contrary to our assumptions, that their traditions have served them well for thousands of years and that our ways are doomed to fail.

Not long ago, the famous Canadian jurist, Thomas Berger, made a tour of Alaskan native villages to document the native viewpoint on subsistence economies (just at the time, the 1970s, the United States was destroying the native economies by converting them to a form of corporate capitalism.) Berger has filled a large report with native praise for traditional subsistence activity. Here is one example of a testimony from Kotzebue, Alaska:

> I came from a subsistence family. I grew up that way. I am very proud of it. I want my children to grow up that way. It brings strength to us as Inupiats (Eskimos). It is something different from going to the store to get meat that comes from Chicago. Our store is millions of acres wide. It brings us pride.

On the rare occasions when Westerners hear such views as these— it was a major point of Berger's study that native people are rarely asked what they think—we tend to relegate the views to ignorance. We are so convinced of the rightness of the Western technological project that we are determined to improve the native condition, even over their objections.

The publication in 1972 of Prof. Marshall Sahlins' seminal work, *Stone Age Economics*, should have exploded the Western myth about native economics for ever. Using extensive field study, and also reports of peoples of the past, Sahlins established that, contrary to prevailing wisdom, primitive societies did *not* work very hard; they had a fairly easy time feeding themselves; they deliberately did not accumulate surpluses; they rarely used their environments to their maximum productive levels; they consciously *chose* subsistence economics; and they had a great deal of fun.

"Hunters and gatherers work far less than we do," says Sahlins. "Rather than a continuous travail, the food quest is intermittent, leisure abundant, and there is a greater amount of sleep in the daytime per capita per year than in any other society."

One study quoted by Sahlins, from aboriginal communities in Western Arnhem Land, added up all the time spent in all economic activity over a span of several months, finding that the average male worked three hours and forty-five minutes per day, and the average female about five minutes more. He goes on to cite work among the Dobe Bushmen showing a work week of about fifteen hours, and that only sixty-five per cent of the population did any work at all.

Here's a quote from Sahlins: "A woman among the Dobe gathers in one day enough food to feed her family for three days, and spends the rest of her time resting in camp, doing embroidery, visiting other camps or entertaining visitors. Meanwhile, the male hunters have a more uneven schedule. It's not unusual for a male to hunt avidly for a week and then do no hunting at all for two or three weeks. During such periods," says Sahlins, "the primary activities of the men are visiting, entertaining and especially dancing."

Stone Age Economics is a huge and impressive work. It speaks about the deliberate *under-use of resources*. Unlike modern industrial societies, the native people chose not to produce at maximum levels. Labor power was underused, technological means were not engaged, natural resources were left untapped, production was kept deliberately low relative to existing possibilities. The work day was very short. The number of days off exceeded the number of work days. And the activities that occupied the greatest part of one's life were dancing, fishing, games, ritual, and sleep.

The immediate environments of most hunter-gatherer communities could easily have supported populations three times the size, but deliberate population control, combined with underused resources, kept the ratio of people to resources impressively small.

As for the idea that native peoples would love to be free of such subsistence economics, the fact is that those who are free to make the choice without outside coercion tend to reject all notions of surplus production. Sahlins quotes one Bushman on this point: "Why should we plant when there are so many mongomongo nuts in the world?"

Marshall Sahlins gives four reasons to explain why native societies avoid surplus production:

First, they are optimistic. They assume that nature is abundant with food, and that you don't need to store it. Nature already has it nicely stored in the form of plants and animals.

Second, hunter-gatherers are nomadic. If they stored food or carried it, they would be slowed down or tied to a specific place. For hunter-gatherers "wealth is truly a burden," says Sahlins.

Third, an economy based on storage would increase the impact on the environment, would threaten mobility and would increase population growth.

Fourth, a hunter-gatherer culture is obviously based on hunting. To accumulate surplus would literally destroy their society.

Sahlins does not suggest that hunter-gatherers are invulnerable to hunger. But, he asks this: "What about the world today? One third to one half of humanity are said to go to bed hungry at night—some twenty million people in the U.S. alone. In the old Stone Age the fraction was much smaller. Now is the time of the greatest technical power, and yet starvation is unprecedented. Hunger seems to increase relatively and absolutely with the evolution of technology."

As for the question of leisure, it is worth noting that leisure *decreases* with the advance of technology. In the United States today, the average work week is forty-seven hours, up from forty hours a decade ago. There has been a 30% increase in the number of people who hold two jobs to survive, just at the same level as they used to with one job.

So the question is this: Have things actually improved? Those of us who enjoy the so-called fruits of the technical juggernaut have more stuff in our lives, we get around more and faster. We are cleaner, and we live a bit longer. But as compared with preindustrial societies, we work much harder, and the time we devote to gathering and caring for commodities has created the great modern paradox: Despite our accumulated commodities, we suffer a shortage of time, a loss of leisure, an increase of stress, a decrease of real security, and we are witnessing the breakdown of the natural world. We are suffering a net *decrease* in the quality of our lives. *So what was it all for?*

The work of Marshall Sahlins, especially when combined with the philosophical writings and observations of such native scholars as John Mohawk, Jeannette Armstrong, Vine Deloria, Dan Bomberry, Oren Lyons and Mililani Trask among others, is absolutely subversive to the paradigms about success that drive the Western technological project. It was the basic premise of technological society that it will prove worthwhile to impact the natural world, to dig it up, pave it over, convert it into commodities, even if we leave behind terrible messes of pollution and destruction, because in the end, life will be improved for all people. This mode of development will make people happier, more fulfilled, offer more leisure, more pleasure, better health and great freedom. But as we have learned, it's not the truth. Instead, this way of life has promoted alienation, drug and chemical abuse, the breakdown of families and communities, while simultaneously leading us to the brink of environmental collapse. *So why are we doing it?*

Sadly, we do it because that's the way the corporations that control society want us to live. They have created an awesome propaganda vision, what I've called "technotopia," and most of us have bought into it, or at least accepted it. Part of that vision is that native peoples who live in another way are inferior to us politically, economically, spiritually, and in every other way. This turns out to be as false as the entire technotopian world-view.

Our only way out of this situation is obviously to recognize the falsity of the current paradigms, attempt in every way possible to unhook ourselves from the growing megatechnological machine, attempt to revitalize small-scale local economic agendas which will promote community self-sufficiency outside the corporate grid, and to fight to help native societies—who want nothing more than to maintain their own successful ways—to fend off the technological juggernaut that seeks to steal their lands and destroy them as viable societies.

This is obviously not going to be easy, but it's not as if we have any choice in the matter. Once we realize that the vehicle we are riding in is heading over the cliff, taking everyone else with it, then the first thing to do is stop it. Seeking viable alternatives and supporting them comes next.

JERRY MANDER is the author of **In The Absence of the Sacred**, *from which this essay was adapted, and* **Four Arguments For The Elimination of Television**.

Reprinted from *Resurgence*, Salem Cottage, Trelill, Bodmin, Cornwall PL30 3HZ, U.K. Subscription: $36.

DHARMA, DEMOCRACY, AND THE INFORMATION HIGHWAY

AN INTERVIEW WITH MITCHELL KAPOR

by HELEN TWORKOV

from TRICYCLE

Mitchell Kapor is the designer of the most widely used computer program in the world, Lotus 1-2-3; the co-founder of Lotus Development Corporation; and the co-founder and co-chair of the Electronic Frontier Foundation (EFF), a not-for-profit organization designed to develop policies to protect democracy and civil liberties on the electronic superhighway. Kapor has pioneered efforts to create dialogues among policymakers, law enforcement officials, programmers, and big business interests in an attempt to civilize the electronic frontier. His work ranges from overseeing projects to make available digital voice, data, and video services at affordable rates to appearances before Congress to testify on intellectual property law and the future of the public telephone network.

Born in Brooklyn, New York, forty-three years ago and raised on Long Island, Kapor received a B.A. from Yale University in 1971 in a self-designed interdisciplinary major, a hybrid of psychology, linguistics, and computer science called cybernetics. After graduation he worked as a disc jockey in Hartford, Connecticut and then became a full-time Transcendental Meditation (TM) instructor. After leaving TM, he studied psychology and then went on to found Lotus. But after a few years Lotus proved so successful—and so demanding—that Kapor felt "like a prisoner of the spreadsheet"; he left to pursue his interest in the public policy and social justice issues at the crossroads of the developments in computer technology.

This interview was conducted for *Tricycle* by editor Helen Tworkov in Cambridge, Massachusetts.

Helen Tworkov: *If there was a key senator who was in a position to influence a major change in government policy about the information superhighway, and you had five minutes to brief him or her about issues surrounding the Internet, what could you say to underscore the enormity of what we're dealing with?*

Mitchell Kapor: One way to start would be to talk about democracy as a kind of self-determination and how we are on the brink of being able to achieve a democratic revolution in media. Instead of a small number of groups having privileged positions as speakers—broadcast networks and powerful newspapers—we are entering an era of communication of the many to the many. And while there will still be editors and intermediaries and people who will be looked to for their wisdom or attractiveness, the nature of the technology itself has opened up a space of much greater democratic possibility. We must not lose the opportunity in this country to run that great experiment.

HT: *And it's up to the government to assure that?*

MK: Yes. Everybody has to be able to get on the system—onto the electronic superhighway. Nobody can be denied the right to connect. Just because you own one of these communication conduits should not mean that you can have exclusive control over what crosses over it. There needs to be open access for people, for creative artists, for entrepreneurs, for teachers and community groups. If you have something to say or do or make that is going to run over this interconnected set of networks, you have a right to be heard. That doesn't mean that people have to listen to you. But it means that you cannot legally be denied access for purposes of creating information or content. Next, you have to respect privacy on this network because that is a fundamental right of the individual.

HT: *You're talking now about concepts, values, mores—not the technology.*

MK: We could wind up building something that is a five-hundred channel nightmare in which all you would have is movies-on-demand

and home-shopping channels and mass-market entertainment; or we could have an open, decentralized system that is faithful to a democratic principle, a system which is going to have plenty of big business and big entertainment and Hollywood, but which will also be a place for the more marginal to participate and find their voice and talk to each other—to communicate. People really do want to communicate: they do not like to be couch potatoes; they do not like being alienated. Online networks offer a medium to find other kindred spirits. We can use the opportunity well, or we can use it poorly. We are at the crossroads.

HT: *You are implying that the information superhighway has the possibility to take democracy to a new level. But sometimes we get the feeling—particularly in the twelve years prior to the Clinton/Gore administration—that the people in Washington don't have democracy as a goal.*

MK: Personally, I worry as much about hindrance from big business as from Congress. The failures of government, which are numerous, arise less out of malice than out of incompetence. At the same time, the value system prevalent in large business is often such that, to an extreme degree, it rewards advancing one's own cause independent of the consequences to everybody else. It glorifies a buccaneer mentality and permits without reproach the kinds of amoral behavior so often seen by very powerful and aggressive corporate forces. We need government to act as a check on the corrosive influence of large private-sector institutions.

HT: *Do we need some kind of check on government control too?*

MK: Government must not be permitted to get in the way of its citizens. There is a middle way between a laissez-faire conservatism, which is morally irresponsible because it does not take a stand to protect public interests, and a total government approach in which the government tries to take the responsibility, to be the provider, the caregiver, the rule-maker in a way that undercuts people's initiative and responsibility. We are finally waking up to that in this country.

HT: *Issues of freedom have been a big concern with you from the time that you were a kid. No matter what you did, whether it was being a disc jockey, teaching Transcendental Meditation or founding Lotus, you were involved in two ideas about freedom: one is an American version of freedom from constraint and the other is some idea about internal liberation. What is the relationship between your preoccupation with freedom of expression and your work—the EFF, computers, technology, free access, open airways— and a more internal idea about freedom?*

MK: There is a more intimate connection between internal and external freedom than one might suspect. I am increasingly coming to realize that internal freedom does not take place in some sphere separate from the world in which we live in each moment. In fact, if "internal freedom" has any real meaning, it's something that would be manifest at each and every moment. So the work that I'm doing now in the intersection of computers and social policy is about trying to create a world which makes it easier for people to realize states of freedom, starting on the outside but for the benefit of the inside as well.

HT: *Does the technology of cyberspace offer us an advanced way to attain internal liberation?*

MK: If you think about how a book or a conversation can stimulate an interest or aid a decision, or how sacred writing can sometimes induce a special state of experience, you're on the right track. But I don't think we know how to tell the story about the relationship between cyberspace and liberation yet. It is an arena in which human experience takes place—so I expect the full panoply of good and evil. To be more specific, I don't know what people are doing in cyberspace now that is leading to liberation. I can envision that when the technology gets a little bit more mature it will be possible to bring people together as a group of co-participants, even though people are not sitting in the same physical space. For instance, it might be possible to have a sesshin [a Zen meditation retreat] without sitting together in a meditation hall. People could actually come together at a particular time without being in the same place.

HT: *Does that signal the end of the spiritual teacher?*

MK: No, I think it adds a new dimension. It might transform the teacher-student relationship, but wouldn't eliminate the teacher. It may be possible to develop a whole new form of groups coming together and, through individual action or meditation, creating some greater collective whole. Is it your experience, for instance, that there is something different about meditating in a group?

HT: *If a fly lands on my nose and I'm sitting alone, I'm more likely to scratch. Suzuki Roshi said something like, "Zazen is all about sitting still and not scratching"—not scratching physically or mentally. When you sit with others the silence can get very loud.*

MK: I wonder whether it would be possible to amplify the quality of silence in individual meditation if people were linked up through cyberspace. That's my intuition.

HT: *To try to comprehend cyberspace I imagine conduits that direct a dynamic already in existence. Since we can be connected at enormous distances through the physics of space and sound and vibration, maybe these cyberspace conduits channel what is already there.*

MK: Yes, in fact it would be fascinating to do some experiments. Suppose people could wear unobtrusive sensors that would monitor certain aspects of breathing or the degree of stillness or motion, and then transmit that? What I notice in groups, live groups, is that there is an enormous amount of completely nonverbal, subtle communication. We do not yet have a scientific vocabulary for this phenomenon, but the things that happen in groups are very real. So here is yet another dimension of the electronic frontier that is a spiritual dimension, which is to say, how can you create a space, in cyberspace, for these types of collective experiences, because they do really bear on awareness.

HT: *If we are talking about the creation of spiritual community in terms of "virtual community," then we are talking about the absence of a particularized teacher-student relationship, or the wisdom of an evolved mind understanding the specificity of any one particular disciple.*

MK: Even in cyberspace that one-to-one relationship is still crucial to teacher/student relationships of all kinds—from elementary school to Zen. Where cyberspace can make a difference is what happens after the teacher leaves town. It's not a replacement for the face-to-face, but rather a supplement to it. It is a way of leveraging a scarce resource: the time and attention of the teacher. But of course not everybody will share this vision, and some people will tend to substitute technology for human contact.

HT: *Do you speak from experience?*

MK: Yes. It was a problem in TM, for example, because they were trying to train teachers on a mass scale, to turn out hundreds and then thousands of them, far more than could be done with any amount of individual attention. And if you have a more powerful technology, it will be used as a substitute. I continue to see more and more of these biofeedback helmets that put you in an alpha state, and they're becoming a whole sort of pseudo-substitute for meditation.

HT: *Is this the natural response to technology?*

MK: Very typically, when a lot of technology comes on the scene, people bring with it a lot of mental baggage such as the impulse to quantify. Because so much of the building of technology itself requires quantification, that technique becomes very prominent and exerts an influence that tries to reduce other phenomena to measurements.

HT: *So here you're getting into self-fabricated prisons, not the technology itself.*

MK: For me there is a very compelling central theme in Buddhist texts: most of us are prisoners of our own minds and no set of changes in material conditions unaccompanied by changes in consciousness is going to achieve real freedom. That sort of story is told over and over again with extraordinary subtlety in the texts of Buddhism. It has been a traditional failing of a lot of progressive politics to not take into account this issue of mental imprisonment, and consequently there has been an overemphasis on just altering material conditions and on the redistribution of wealth. All we have to do is to look to the great American middle class—which enjoys a standard of living higher than any people of any time anywhere in the history of the planet—and see the peculiar new forms of spiritual and psychic disease and alienation and nihilism and substance abuse to understand that material circumstance alone won't do it. If everybody were poor and starving and dying of diseases, you could say, Well what we really need to do is just to cure diseases and give people a place to live and food to eat. But we have done it in a way that doesn't make the majority of middle-class people genuinely at peace. And we have also done it in a way that continues to exclude very large numbers of people, and our success rides on their backs.

HT: *Can that sort of mental imprisonment be addressed by the outside?*

MK: Yes, in part. The nature of reality is suffering, and reality is a pretty big place, so there is a lot that can be said and done about suffering. If you have a broad view of suffering, in its internal and external varieties, it creates a pretty big field of opportunity for action. I like the idea of engaged Buddhism, the notion that one builds one's life around a commitment to relieving suffering wherever and whenever possible.

HT: *It seems that the material you've been involved with has addressed issues of internal and external freedom and also has an entrenched wariness of authoritarian rule. Is this perspective influenced by your experience with Maharishi Mahesh Yogi and TM?*

MK: My dislike for authoritarian structures goes back as far as I can remember. If I could remember past lives, I'm sure my memories would extend there, too. But my experiences in Transcendental Meditation ultimately really deepened my commitment to anti-authoritarianism.

HT: *How did you get into TM?*

MK: Well, my experience was typical for my generation. I had gotten to college in the sixties and started experimenting with marijuana and psychedelics, fairly heavily. I had some distressing experiences with LSD. Bad trips. So I stopped doing drugs and then started getting acid flashbacks. I decided to give meditation a serious try to see if that could have some calming effect. I got hooked into TM and eventually made the decision to go through advanced training to become an initiator, an instructor.

HT: *How long did you stay involved with TM?*

MK: I was involved for seven years. It all ultimately came to a head in 1976. The movement went into a new phase and Maharishi started talking about siddhis, powers, and techniques for doing levitation and other things. This created so much cognitive dissonance in me that I didn't know what to do. I had to find out if it was real or not, and I wanted to believe that it was real, but something in me said that it couldn't possibly be real. People weren't really going to levitate. So I went to Switzerland for the six-month course on "powers." I went and I fell apart. They were using us as experimental subjects. There was fasting involved and various austerities that come out of Hindu traditions, enemas and various bizarre food-combining rituals. A lot of madness got released. After five months of this I said, Whatever problems I might or might not have, TM is not making them better, it is making them worse. And I decided to leave. This was like leaving everything, because I had severed all of my other ties and relations: no job, no career, no marriage, and no prospects. I got up in the middle of the night and walked to the train station. I felt like I was crossing from slavery into freedom, from one intolerable situation into the great unknown. By the way, no one really levitates. I fully satisfied myself as to that.

HT: *How did you go from TM to Lotus?*

MK: I was on my way to getting a doctorate in psychology when personal computers first came out. I had sporadic run-ins with computers in high school and in college, but that was in mainframe computer days, big boxes that sat in their own room with a raised floor, tended by a priesthood of systems programmers. As a user of computers one was of low caste, and one had to deal with the priestly intermediaries to get anything done. There was no direct communion between the user and the computer. The computer was in the ark, and only the priests could open the ark. But I had the intuition, as a lot of others had, that if that ever changed, it would be really cool. Finally, by the mid-seventies, personal computers, PCs, came out. These were things that you could buy, that you could play with—that you could relate to on an intimate level. In between the time I decided to go back to graduate school in 1978 and when I was supposed to go, the fall of 1979, I started doing consulting work for personal computers, hiring myself out at five dollars an hour. I wrote little programs and I parlayed one thing into another.

HT: *What a grand understatement.*

MK: Nobody had any idea that it was going to amount to something this big. All I knew was that this was fun and I had finally found something to do that I was good at. So for the next three and a half years I learned as much about personal computers and software as anybody on the planet. I got that if you could put one of these programs on a desktop, hundreds of millions of people would want them. I went to MIT Business School and they thought I was nuts. I wrote a business plan for a course in entrepreneurship. I got a B in the course—because it wasn't a very good business plan, as they go—but I said we should just do it!

HT: *Where did Lotus 1-2-3 come in?*

MK: There had been a spreadsheet program before ours; 1-2-3 was really a second-generation spreadsheet. It made a number of fundamental improvements on the basic model, which then sparked a massive adoption of the personal computer as a tool by the business community.

HT: *How big did Lotus become?*

MK: We thought in our first year we might do three to four million dollars in sales, and that would have been a big success. We did 53 million. And then 156 million the next year, and 225 million the year after that, and the year after that I burned out. I was miserable.

HT: *Did the ideas that have informed the EFF—the concerns with democracy and free speech—figure prominently in your work at Lotus?*

MK: Not on the surface, but as we were building the business, I started getting involved with some of the public-policy issues that arose in the software business. The first one was copyright problems. I found that I got a tingle from working on issues where my knowledge of technology made a material difference, but that were about something besides the technology itself, that somehow reached out and had an impact on people's lives in a broader way.

HT: *Were there discussions in those days about the possibility of free access or democracy in terms of information highway technology?*

MK: Only to a very limited extent. The first wide-area computer network, called the ARPAnet, was started in 1969 by the Defense Department and eventually evolved into the Internet. But in the seventies, the number of people using that was very small—a dozen campuses at most. In the late seventies computer networks started to expand; computer bulletin boards began to appear, and the first online services like CompuServe and The Source started out. In general I had a sense of great possibility, but I had a lot of disdain for the ARPAnet in particular. I thought it was very elitist. You had to prove you were worthy to get an account on it. When I was at MIT, I said, Oh cool, I'm an MIT student, I can get on the Internet now. MIT had open access, so open that local high school students used to pass around the phone numbers to dial in and get access. But I said, I am not going to do that. That is cheating. That's not what the policy is. And to make people cheat to get access sends the wrong message. So I went to MIT and said, I want an account on the Internet. And they said, Why? And I said, I just want to play around and explore. I told the truth. And they said, that's not one of the qualifying reasons on this list. You can't have that account. So I left, got mad, and stayed mad for a long time. That's the kind of bureaucratic closed-mindedness we're trying to get rid of. It was only after I'd left Lotus and several more years had gone by that these issues were on the center of my plate, because of some personal experiences that I had.

HT: *Such as?*

MK: In December 1989 I spent two weeks exploring an online system called The Well [Whole Earth 'Lectronic Link], which is in Sausalito, California, and which was started by Stewart Brand. I fell in love all over again, just like I fell in love with the Apple II in 1978. It was a transforming experience. Here was a place, a virtual place. What I was reading was the record of conversations between groups of people on a very wide range of topics that had been collected over a period of time about everything from politics to media to current events. But it was also about the whole phenomenon of "virtual communities." That's the first place I ever heard that phrase. I said, Hey, these are interesting people, these are people I would like to get to know in the real world. I want to communicate with them. They're smart; they're interested in the things that I'm interested in; they care about those things. I got hooked.

HT: *The idea of a "virtual community" was new?*

MK: Yes. The Well was one of the few places where it was taken seriously. Until then, people who had been on networks had been interested in technical topics only; or they were hobbyists, like ham radio people. Some people relate to computers the way hams relate to ham radios; all they want to do is talk about their equipment, which is a perfectly nice hobby, but my appetite for that was limited. On the Well you had a set of people who were interested not in the technology in and of itself, but in what it meant.

HT: *Was there a specific situation that prompted you to found the EFF?*

MK: I met a person on The Well named John Perry Barlow who is an integral part of this story, a sometime Wyoming cattle rancher, lyricist for the Grateful Dead, former Republican county chairman, and self-confessed acid head and amateur Buddhist. Later we met in physical space when he came to interview me for a computer publication: one of the other hats he sometimes wears is journalist. We hit it off. He knew some of these kids, some hackers; he'd met them online and gotten to know them. He formed a picture that they were not spawned by the devil, they were teenagers who were doing what teenagers had always done, which is to cross lines that people have drawn. They were misunderstood, and those people, the ones that he knew, were relatively harmless.

HT: *These were the kids who were getting busted because they were breaking into government files?*

MK: Yes. they were alleged to be undermining national security and were facing lifetime jail sentences! There was a demonology at work. What the press and the Secret Service were saying and what we thought was true amounted to the difference between day and night. John [Barlow] and I both had our personal taste of this because we had been interviewed, separately, by the FBI in a matter related to the same case, the theft of some source code for Apple's operating system—the instructions that make the Macintosh what it is. The problem was, at that time, the FBI didn't know a microchip from a cow chip. When I had my interview, I wound up feeling sorry for these guys, and gave them a computer tutorial. It was clear that the legal system didn't have a clue what to do with these hackers. And then there were these kids, whose lives were getting caught in the gears and who were about to be chewed up.

HT: *So you identified with the kids?*

MK: Yes. If I'd had a chance to be a hacker when I was a kid, I would have gone for it. And maybe I would have needed somebody to take me back behind the woodshed or slap me on the wrist, but felony charges and long jail terms—no way! Not for what they did. So John came to me because Lotus had left me with a lot of money. Our initial construction of this was as a civil liberties issue, saying computers represent a new medium of information and the specific problems were violations of the first and Fourth Amendments: seizures of equipment, unreasonable searches and seizures, and interference with the rights of free expression—cases involving Steve Jackson Games, a game manufacturer in Austin, Texas, and he wasn't a hacker at all but got confused for one. They practically shut down his business. So we thought we would have a sort of legal defense fund and hire some sharp New York civil liberties attorneys.

HT: *You saw that these weren't isolated instances.*

MK: We understood that these cases were symptomatic, the tip of a much bigger iceberg. We felt that it would be a good idea to create an organization that would try to help civilize cyberspace, to raise issues before they get to be problems, to seek to help society understand what kinds of policies we ought to have—public policies on the law side but also the broad issues of ethics and morals and civil liberties, and thus was born the Electronic Frontier Foundation.

HT: *But your motivation was more complex than just to protect a few individuals, wasn't it?*

MK: It was an issue of the destruction of community. This new good thing that was developing in cyberspace, communities of people online, was in danger of being disrupted and ruined. I think that that was something we were not very clear about and because of that, we were cast into the role of pure civil libertarians, which I found to be an uncomfortable suit of clothing. While free expression issues matter enormously, they are not the only issues that matter.

HT: *For example?*

MK: Well, for instance, it seems a very poor species of liberalism that is only interested in protecting the right of neo-Nazis to march in Skokie. That is certainly important, but the real question is, how do we have a society in which those evil seeds cannot take root? You cannot achieve that simply by enforcing the first Amendment. If you have a hundred units of resources to spend, how many of them do you spend in getting them their permit, and how many of them do you spend on building the kind of society that makes it less likely that such a thing would ever emerge? Some people want to spend a hundred units just on getting the permit. We wanted to have a kind of balance expenditure, but the problem was that we had a very specific program for half of it—for the civil liberties part—which was to hire some lawyers to defend rights in these cases, so we could immediately engage in the specific programs; hire a staff attorney to help educate BBS [Bulletin Board System] operators and users of BBSs in the law enforcement community on the nature of these legal issues.

HT: *Why have you been referred to as the Thomas Jefferson of the Internet?*

MK: Well, he was a decentralist, that's my term; he was suspicious in the extreme of the power of large institutions to oppress, and he came to believe that the proper form of government would be a ward-and-council system at the local level. He thought that individuals and communities ought to control themselves, not some abstract, distant, remote, uncaring, inefficient entity. He said, "If we had to depend on Washington to defend our crops, we would never harvest anything." The view that prevailed, however, was a Federalist view that emphasized a stronger central government. He would have been opposed to big companies on the grounds that larger, powerful institutions would dampen and demean the human spirit. So what is Jeffersonian about my view of cyberspace is that there will be similar battles for control of it: Will the rules be made centrally? Will the use of the resources and accesses to them and the determination of who can say what or who can say anything at all be made by some centralized authority, private or public? You need to decentralize technology and decentralize the set of policies, and that is very Jeffersonian.

HT: *And that is at the heart of the EFF?*

MK: The broad concern is to decentralize a lot of the power in this society. To have more of a balance and to have individuals in small groups to be less disadvantaged vis-à-vis large institutions, whether they be private or public. What makes EFF what it is politically is not that it's particularly left or right but that it's decentralist, as opposed to authoritarian.

HT: *How did moving the EFF offices to Washington affect your work?*

MK: Many people on the Internet thought that by relocating entirely to Washington, which we did a year ago, we were selling out our constituents. We went through an identity crisis and decided that we didn't

have constituents in the formal sense. We were not trying to set ourselves up as the provisional or territorial government of cyberspace.
Some people assumed that we were doing that!

HT: *The "government of cyberspace" seems to contradict the very quality that cyberspace is about.*

MK: It's only an apparent contradiction. We were grappling all
along with the fact that you couldn't keep cyberspace in a "state of nature." Willy-nilly, it would be civilized after some fashion, because large
and established interests would come in and seek to establish claims: "We
own this piece" or "We will make the rules on this network." That courts
would make interpretations for cyberspace to remain extraterritorial for the
long term was actually a foolish and romantic wish. So the notion of a government in cyberspace is not as completely peculiar as it first sounds.

HT: *And you were supposed to be the elected officials of cyberspace?*

MK: Some network users did look at us as their representatives,
that somehow we had established a moral obligation to represent their
interests. We ultimately decided that we wanted to be part of the democratic process, but we didn't want to be the process itself. We wanted to
be able to disagree with people, to stand up for what we thought was
right, to find other people to work with on issues. But we didn't want to
become a representative body pushed in that direction. And people felt
we had sold out, that we had been captured by the lure of playing power
politics inside the Beltway.

HT: *I gather that Gore understands the policy dilemmas, but I also
understand that there are many senators who don't even know what being
online means.*

MK: Out of the 535 senators and representatives, a handful get it.
Members of Congress tend to look for simple ways to understand complex problems and they try to support approaches which are consistent
with their general approach to political life. It would be easier and better
for us if there were the time to really get everybody to understand all the
issues—that would be like heaven. But as it is now, you have to market
your ideas. That introduces the possibility, if you are an interest group,
whether commercial or public, of the risk of falsification, of the advertising
pitch taking over from the substance. So it introduces an additional risk
and problem: How do you stay faithful to your own principles and truth
when the people that you need to persuade are actually not dealing with
things at the level of truth?

HT: *Is the level of truth obscured by information overload?*

MK: Yes. Data shock. The information highways are in reality still mostly unpaved. The cost of acquisition of information is really high. Information is not well organized. The Internet is like a gigantic library whose card catalogue has been spilled on the floor. A lot of that is a function of its immaturity and over time it will evolve to become simpler. But there is a larger ontological problem lurking behind it; it has been reported to me that Marvin Minsky, one of the gurus of artificial intelligence, has said that he prefers virtual sunsets to real sunsets—a virtual sunset meaning a representational image done in a computer graphic—because it's perfect and you can have it whenever you want it. I would say that if we lose our ability to prefer the real over the virtual, we have a sickness of the soul that will be far greater than anything that has been previously imagined. Reality—and I'm just talking about the physical world, the part of "isness" that manifests itself—is deep. It is mysterious. It is complex. It is always changing. And a real sunset or a real anything is always going to be real in a way that any representation of it is not, and the representation is going to lose something. We really are in danger of losing that distinction to the point where people are not even aware that there is a distinction to be made—and that would be terribly dangerous. It requires a kind of higher wisdom to know both at the social level and at the individual level how to use the tools of technology and to use these new digital media appropriately.

HT: *Can the new technology itself be used to cultivate that higher wisdom?*

MK: There is no guarantee, and we can't rely on the technology itself to do that and we can't escape from the necessity of making choices and living with the consequences of those choices. I can see a fork in the road, two different kinds of outcomes and uses, which will no doubt be mixed up together, but I worry about which will predominate. You can learn to use the technology in a way that enhances your human contact, such that your interactions with people online have the same character and take place in the same moral universe as your actions with people in the real world. And the great thing about it is that you can leverage a modest amount of face-to-face contact with a lot of electronically mediated contact if you go about it in this spirit. So there are people I have met with whom I am in correspondence: they're part of my universe, we share information, we do things together. But it is in the spirit of the notion that we are all kind of connected in the real world. If you go about this as some play universe in which it doesn't matter what you do ultimately, in which there is no connection to it, in which it is kind of an escape, then it's a sort of addiction to not dealing with things. That potential is clearly there, and it's there in spades. So we make one set of choices now about whether we build a system that is biased toward that or not. I don't think we should build a system that is biased toward turning people into interactive, virtual-reality couch potatoes. We have choices.

HT: *How does the two-way system in itself function as a corrective to the human inclination toward delusion?*

MK: A system that is a two-way interactive lets people be their own originators and creators, and that is necessary but not sufficient. Ultimately, we have to look outside the technology and outside its possibilities and ask ourselves a more fundamental set of questions, like: what is the purpose of existence? How are we trying to reduce suffering?

HT: *What sounds more plausible is that a lot of people who go online will prefer an artificial sunset.*

MK: Historically, it has often been the case that elites have underestimated the ability of the mass of people to respond positively and favorably to some kind of change. There are lots of people who said that American democracy would never work. I come from a background where the impossible happened more than once, so I can't help but be an incurable optimist. But part two, suppose you're right, what are our options? To roll back the technology? Not a chance. So what we have to do is pretty much what we are trying to do, which is to re-embed the technology in a broader moral and spiritual universe, because that's the only hope. Let us have the kind of society which, when we think about the choices that we are making in these regards, is informed by a moral and spiritual sense.

HT: *How are we going to go about this?*

MK: We can build a system that is decentralized, that is not highly controlled, that enables individuals and groups with very marginal ideas to have ready access to it.

HT: *Why do you think that's a good thing?*

MK: Because if you look at history, things that we now take for granted, like women's suffrage, started out as very radical, totally marginal ideas. There is a process by which the surviving ideas work their way toward the center over a period of time.

HT: *I don't know what to make of your optimism.*

MK: It's a chronic disposition, and therefore something to be worked with and refined. Used poorly, it blinds one to suffering, but used well, it inspires, gives hope, and sees possibilities. To make progress on something in society, to get answers, you have to frame questions. I think that the time is really ripe for a general moral and spiritual revival or renewal. I think that people increasingly sense that something is missing and are prepared to look seriously at what that might mean in their individual lives and their family or community. I think this new medium could be a wonderful channel for that exploration and discussion because it is open and democratic and it does not depend on the buy-in of any elites to sanction it.

HT: *And what about the groups that preach hate and separation?*

MK: In general, the Net should be equally available to the skinheads and the Nazis and purveyors of "filth." While there ought to be limits on speech, such as on child pornography, they should be very narrowly drawn.

HT: *It "should be" that way because it has to be.*

MK: Right. Because all the other arrangements that we know about are far worse in their consequences. The Net is an obvious win for free speech, but its value as a seedbed for community is more problematic. I think we are fundamentally stuck, as a society, grappling with questions about happiness and suffering, and we've gotten deeply off on the wrong track. So deeply that it has become illegitimate in many quarters to talk about that.

HT: *Do you ever wake up in the middle of the night and feel that there is a possibility that you're like a member of the Manhattan Project, working on something that you think is really wonderful only to discover years later that you have contributed to a monster?*

MK: Sometimes. I try to confront that as best as I know how. Being human and being fallible, there is always a distinct possibility of coming to conclude that one's actions were in error. Even if our vision is not really correct, it's better than the five-hundred-channel nightmare. But sure, I may likely decide that there was too much misplaced optimism and hope on my part in the ability of the technology itself to have social value, and what was really going on was simply my own excitement about new things operating in this domain with a sort of lack of discipline and judgment. From the first waves of religious revival in pre-revolutionary

America to the millennial impulse, enthusiasm is chronic in American history. I think there is now another wave of this in cyberspace; people see it as some omega point of development, and that's a very ahistorical view. But that aside, it does pay for us to look into the creative possibilities inherent in the new medium, to look for what it can help contribute to the liberation of the human spirit. That's the whole point. Why else would one be interested in it?

e-mail: info@eff.org *for information about the Electronic Frontier Foundation.*
e-mail: mkapor@eff.org *for contact with the author.*

Reprinted from *Tricycle*, TRI Box 3000, Denville, NJ 07834, 1-800-950-7008. Subscription: $20/year.

A PATH UNCOVERED

by DAVID A. COOPER

from COMMON BOUNDARY

A large number of Jewish people these days think of themselves in divided terms: There are Hin-Jews, Su-Jews, Tao-Jews, and Bu-Jews (or Ju-Bus), representing the syncretization of Hindu, Sufi, Taoist, and Buddhist traditions with Judaism. Rabbi Zalman Schachter-Shalomi refers to these people as "hyphenated Jews." Some Jews have rejected their birthright altogether, preferring to identify fully with a new spiritual path or no path at all. Many of these and other Jews have suggested to me that Judaism is not "spiritual" enough. What they don't know is that there is an established way into Jewish spiritual life through contemplative insight.

Examples of meditation practices in Judaism exist that are equivalent to chanting mantras, gazing at mandalas, engaging in one-pointed concentration, and utilizing visualizations. There is a devotional practice similar to *bhakti* yoga, an intellectual practice similar to *jnana* yoga, and a practice of attaining what is commonly called automatic writing or automatic speech—on higher levels, called prophesy—through *ruah hakodesh* (holy spirit). There is a series of practices, described in the Talmud, that guide one on the path of the *tzaddik* (a being with saintly behavior), just as in Buddhism there are directions on how to become a *bodhisattva.* Different forms of meditation appear in the Talmud and the Bible—some leading to ecstasy, others to equanimity, still others to cosmic consciousness. Upon inspection we discover that Judaism is filled with contemplative techniques.

From its inception, Judaism has possessed a strong subcurrent of contemplative, spiritual practice, revealed clearly when its oral tradition was committed to a written form almost 2,000 years ago. The Talmud refers often to the "secrets of the Torah," which are generally understood to be the kabbalah, a body of teachings that delved into the esoteric meanings of scripture and the hidden purpose of the "commandments" that guided Jewish life. The kabbalists suggest that the fundamental reason to observe the commandments is not merely because a divine authority demands it, but because once we are attuned to the impact each of our actions has on the universe, we gain a deep understanding committing us to living a life of full awareness.

The earliest Jewish texts, and even scripture, refer to what is known in kabbalah as the "Works of the Chariot," the metaphysical vehicle through which one is transported from the physical world to higher levels of awareness. One of the primary objectives of kabbalistic inquiry is known as "descent into the chariot," which requires altered consciousness. The only way this state of mind can be achieved is through devoted contemplative practice.

While rabbinic Judaism has relied consistently on *halakhah*—the body of Jewish law—as the foundation of the outward expression of the religion, kabbalists have always sought to pierce the meaning of the inner experience. The kabbalists behold the Torah not only as the source of law for the Jewish people, but as a revelation of cosmic principles. They view it as the "mind of God," revealing the mysteries of Creation and all of nature. As far as the sages were concerned, the only way the kabbalah could be truly appreciated was by fully experiencing the life of Jewish practice.

The insistence of the kabbalists to remain hidden, purposely obscuring the teachings in mysterious symbols and coded language, effectively cloaked this body of wisdom from the world for most of the last 2,000 years. In fact, many practicing Jews —including rabbis—are still unfamiliar with deeper kabbalistic knowledge. As a result, contemporary Jews interested in spiritual exploration have been turning to other traditions where esoteric principles and practices are more readily accessible.

In the last 20 to 30 years, however, many kabbalistic teachings have been translated and published. Indeed, the beginning of a counter-trend has been observed in which many people are turning back to their Jewish heritage. They are focusing on the contemplative aspect of the tradition and attempting to integrate ancient Jewish practices into modern daily life.

Aryeh Kaplan's book, *Jewish Meditation*, points out that there are three basic types of contemplative practice in Judaism. One is called *kavannah*, which means "concentration," "feeling," or "devotion" but is commonly translated as "intention." Kaplan notes that the word comes from the root *kavan*, meaning "to aim." Thus, *kavannah* has to do with the conscious effort to develop a spiritual frame of reference when engaged in any act. In many ways, *kavannah* is the pulse beat of Jewish spirituality.

Kavannah covers a wide spectrum of practice, from acute awareness of the simple act of moving the body, speaking a word, or thinking a thought to intense, transformative meditations in which one elevates the mind from one level of light to another until attaining the highest realization of what is called the "Infinite Light."

In the daily practice of *kavannah*, we constantly invite awareness into our consciousness. It is similar to the experience of Buddhist meditation, in which we are instructed to observe our breath or parts of our body at all times. Using *kavannah*, we observe our intentions, the "who" behind the act, the possible ramifications of the act, and how the act would be measured in comparison with the advice of Jewish sages recorded and transmitted over the centuries. Obviously, this form of practice is a tall order, considering that each human being is a vehicle for tens of thousands of daily acts. Yet, as a contemplative practice, each effort toward moment-to-moment awareness is a step closer to the major goal in Jewish life: expanded consciousness, ultimately leading to a paradigm shift in which a new era of peaceful human relations will reign.

Kaplan notes a second type of contemplative Jewish practice known as *hitbonenuth*, which means "self-understanding," in which one constantly reflects upon how he or she fits into the drama of unfolding Creation. As opposed to casual gazing, daydreaming, or even one-pointed meditation, this process invites an appreciation of the continuing presence of the Divine that penetrates each of our thoughts and actions. This kind of contemplative reflection opens a profound level of understanding and leads to a new sense of purpose. Out of this process comes the motivation for a central feature of Judaism: *tikkun olam*, the obligation upon every Jew to repair the broken aspects of the world.

The third form of meditation mentioned by Kaplan is *hitbodeduth*, which translates as "self-isolation." This involves not only practicing occasional silence and solitude but also learning the process of *internal self-isolation*, to cleanse the mind of all the chatter and find the center of stillness within. Many of the greatest kabbalists went on solitary retreat for weeks at a time, some for longer. In fact, Isaac Luria (known as the Ari), who transformed Judaism with his kabbalistic insight, reputedly sat on silent retreat for seven years, coming out only once each week to celebrate the Sabbath.

Rebbe Nachman of the Breslev sect is famous for teaching his version of the practice of *hitbodeduth*, in which the practitioner is advised to go into the woods alone to speak with God—using any form of prayer that comes to mind. Many Hasidic members of Breslev today continue this practice, while other people have found that spontaneously communing with the essence of the Divine—in their own home or any place of solitude, as a respite from the intensity of daily life—has healing qualities and is a source of personal empowerment.

Kaplan, who was a Jewish scholar of great genius, pointed out that many commentators missed the meditative and contemplative side of Judaism because of mistranslation and misunderstanding. He says: "One can read a Hebrew meditative text and not even be aware of the nature of the subject. . . . The general impression one gains from studying these texts is not only that meditation was practiced by Jews but that for quite a number of centuries it was a very important ingredient of Judaism."

The failure of mainstream Judaism to appreciate the contemplative dimension over the last few centuries surely has contributed to some of the erosion the tradition has experienced. Obviously, there are many other factors at work. But continuing to ignore the growing need for meditative practice—a need clearly expressed by the tens of thousands of Jews engaged in other contemplative forms—may have serious consequences.

Most contemporary Jews relate that entering an ordinary prayer service in synagogue is often a daunting, alienating experience. Many feel enormous confusion, especially when the prayers are read at great speed—a common practice. Regarding prayer, the Talmud teaches that *"the ancient ones used to wait an hour [in preparation], pray for an hour, and then wait again for an hour [in reflection]"* (Berakoth 32:b). As the Talmud is a couple of thousand years old, we can only imagine who the "ancient ones" are. The point is that this source—at the heart of Judaism—teaches us that daily prayer requires a meditative mode.

Mainstream Judaism is terrified that other traditions will convert Jews away from Judaism—and with good reason, because it is happening. But the spiritual richness of Judaism, if allowed its rightful place in the tradition, will be sufficient to hold its own once its true value is established. This is why many people are beginning to take a second look at Judaism. In fact, some of the best teachers in Judaism are those who have experienced other paths and have returned to bring new vitality into the tradition.

Judaism offers a broad spectrum of possibilities and presents a constant challenge to anyone who seeks to plumb its depths. Once Jews taste the nectar from its mystical orchard, they will discover that their own tradition is as rich as any other authentic path of enlightenment in the world today.

RABBI DAVID A. COOPER lived and studied in the Old City of Jerusalem for eight years. He and his wife now live in the Colorado mountains, overseeing a facility for people engaged in individual spiritual retreats. His books include **Entering the Sacred Mountain: A Mystical Odyssey***;* **Silence, Simplicity, and Solitude: A Guide for Spiritual Retreat***; and* **The Heart of Stillness: The Elements of Spiritual Practice***.*

Reprinted from *Common Boundary*, PO Box 445, Mt. Morris, IL 61054, 1-800-548-8737. Subscription: $22/year.

GRACE IN THE MIDST OF FAILINGS

by ROSEMARY RADFORD RUETHER

from SOJOURNERS

I am frequently asked, "How can you stay in the church?" Some who ask this are expressing amazement that anyone seemingly so intelligent could remain connected with such a benighted institution as the Christian church. They want to know why I don't leave, much as an impatient social worker might ask a battered woman why she can't bring herself to leave her abusive husband. Many other questioners desperately want to continue in relation to the Christian church, but are finding it hard to do so. They want to know if I have some clue that has escaped them on how to remain a Christian without being demoralized or depressed.

I am not sure I have a satisfactory answer to the question from either of these contexts. But I can unpack my own thinking on the problem, which I define as how to remain faithful to Christ in a sinful church.

Dismay at the public and private behavior of church leaders and their governance of the church is hardly new. Such criticism can be found in some form from the earliest days of Christianity. In our own time, revelations of sexual abuse of children and youth by clergy have dominated the news, probably less because this is a new occurrence in

Christian circles than because it is now being prosecuted in secular courts. Such revelations are causing a significant crisis in the credibility of church leaders, both among lay people and in the society at large.

However, reformers have also been cognizant of other failings. At least since the late 18th century, secular critics, as well as Christian reformers, have called for transformations of society that would overcome gross injustices: the vast gaps between wealth for the few and grinding misery for the many; the denial of human and civil rights to those without property, to blacks and Indians, to women.

Christian liberalism, the social gospel, and liberation, black, and feminist theologies have been ways of reconceiving a prophetic vision that makes transformation toward social justice intrinsic to the promise of salvation. If one believes this vision, then the Christian church should be at the forefront of the movements for liberation and justice. But the majority of churches have functioned to sacralize the social status quo; church teachings have promoted and justified the very evils that they should be denouncing.

From New Testament times to the mid-19th century, the continuous teaching and practice of most of the Christian churches condoned slavery. Likewise, Christian churches in the United States and elsewhere into the 1960s acceded to and at times theologically justified racial segregation. Those church leaders earliest to denounce slavery and segregation usually came from outside the mainline churches—Quakers, Baptists, and Methodists.

Anti-Semitism also has its long and evil history in both church teaching and practice. Theological diatribes in the ante-Nicene church fathers became institutionalized in the Constantinian era as theologically justified discrimination and sometimes even violence against the Jewish communities. This continued through the Middle Ages into modern times, reaping its horrendous fruit in the Nazi Holocaust.

The Deutero-Pauline texts define women as second in creation and first in sin and call for silence and subordination as women's path to acceptability in the church. A continual line of theologians, from Tertullian and Augustine through medieval scholastics and 16th-century Reformers, backed by canon law, continue the exclusion of women from ordained ministry and public preaching.

Even 20th-century theologians, such as Karl Barth, opined that the subordination of women to men is intrinsic to the order of creation. Needless to say, women in seminaries and churches remain surrounded by conservative church leaders and members, men and women, for whom the continuity and weight of this tradition are definitive proof of its truth, even after church bodies have voted to admit women to ordained ministry.

Women seeking ministerial roles are caught between two equally daunting possibilities. Either this tradition is true precisely because it has been continuously taught, enforced, and re-enforced, and therefore aspiration to ministry and existence in the ministry is contrary to God's will and Christ's intention for the church. Or the church has been deeply apostate, denying to women—who have probably been in every age more than the majority of faithful Christians—full membership in the body of Christ and thus full recognition of that equal redemption won them by Christ.

IF THIS IS THE CASE, THEN THE ANCIENT "RULE OF FAITH"—that what has been continuously taught by the church, at least most of the time and in most places, is a trustworthy guide to true doctrine—is not so. Then the church can publicly err in its dominant and continuous teachings much more massively than even most non-infallibilist Protestants have cared to admit. Nor can one take refuge from an erring church in an inerrant Bible, since it is precisely here that we find the root of certain teachings of women's subordination, as well as those that condoned other evils, such as slavery.

One traditional way of dealing with revelations of sinful and scandalous behavior on the part of church leaders is to separate the private from the public, the personal from the institutional. Church leaders in their personal lives and morality may err, but this does not jeopardize the church institution's reliability in solemn and official teachings: The sustaining power of the Holy Spirit preserves it from corporate error.

But this kind of saving apologia does not suffice to deal with contemporary consciousness of the crisis of reliability of church authority. Even in cases of sexual abuse by clergy we are not just dealing with individual sin, but with corporate cover-ups of such sins by the clergy, legal hardball by ecclesiastical lawyers to silence complaints by the abused, refusals to deal directly and honestly with the problem, even efforts to get churches to raise the money to pay for the litigation. All of which compounds the sense that we are dealing here with corporate perversity and hardness of heart, not just individual weakness.

Yet even this disheartening revelation of institutional lies and power plays in self-defense stops short of actually teaching officially that clergy have a right to abuse women, youth, and children sexually. In effect, all parties agree that this is wrong.

However, in the case of the denial of women's full membership in the body of Christ, as well as earlier, now more or less discarded teachings justifying slavery, racism, and anti-Semitism, we have not only corporate institutional abuse of large groups of people, but official teaching justifying such abuse. It is claimed to be the will of God, to be in accord with the intentions of Christ.

Not furtive sinners, but serious churchmen—in the full solemnity of their teaching office—proclaimed, taught, and re-enforced such views, not here or there in odd moments of particular crisis, but continuously, in some cases over most of the 1,900 years of Christian history. Since the mission of the church is to proclaim and promote salvation, the salvation made known in Christ, we are also talking about a fundamental apostasy to its vocation as the church of Christ. If such teachings are records of continuous apostasy, the teaching of error and moral evil, then what do we make of the reliability of church teaching authority, and the sustaining presence of the Holy Spirit in that teaching?

IN MY VIEW THERE ARE ONLY TWO OPTIONS: Either such teachings *do* represent normative Christianity, in which case this is a religion that sacralizes evil, and we should get out of it posthaste. Or else prophetic truth and justice is preserved in biblical and Christian history more in the minority communities and the critical edges of the Christian churches than in the mainstream. This does not mean that an idea is true simply because it is a minority opinion. But we must give up the long-held assumption that the majority tradition has a guaranteed likelihood to be right.

How can such apostasy be reckoned with and still talk about the church as body of Christ? In earlier eras, when reformers glimpsed such a deep hiatus between the vocation of the church as agent of salvation and its historic perversion as agent of evil, they called for deep corporate repentance. Failing to achieve such repentance, they dealt with it by schism.

This church, they said, is no longer the church of Christ, but the whore of Babylon, the seed of the anti-Christ. By shaking the dust of this fallen church off our feet, and regathering a remnant of those faithful to the true vision of the gospel, we will repristinate the true church risen from the ashes of the fallen one. That bad group is *not* the true church; *we are* the true church.

Although forming new church institutions has sometimes been necessary to articulate authentic visions that otherwise would have been silenced, dualizing schism as the separation of the true church from the false one itself falsifies the problem. Even worse, it creates a self-righteous triumphalism that repeats the same error: believing oneself preserved from error by virtue of possessing an organizational mónopoly on God.

The real question is how to live by faith in the midst of error and sin—not the errors and sins of others with whom we do not identify ourselves, but the errors and sins to which we ourselves are prone. How do we hold on to a sense of God's grace at work in our lives, even in the midst of evidence not only of failings of individual Christians, but of institutionalized crime and deceit in high places?

This is possible only if we take much more profoundly and seriously that faith is trust in God rather than in ourselves. The good news that God loves us and is at work transforming our lives in Christ did not just enter the world once long ago. It enters a world 2,000 years later that continues to seize upon each new prophetic breakthrough of God's grace only to distort it into a way of justifying its apostasy. The majority of the church and its corporate tradition and practice is apostate, because most of the time individual and corporate humanity wishes to remain in distorted ways and justify them as God's will, rather than be open to real conversion.

The breakthroughs of authentic love, justice, mutuality, and reconciliation are constantly there also. And when they touch us we know that way of being as our true "natures," our authentic calling. But the gracious and redeeming presence of God is there at the point when we give up trying to possess it, institutionalize it, and guarantee it as something that we can deliver by the means that belong to us. This is another way of saying that it is, and remains, grace.

I SUSPECT THAT PART OF OUR DISMAY AT recognizing the fallibility of the church is our reluctance to grow up, and the way in which certain kinds of ecclesial "spirituality" operate as spiritual infantilization, rather than maturity in faith. We are shocked at clerical and corporate ecclesiastical evils a little the way children are shocked and demoralized to discover that their parents are fallible.

We can depart in sorrow looking for another impeccable father (or mother), perhaps in an all-wise guru or a preacher of an inerrant Bible. Or we can grow up and become responsible for the church of Christ as our beloved community, to which we must seek to give our best insights even as we recognize one another's fallibility, acknowledging that our assurance lies in being ever open to a grace that is both beyond and unfettered by any institutionalized guarantees.

To live by faith is also to live by repentance. God's redeeming presence is at the same time the power to face and shake off the way we cling to privilege and self-deception. We can look steadily and without any denial at the records of our corporate apostasy, not as the defeat of the gospel, but as the revelation of God's amazing power to deliver us from even our most monumental efforts to defeat God's grace.

We might recall that the hymn "Amazing Grace" ("how sweet the sound, that saved a wretch like me") was written, not by a punctilious Christian beating his or her breast over small peccadillos, but a ship captain who once profited by ferrying slaves from Africa. He found in Christ the strength to repudiate this profitable but evil way of life and become instead a champion of the abolition of slavery.

Grace is the power to live by repentance. The church remains faithful not by being perfect, but by keeping that message central in a way that is concrete and ever truthfully applicable to our real personal and corporate lives.

The sin against the Holy Spirit is trying to evade that good news of God's gift of repentance by claiming that we have certainty and impeccability in our own hands—that we are Christ's church and so are preserved from serious error and corporate sin. This is where the church as institution circles its wagons against the threat of grace, the threat of the Holy Spirit, the threat of repentance. We build our fortifications ever higher, claiming that anything we have taught a long time cannot be wrong. We justify our sins by their longevity.

This is a big challenge to God, but from time to time the Holy Spirit manages to sneak through even the highest barriers the church builds against her, playing havoc with our certitudes, revealing the absurdity of our self-deceptions, the pathos of our power, but also breaking the death grip that seals us up against new life. She gives us the gift of tears, the grace to weep profoundly at the sight of our tragic errors and the sufferings they have caused so many. She also gives the gift of explosive laughter that dissolves pomposity and liberates us to be, not infantilized zombies, but living children of God.

Perhaps with the 19th-century sea captain converted from the slave trade, we too can sing "through many dangers, toils, and snares, we have already come; 'tis grace that brought us safe thus far and grace will lead us home."

ROSEMARY RADFORD RUETHER is Georgia Harkness professor of applied theology at Garrett-Evangelical Seminary in Evanston, Illinois, and the author, most recently, of **Gaia & God: An Ecofeminist Theology of Earth Healing**.

Reprinted from *Sojourners*, 2401 15th St. NW, Washington, DC 20009. Yearly subscription rate: $30/year.

COMPARATIVISM IN A WORLD OF DIFFERENCE

THE LEGACY OF JOSEPH CAMPBELL TO THE POSTMODERN HISTORY OF RELIGIONS

by DAVID MILLER

from THE JOSEPH CAMPBELL NEWSLETTER

I have been asked to initiate a discussion on the question of the importance of the work of Joseph Campbell to the future of the study of the history of religions. To be sure, this is a controversial topic. On the one hand, there are those perhaps Romantic enthusiasts (mostly persons who are not professional scholars teaching in graduate centers of the history of religions) who affirm the relevance of Campbell's work because of the insight of its comparativist hermeneutic, as well as its geographical and temporal scope. On the other hand, there are those perhaps Classic and sometimes historicist detractors (mostly professional scholars teaching in graduate centers of the history of religions) who decry the relevance of Campbell's work precisely because of its comparativist hermeneutic and its impossible attempt to be broad. There is something naïve about both of these positions. In the case of the enthusiasts, there is a naïveté about scholarship and about the postmodern condition. Among the detractors, there is a naïveté about Campbell's work and a curiously unscholarly lumping together of Eliade, Jung, and Campbell on the issue of archetypes and universals, a comparing of comparativists that simply will not bear close analysis. The academics, I believe, are as naïve and as unscholarly in their reading of Campbell as are the anti-academics.

My own position differs from both. It agrees with the first group about the relevance of Campbell to the future of the study of the history of religions, even if not for that group's reason. Rather my position concurs with the reasoning of the second group concerning the irrelevance of a certain kind of universalizing, archetypal comparativism. However, my disagreement with the second group is in their attribution of this comparativism to Campbell. A careful reading of his whole corpus demonstrates that he simply was not the comparativist that either the enthusiasts or the detractors imagine in their polemical and ideological apologetics, whether pro or con.

THE KEY TO ANY FUTURE STUDY OF THE history of religions has to do with the affirmation of the value of difference and otherness. The sins of academic and intellectual colonialism have been both of commission and omission. Edward Said and Charles Long, not to mention the many permutations of Foucaultian and feminist perspectives, have sensitized all to the witting and/or unwitting reduction of the thousand faces of multicultural religiosity to one monomythic understanding. The four-thousand-year Platonic and Aristotelian experiment with meaning as identification, as *adaequatio intellectus et rei*, as *homoiosis*, as *correspondentia*, as *analogia*, as a meaning being like that which it is like, is ended, smashed to smithereens, not only by Nietzsche, Heidegger, Derrida, and the deconstructionists, but also by the postmodern social facts of a planetary politics of cultural diversity, each small unit of which, not only seeks, but is willing to kill for its difference. *Différence*—as Derrida has put it neologistically—represents differences demanding the foreclosure of closures of signification, deferring identifications and comparisons in the global melting pot where no one melted. For the time being in the study of religions the experiment will be, not with identity, but with difference, not with similarity, but with otherness.

Our question, of course, is how Campbell's work, itself so identified with identity, similarity, and comparison (as it has been by blissful followers and carping critics alike) is fated in such a future, that is, its serious future in the scholarly study of the history of religions, not its future in the New Age marketplace which will always cling hysterically to a Romantic perspective that produces the very nihilism it wishes angelically to transcend.

The comparativist matter is complicated, as is indicated by the mis-understanding that leads to the uncritical lumping together of Jung, Eliade, and Campbell to which I have already alluded. Robert Segal has questioned this before me, though few seem to have noticed. Perhaps an account of an incident involving Jung and Eliade in 1955 may more poignantly make the point concerning comparativist confusion and misunderstanding. In the context of their friendship at the Eranos Conferences, Eliade had sent Jung a copy of his then new book on Yoga in which the former speaks about the archetypal significance of mandala images and quotes Jung in support of the point. Eliade thought he was agreeing with what he took to be Jung's universal and comparativist point on such imagery in his patient's drawings. Much to his surprise, instead of receiving a pleasant thank-you note, Eliade received in reply a diatribe that indicated a profound difference between a philosophical (Platonic/Augustinian) use of the notion of archetype in a phenomenology and a depth psychological use of what many take to be the same notion.[1] So crucial is the difference that it seems nearly to have destroyed the personal friendship between the two men until Eliade changed the citation of Jung in a later edition of the work and wrote an apology in the introduction to another work.[2]

The difference between an observation of apparent phenomenological likeness and an observation of similar psychological functions of events or structures of meaning that are unlike each other in appearance is somewhat of the same order as Plotinus' noting a difference between likenesses of like things and likenesses of unlike things, the later of which the Neoplatonic philosopher thought more important.[3] In these terms, Eliade is closer to Plato and Jung to Plotinus. But Campbell's work, in the main, represents yet a third position. It is like Eliade in its phenomenology of mythic image and narrative, but it is like Jung in stressing unlikeness, as I shall attempt to demonstrate against common opinion both pro and con. That is, Campbell is neither Eliadian nor Jungian, in spite of his regard for and knowledge of both men's work. This means that a discussion of Campbell's importance for the future of the study of the history of religions should be distinguished from a discussion of the importance of Eliade and Jung for the same. To refer to Campbell as Jungian or to refer to Eliade as Campbellian so as to dismiss one or the other is simply the name-calling opprobrium of an uninformed ideologism which ironically would dismiss all comparativism by using a comparativist logic.

ONE MIGHT HAVE NOTICED THAT even in the title of Campbell's early work, the phrase did not read the thousand heroes with one face, even if one were unable to take seriously what is always ignored in reading of *The Hero with a Thousand Faces*: namely, the radical literary theory regarding humor and the comedic at the beginning and the Nietzscheanism so beloved by postmodern thinkers at the end wherein Campbell speaks directly about diverse modulations in the human face. Indeed, Campbell's major work was about masks (plural differences), not mask (singular meaning). If the diction of his writing often seems by contemporary tastes archaic and patriarchal in matters of gender and race, nonetheless Campbell knew full well that mythology has often— alas!—functioned repressively and oppressively with regard to race, religion and gender by making stereotypes seem archetypal by way of the power and beauty of mythic narrative and image. He knew that mythicizing the archetype has given the status quo metaphysical sanction and has supported political atrocity (as he wrote, for example, about Tibet). He knew that comparativist method colonializes in the name of the dominant group and can blur historical distinctness and particularity, even rationalizing scapegoating by refusing to problematize victimage and violence. He knew, too, that the study of mythology, if appropriated by certain forms of spirituality, refuses moral engagement and responsibility, and becomes a defense against the realities of those suffering an apocalyptic culture and life. In short, Campbell was not blind to the latter day insight of such recent mythoclasts and anticomparativists as Naomi Goldenberg, Carlos Ginzburg, Jürgen Habermas, Roland Barthes, Wendy Doniger, Marcel Detienne, René Girard, Alan Dundes, Charles Long, Michel Foucault, and others. Campbell, like these, knew that the danger of following one's own bliss intellectually, as well as fundamentalistically in faith and action, is that it may, even without malice or intention, keep someone else from following his or her equally valid and mutually exclusive bliss.

In the 1959 edition of *Masks of God: Primitive Mythology*, Campbell forcefully argued the case that the modern study of mythology grew out of a Northern European, Romantic intuition about Aryan language and culture that became an intellectual rationale and mythic support for the antisemitic politics of Nazism. At the end of this historically explicated argument, Campbell mythoclastically warned: "Clearly mythology is no toy for children, nor is it a matter of archaic, merely scholarly concern, of no moment to . . . action . . . The world is now far too small, and [the] . . . stake in sanity too great, for any more of those old games of Chosen Folk . . . by which tribesmen were sustained against their enemies in the days when the serpent still could talk."[4] At the Eranos Conference in 1957, Campbell began by asserting that ". . . one of the main themes of my subject is to be that of the provincial character of *all* that we are prone to regard as universal," and he added that his own presentation would be "an illustration of its own thesis."[5] Campbell's enthusiasts and detractors alike are joined in not attending to such statements, let alone in taking them with any seriousness.[6] Yet serious utterances such as these, aligned as they are in advance with postmodern insight, might be a clue that the importance of Campbell's work for the future study of the history of religions does not lie in the TV series, the video- and audio-tape interviews, the popular workshops, as much as it does in the sites of Campbell's serious scholarship. After all, who of us has not spoken to lay groups with enthusiasm and in uncomplicated ways?

THE ERANOS LECTURE OF 1957 CAN SERVE as an example of Campbell's serious work, little known by enthusiasts, and ignored by critics. The lecture was entitled "The Symbol without Meaning." In it Campbell argued that there have been two ways of understanding mythic discourse and thinking: (1) as a symbol functioning for engagement, reference, and iden-tification; and (2) as a symbol functioning for disengagement, transport, and differentiation. "When the symbol is functioning for engagement, the cognitive faculties are held fascinated by and bound to the symbol itself, and are thus simultaneously informed by and protected from the unknown. But when the symbol is functioning for disengagement, transport, and meta-morphosis, it becomes a catapult to be left behind."[7] In hunting societies (paleolithic and contemporary), religious meaning is focussed on the indi-vidual—the individual fast for the gaining of vision, or on hierophantic realizations. This does not imply a rupture with society and world, as critics of Campbell assert incorrectly that he argued. Rather it is a separating of oneself from the "comparatively trivial attitude toward the human spirit and the world,"[8] a conversion in myth and ritual from family to universe, from particular tribe to deep structures. Meaning is in dis-engaging from the collective sociological unit; the particularity has a different site, a location in otherness.

But all this changed, Campbell argued, at the time of the agricultur-

172

al revolution in different portions of the world. In neolithic planting societies, one imagined a falling out of Edenic existence, out of the universal, into history and time. Now the sociology of the collective unit (family, religion, tribe, state, nation) dictated religious meaning. Conversion was no longer from family to cosmos and planet; it was from family to tribe or religion or nation. In this there was little room for individual deviation and variation in the religious realm. Spiritual significance now was in relation to neighbor (not other), to village life (not world), to calendar (not cosmos or eco-sphere). *Extra ecclesium nulla salus*: outside the particular group there could be no salvation. In this way religion and myth engage literalistically and fundamentalistically in a particular literalism without—as Campbell's literary theory stressed—humor.

Campbell adjudged that people today no longer live in the neolithic agricultural paradigm of meaning, though they repeat it by unconscious habit. I spent seven years with Campbell as an officer of the Society for the Arts, Religion, and Culture in New York City discussing in private and in public the topic of "what are the myths of a mythless time." Like the American poet, Wallace Stevens, Campbell knew that "here / in Connecticut, we never lived in a time / when mythology was possible." As he put it to Bill Moyers on public television: "What we have today is a demythologized world."[9] The so-called "death of God" and the death of the gods was axiomatic for him. Campbell was postmodern before his time.

This is especially obvious in the conclusions Campbell drew at Eranos in 1957. In a world of science and computer bits and bytes, a scattered world of multicultural chaos, the meaning of "meaning" that implies an engagement, an attachment, an identification, and a comparison is now, as he put it, "like the carapace of a crayfish or cocoon of a butterfly that has been cracked, sloughed off and left behind."[10] Today, religious signification is semiotic and paratactic, functioning, as Campbell said, like a bow. "The bow, in order to function as a bow and not as a snare, must have no meaning whatsoever in itself . . . beyond that of being an agent for disengagement from itself."[11] If religious and mythic discourse is thought to "mean" something, it serves for engagement of energy and consciousness to itself, and can become the religious and theological basis for mean-spiritedness and, in extreme cases, terrorism. More appropriate to a future world order, would be to see such discourse as mythic, pointing to the unknown and the unknowable, such that foreclosure of signification is withdrawn, so that, like a bow, it can send the arrow forth from itself. In this view, as Campbell said: "The world, the entire universe, its god and all, has become a symbol without meaning. . . . Our meaning is now the meaning that is no meaning; for no fixed term of reference can be drawn."[12] Or, as Campbell told Moyers thirty years later: "People say that what we're all seeking is meaning for life. I don't think that's what we're really seeking. I think that what we're seeking is an experience of being alive."[413] "What," Campbell asked Moyers, "is the meaning of a flower, and having no meaning should the flower then not be?" "There's no meaning. What's the meaning of the universe? What's the meaning of a flea? It's just there. That's it."[14]

THIS IS, OF COURSE, RADICAL IN THE EXTREME . . . as radical as Angelus Silesius' "rose that is without why," or the Zen master's one-hand thunder-clap, or Meister Eckhart's prayer to God that he may be rid of "God." It is the perspective that would permit Campbell to demonstrate the anomaly of certain ideologies and theologies in a postmodern time by contextualizing the Assumption of the Blessed Virgin astronomically.

> Is one to image a human body rising from this earth, to pass beyond the bounds of our solar system, beyond the bounds, then, of the Milky Way, beyond the bounds even of what may lie beyond that? If so, then—please!—at what velocity is this body moving? For it must still be in flight! Having been launched less than two millenniums ago, even if travelling at the speed of light (which for a physical body is impossible), both the body of our Lord Jesus Christ (which began its own ascent some fifteen years earlier) and that of His Most Glorious Virgin Mother Mary, would now be only some two thousand light-years away—not yet beyond the horizon of the Milky Way.[15]

The image is, of course, ridiculous, bordering on blasphemy. That is Campbell's point, of course! To attempt to sustain anachronistic, neolithic theological perspectives on identifiable meanings is a form of comparativism that is absurd and that does an injustice to one's own and another's mythos.

Campbell is even firmer about this point, though not less humorously, when at the end of his last book, the second volume of the *Historical Atlas of World Mythology*, he writes:

... there was no Garden of Eden antecedent to the Lower Paleolithic finds of c. 3 to 4 million years ago, no time when the Serpent could talk, no Fall, no Exile from such a Paradise with sword-bearing cherubim at its gate: the unequivocally documented history of the evolution of life and mankind on this planet has wiped that fairytale off the map. And if there was no Fall, what then of the need for Redemption? What god was offended and by whom? (Some especially touchy cave bear whose skull had been improperly en-shrined?) What devil then took [hu]mankind in pawn, so that we all had to be redeemed? And there was no Universal Flood, no Noah's Ark, no Tower of Babel, no scattering of the peoples, after Babel, all over the planet, no Seven Plagues of Egypt, no drowning of any pharaoh and his army in the Red Sea, and no stopping of the sun and moon so that Joshua, God's special friend, might finish off in a battle the residents of a neighborhood he was invading. It is not the sun that moves in the sky, but the earth that revolves on its axis, and if this spinning had been suddenly stopped, every man, woman, and child, and every dog, elephant, and giraffe, would have been sent flying in trajectories east at a speed of some 1,500 feet a second, like Aunt Sarah through the windshield when her Cadillac hit the tree. So let's be serious! [16]

This is Campbell being, not only serious, but also postmodern before its time. It implies a hermeneutic beyond meaning and meaninglessness, not unlike Derrida's notion of scattered epistemological reference through dissemination, or Lacan's radicalized version of Saussure's semiotics in which language functions as a floating arbitrary signifier deprived if any necessary signified. But these references that I have made to Campbell's serious methodological work are not only instances of his being *au courant* forty years before the flow of critical theory from France; they also imply his work's importance for the future study of the history of religions.

Campbell knew that historicism is not a possible way to go following upon the nihilistic collapse of Romanticist religious and mythological hermeneutics. Though he did not put it in the terms of the postmodern lexicon, Campbell had learned this post-Kantian lesson well enough to know that there is no *dehors texte*. That is to say, that he knew that one does not get rid of myth's ideologism by getting rid of the comparativist study of myth. Mythos will be there, always and already, even in mythless times and methods. Turning to Annales-like historicism, Girardian ritualism, or Von Rankean literalism in the study of the history of religions only drives mythic ideologism underground and possibly renders it thereby even more stereotypically demonic by reason of its being unconscious. Historicism and particularism are mythologies and ideologies, too. Ask Aunt Sarah. She knows that the social scientization of the study of myth and religion is as naïve about the transparency of mythic language to human meanings as is Romanticist comparativism. That is why Campbell said at the beginning of his Eranos lecture that all statements about myth and religion betray the provincialism and ideology of their authors . . . and he knew that that includes this statement, too.

It is out of the humility that such an insight produces that we are permitted to go forward into the future of the study of the history of that whose object will always already be unknown and unknowable. Into the opening provided by that humility, both historical studies and comparative studies may and surely will proceed, but hopefully with a difference. For though Campbell knew the fascist and colonializing risks, though he knew that there would always be literalist and fundamentalist enthusiasts, even in myth-studies, it did not deter him from continuing the work of historical particularity, as for example in the Atlas, as well as the work of comparativism based, not on likeness, but on difference. And in this going forward in a postmodern context, Campbell demonstrated the dialectic of there being no particular judgments without implied comparisons and there being no identification of comparisons without assumptions of individual difference.

In this, Campbell was a forerunner to what is just now aborning in the history of religions. I mean the new comparativism based on difference—a sort of post-postmodernist hermeneutic, if the phrase may be permitted—exemplified, for example, in Jonathan Z. Smith's *Drudgery Divine* and his "Differential Equations: On Constructing the 'Other,'" and, to give another example, in Howard Eilberg-Schwartz' *The Savage in Judaism*. Campbell's importance to this new work is to help those of us who are enthusiasts to keep in mind that all comparativism is not the same and to help those of us who are critical theorists to remember that comparativism by any other name (such as historical non-comparativism) may not be as free of ideological stench as it imagines. Indeed, it may not smell as sweet as Angelus Silesius' rose which is without why.

NOTES:

1. See Jung, *Letters*, II (19 January 1955),
   pp. 210-12.
2. See Eliade, *Yoga*, pp. 219-27; also *Cosmos and History,* Harper & Row, Torchbook edition, 1959, pp. vii-ix.
3. *Enneads*, I.ii., 2-6.
4. *Masks of God: Primitive Mythology*, p. 12.
5. *Flight of the Wild Gander*, p. 120.
6. See dismissal of the Eranos opening by Campbell's biographers: *Fire in the Mind,* p. 431.
7. *Flight*, p. 169.
8. *Primitive Mythology*, pp. 229, 242, 252-54, 263, 348.
9. *The Power of Myth*, p. 9.
10. *Flight*, p. 130.
11. *Flight*, p. 178.
12. *Flight*, p. 190.
13. *Power*, p. 5f.
14. *Power*, p. 6.
15. *Flight*, p. 125.
16. *Historical Atlas of World Mythology*, Vol. 2, Part 1, p.111.

DAVID L. MILLER is Watson-Ledden Professor of Religion, Syracuse University and Chair of the Joseph Campbell Foundation's Advisory Group in Mythology and Higher Education. Miller has been a regular contributor to the Eranos lectures and author of numerous studies on religion, myth, and literature.

Reprinted from *The Joseph Campbell Foundation Newsletter*, PO Box 457, Madison Square Station, New York, NY 10159-0457, (212) 678-0545. Newsletter subscription with Foundation membership: $25/year.

BORDER CROSSINGS

by LAUREL THATCHER ULRICH

from DIALOGUE

It happened again as I was walking through the New Hampshire woods with a woman I knew only slightly. We had been chatting amiably when the words "Mormon feminist" escaped my mouth. From the expression on her face, I knew exactly what she was going to say.

"Mormon feminist! That sounds like an oxymoron!"

I bristled, though I didn't mean to, annoyed at having to explain myself once again.

Yes, I am an active, believing Mormon. I was baptized at the age of eight, graduated from seminary, and married in the Salt Lake temple. For thirty-five years I have tried to remain true to my temple covenants, including the one about consecrating time and talents to the church. I have taught early morning seminary, written road shows, edited the stake newsletter, and picked apples, plums, peaches, and pears at the stake welfare farm. With my husband, I recently completed my third stint as Gospel Doctrine teacher in our ward.

And, yes, I am a feminist. I deplore teachings, policies, or attitudes that deny women their full stature as human beings, and I have tried to act on that conviction in my personal and professional life. I have written two books and more than a dozen articles in women's history. I give money to the day care coalition in my town and the women's political caucus in my state. I helped draft my university's non-sexist language policy.

I am quite aware that some people consider these commitments incompatible. A couple of years ago, a member of the Women's Commission at my university, learning that I was Mormon, said in astonishment, "I am surprised your church hasn't thrown you out long ago."

"Thrown me out!" I gasped. "I'm a pillar of my congregation." The very same day I was queried by a Latter-day Saints (LDS) acquaintance I had not seen for several years. Hearing about my awards for feminist scholarship, she asked earnestly, "Do you go to church? Do you bear your testimony?" I groaned and told her, tongue in cheek, that I was an agnostic Gospel Doctrine teacher.

Perhaps my disposition to stand apart is genetic. Elsewhere I have written about my Thatcher pioneers who regularly disagreed with church authorities. I have said less about my maternal ancestors, the Siddoways. In my mother's home town, I am told, there are still three ways of doing things—the right way, the wrong way, and the Siddoway. Graduate school compounded what family inheritance and eight years of high school and college debate began. I am afraid I fit the definition of an intellectual as "a person who thinks otherwise." Hence when I began this essay more than a year ago, I entitled it "Confessions of an OxyMormon." According to my dictionary, the prefix oxy means, "sharp, keen, acute, pungent, acid," not a bad description for one given to critical thinking. I admit to preferring vinegar to honey, being less interested in catching flies than in rousing the faint.

Yet I am not so sure I want to admit to all the implications of the epithet. Acid can burn as well as cleanse, and in my dictionary, the word "keen" slides along an enticing but slippery lexical path from "wise, learned, clever, and brave" to "proud, forward, and insolent." Against such dangers my Mormonism buzzes: "O the vainness, and the frailties, and the foolishness of men! When they are learned they think they are wise, and they hearken not unto the counsel of God" (2 Ne. 9:28). As an intellectual I am forced to question my questioning. As a Latter-day Saint I acknowledge my foolishness.

Last winter the Boston *Globe* ran a story on *Exponent II* under the headline "Challenging the Mormon Church." The author, free-lance writer Suzanne Gordon, had worked hard on her essay, interviewing members and non-members, scholars and activists, and attending at least one meeting of the newspaper staff. "To an outsider," she confessed, "the very act of understanding these women requires a minicourse in cross-cultural studies." Building on interviews with two non-LDS historians, she concluded that the editors and writers of *Exponent II* were not only risking censure in this world but salvation in the afterlife. In the context of Mormon theology, she concluded, "any talk about a female identity outside of the family, or critical consideration of the problems of family life, can be taken as a fundamental challenge to the very foundation of Mormonism itself."[1] My youngest son, a man of quiet good sense who lives in a converted warehouse in the heart of bohemian Boston, said that while he enjoyed the article, he thought the author "exaggerated the rebellion." He was amused that the sturdy Mormon mother he knew, a habitual reader of scriptures and monitor of hair length, could be seen as shaking the foundations of the church.[2]

He is right. I am not an oxyMormon. I am a Mormon. And a feminist. As a daughter of God, I claim the right to all my gifts. I am a mother, an intellectual, a skeptic, a believer, a crafter of cookies and words. I am not a Jack (or a Jill) in one box, ready to jump when the button is pushed.

Perhaps I am comfortable wearing the feminist label because as a Latter-day Saint living in the east I have had so much practice being an oddball. Shortly after we moved to Massachusetts in 1960, I succumbed to the entreaties of the missionaries in our ward and agreed to help them with a telephone survey. We were to ask each person on our list the Golden Questions: What do you know about the Mormon church? Would you like to know more? One man silenced me by responding, "I don't know a thing about the Mormon church, but I shall look it up in the *Encyclopedia Brittanica* immediately." His smug tolerance put me in my place—in the Ms, somewhere between moonbeam and moron.

I doubt his encyclopedia had an entry for feminism. Although the word was in common use in the United States between 1895 and 1930, it fell out of fashion before World War II, not to be revived again until the 1970s. My *Compact Oxford English Dictionary*, copyright 1971, defines feminism as "The qualities of females." Until 1977, the index to *The Reader's Guide to Periodical Literature* cross-referenced the word under "Woman—social and moral questions." It is really rather startling to think that in July 1974 a group of Massachusetts housewives could launch a quarterly newspaper, *Exponent II*, "on the dual platforms of

Mormonism and Feminism." We did not think we had committed an oxymoron.

Today the computerized catalog at the University of New Hampshire library lists 777 books under the subject entry "Feminism." Obviously, any movement as large, as fast growing, and as complex as this one cannot be reduced to a simple definition. When I hear people rail against feminists I always wonder who they mean. Scholars have differentiated among radical feminism, liberal feminism, Marxist feminism, Christian feminism, lesbian feminism, and more. Pushing the concept back in time, they have coined terms like domestic feminism, social feminism, material feminism, relational feminism, and proto-feminism.[3] Long before there was an organized women's rights movement, there were women who struggled against arbitrary limits on their humanity. Though my dictionary doesn't have a definition for feminism as we know it, it does have an entry for bluestocking, a term coined about 1750 and applied "sneeringly to any woman showing a taste for learning."

When I say that I am a feminist, I identify with women across the centuries who have had the courage to claim their own gifts. Theologically, I don't have much in common with the Puritan poet Anne Bradstreet, but having been raised in a culture that simultaneously nurtures and mistrusts female achievement, I can identify with her words:

> I am obnoxious to each carping tongue
> Who says my hand a needle better fits...
> For such despite they cast in female wits;
> If what I do prove well, it won't advance,
> They'll say it's stolen, or else it was by chance.[4]

There was no organized women's rights movement in seventeenth-century Massachusetts, but there was something like feminism.

As a Mormon, I embrace ideals of equality and a critique of power that also shaped early feminism. Abigail Adam's "all Men would be tyrants if they could"[5] is not far removed from Joseph Smith's "We have learned by sad experience that it is the nature and disposition of almost all men as soon as they get a little authority, as they suppose, they will immediately begin to exercise unrighteous dominion" (D&C 121:39). Mormonism rejects the Calvinist notion of predestination as well as the monarchical notion of a great chain of being in which each person is subordinate to the one above. Listen to Lehi: "And because that they are redeemed from the fall they have become free forever, knowing good from evil; to act for themselves and not to be acted upon" (2 Ne. 3:26). Lehi's formulation is surprisingly close to the modern distinction between subject and object. That each person be free to think, speak, and act for herself is both a feminist and a Mormon dream. As a Latter-day Saint, I say with Mary Wolstonecraft, "Let not men then in the pride of power, use the same arguments that tyrannic kings and venal ministers have used and fallaciously assert that women ought to be subjected because she had always been so."[6]

Yet my commitment to the Church of Jesus Christ pushes me beyond a mere concern for "rights." As a feminist I know that structures matter, that formal authority makes a difference in the way people think as well as behave, that institutional arrangements can lock in prejudice, yet I also know that legal protection is hollow without spiritual transformation and that the right spirit can transform a seemingly repressive system. My daily experience as a Latter-day Saint confirms the words of Margaret Fuller, a nineteenth-century feminist and contemporary of Joseph Smith: "Were thought and feeling once so far elevated that Man should esteem himself the brother and friend, but nowise the lord and tutor, of Woman,—were he really bound with her in equal worship,— arrangements as to function and employment would be of no consequence."[7] I have tasted equal worship in the Church of Jesus Christ of Latter-day Saints. Unfortunately, I have also observed the smug condescension of men who believe they have been called as lord and tutor. Against such behavior I assert both my Mormonism and my feminism.

To claim multiple identities is to assert the insufficiency of any one label, including Mormonism. According to my *Compact Oxford English Dictionary*, an oxymoron is not simply a self-contradictory expression like "freezing heat" or "swampy desert." It is a rhetorical figure in which contradictory or incongruous terms are intentionally joined in order to complicate or enlarge meaning. Although in current usage the word is "often loosely or erroneously used as if merely a contradiction in terms," a true oxymoron is "an expression in its superficial or literal meaning self-contradictory or absurd, but involving a point." The phrase "Mormon feminist" can work that way. Those who assume Mormonism is inherently hostile to women or, conversely, that feminism undermines faith, sniff at the phrase. But when confronted with a real person claiming to be both things at once, they are forced to reconsider their assumptions. Feminism may be larger than they imagined and Mormonism more flexible.

As biologist Stephen Jay Gould has written, "We must categorize and simplify in order to comprehend. But the reduction of complexity entails a great danger, since the line between enlightening epitome and vulgarized distortion is so fine."[8] The Boston *Globe* crossed that line when it described the Church of Jesus Christ of Latter-day Saints as "quintessentially misogynist."[9] But when anxious church leaders denounce feminists they compound the distortion. Each group reduces the other to its own worst nightmare, and the war is on. In such a climate it is tempting to run for shelter, saying less about feminism among Mormons and less about Mormonism everywhere else. But a silence based on fear is no solution. As long as the issues are there, unacknowledged and unresolved, the anger and hostility will remain. I think it is better to gently but consistently tell the truth. I am a Mormon and a feminist.

I remember as a teenager standing up in my ward in Sugar City, Idaho, to repeat the Mutual Improvement Association (MIA) theme of the year: "Let no man despise thy youth: but be thou an example of the believers, in word, in conversation, in charity, in spirit, in faith, in purity" (1 /Tim. 4:12). I am grateful for a religious education that taught me how to be different, though I had no idea it would sometimes make me feel like a stranger among saints. In my generation, being an example of the believers had a lot to do with the Word of Wisdom. In Sunday school and MIA we learned about the Mormon lad who resisted a proffered cup of coffee or a drink only to be rewarded with a promotion. (Nobody told us the promotion might be the biggest danger of all!) Fortunately, in the old seminary room above the Sugar City Theater, a mandolin-playing teacher named Ken Brown taught a more complex ethic. Gently and with humor, he led us through the New Testament, helping us to see the dangers in the Pharisees' attempt to separate themselves from the ungodly. The harder they tried to behave as "Abraham's children," the less they were capable of receiving the Messiah when he came.

A few years ago I attended an invitational conference in U.S. women's history. The organizers, fully committed to diversity, had gone out of their way to include women from large and small colleges, from every part of the United States, and from many minority groups. When one scholar expressed surprise that no one from BYU had been invited, a well-known nineteenth-century historian responded, "Oh, we don't want them!" Orthodoxy feels the same wherever it is found. Certainly there is a need for boundaries, for rigorous defense of ideas and ideals that matter, but defenders of every faith too often violate their own ideals in the very act of defending them. The gospel of Jesus Christ teaches us that light falls across borders, that the sun in its revolutions brightens both sides of a wall, spilling through the spaces in our fences. Mormon intellectuals should not forget that Jesus gathered his disciples from among sinners, publicans, *and* pharisees, even zealous pharisees like Paul, a man who knew what it meant to live in a multi-cultural world. To the saints at Ephesus, Paul wrote: "For he is our peace, who hath made both one, and hath broken down the middle wall of partition between us" (Eph. 2:14).

Recently I assigned Tzvetan Todorov's *The Conquest of America* to my students in early American history. Reading it again I found personal meaning in the closing section which relates the story of the Spanish conquest to the problems of pluralism in our times. In Todorov's view, one of the few Spaniards who was able to transcend the brutality and condescension that characterized early Spanish treatment of the Indians was Cabeza de Vaca, an explorer who spent eight years lost in the interior of North America. It wasn't only that Cabeza had experienced both cultures from within, it was that after his exile he never fully belonged to either. Without becoming an Indian, he "was no longer quite a Spaniard." For Todorov, Cabeza illuminates the mysterious words of Hugh St. Victor: "The man who finds his country sweet is only a raw beginner; the man for whom each country is as his own is already strong; but only the man for whom the whole world is as a foreign country is perfect." Todorov's insight helped me to reassess the dislocations in my own life. I have sometimes felt like a woman without a country. Perhaps the experience of "otherness" can be a source of strength. We are all prisoners of our culture, bound not by visible laws but by a net of assumptions and prejudices we cannot see. In the space between competing identities, I seek Lehi's freedom.

I do not apologize for what I am—an intellectual who reveres the scriptures; a Sunbeam teacher who would sooner write than eat; a transplanted westerner at home in the east. I can no more deny my religious identity than I can divest myself of my Thatcher freckles or my Rocky

Mountain accent. Nor would I discard my feminist values. The women's movement has refreshed my life like the "sea change" that sometimes hits my town in those steamy, grey days so common on the east coast in mid-summer. At such moments a blue, almost Western, sky breaks through the haze.

NOTES

1. Suzanne Gordon, *Boston Globe*, 25 Mar. 1993, reprinted in *Exponent II* 17 (4): 5-7.

2. Ibid., 6.

3. For a useful discussion of the historical origins of the term feminism, see Nancy F. Cott, "What's in a Name? the Limits of "Social Feminism': or, Expanding the vocabulary of Women's History," *Journal of American History* 76 (1989): 809:29. Although I agree with Cott's plea for an expanded vocabulary for female activism, I can think of no substitute for "feminism" when used in a broader context.

4. Anne Bradstreet, "The Prologue," *The Norton Anthology of Literature by Women*, ed. Sandra M. Gilbert and Susan Gubar (New York: W.W. Norton, 1985), 62.

5. Abigail Adams to John Adams, 31 Mar. 1776, in *The Feminist Papers*, ed. Alice S. Rossi (New York: bantam Books, 1973), 10.

6. From *A Vindication of the Rights of Women*, excerpted in *Feminist Papers*, 58.

7. *Feminist Papers*, 164.

8. "Triumph of a Naturalist," *New York Review of Books*, 19 Mar. 1984, 58-71, quoted in Cynthia Fuchs Epstein, *Deceptive Distinctions: Sex, Gender, and the Social Order* (New Haven: Yale University Press, 1988), frontispiece.

9. Suzanne Gordon, "Herstory in the Making," *Boston Globe Magazine*, 31 Jan. 1993, reprinted in *Exponent II* 17 (4): 4.

Laurel Thatcher Ulrich is professor of American History at Harvard University and author of **Midwife's Tale**.

Reprinted from *Dialogue: A Journal of Mormon Thought*, PO Box 658, Salt Lake City, UT 84110-0658. Subscription: $25/year.

A Faith to Move Mountains

Shaking the Foundations
of Power in Mexico

by Jeff Shriver

from Sojourners

Winding our way up through the thick pine-trees of the Chiapas highlands and past the military blockades, we arrive in the treasured colonial city of San Cristóbal de las Casas. The main square is awash in fresh blue and white paint, an attempt to hide the black rebel graffitti sprayed on public buildings only a month ago. Vegetarian restaurants, cappuccino bars, and quaint bookstores dot the city's cobblestone streets.

Chiapas feels more like an ideal spot for a honeymoon than the site of a guerrilla war. Indeed, it is both; San Cristóbal typifies the paradox of wealth and poverty that exist back-to-back in the rest of the state.

In early 1992, 400 Mayan Indians from the state of Chiapas marched from Palenque to Mexico City—a six-week, 625-mile walk—to petition against land evictions and local government corruption. Upon arriving on the outskirts of Mexico City, they were met with a military blockade to the city center; 100 people were arrested and several were beaten. The Indians turned back, once again frustrated and angry at a government that wouldn't listen.

Two years later their tactics changed. Tzeltal, Tojolabal, and Tzotzil Indian farmers with communities within or around the Lacandón Rain

Forest organized with a handful of urban Mexican Latinos to establish a rebel army. The Zapatista National Liberation Army (EZLN) declared civil war the first day of January 1994 in the Chiapas highlands.

Initially, Mexican authorities attempted to crush the uprising and intimidate the population, reminiscent of Central America in the 1980s. About three hours east of San Cristóbal in the small indigenous village of Morelia, the people told us of beatings, torture, and disappearances on January 6.

"They [the army] put all of us in the basketball court for eight hours," a community leader explained. "They beat us with gun butts, they kicked us with military boots. They grabbed our heads by the hair and slammed our faces into the ground." Two hundred men and young boys in all were ordered to the basketball court. Six weeks later, community members found only the bones of their three disappeared laying in a nearby cornfield.

After clashes with the army forced the rebels out of the cities, a battle of the pen intensified. A flurry of rebel communiques and press releases issued from EZLN communities in the Lacandón jungle. Sub-commander Marcos, the articulate and sarcastic rebel who has achieved a kind of cult following, responded to early government statements that identified the EZLN as a political force "in formation," irrelevant to the national agenda:

> What does this mean? That the misery of indigenous people does not exist but is rather "in formation"? Why did the federal government take away the agenda in our dialogue that pointedly refers to national politics? The country wants Chiapan oil, Chiapan electric energy, premium Chiapan materials, the strength of Chiapan workers, in the end, Chiapan blood, but not the opinion of indigenous Chiapans regarding the path of the country?

In just 12 days, EZLN regional and national demands won legitimacy and a cease-fire was called; the Catholic Church flipped from presumed revolution instigator to peace mediator; and the Mexican government sent the moderate Manuel Camacho Solís to negotiate directly with the rebels.

The events in Chiapas caused an uproar over the political and economic direction of Mexico. The foregone conclusion that Salinas' neoliberal economic reforms were well-equipped to usher Mexico into the chande-liered ballroom of the first world was suddenly thrown into question. International investors wondered when peaceful social conditions, so necessary for stable business practice, would return to Mexico. In the United States, the uprising gave reason to rethink NAFTA's effect on Mexico's 40 million poor people.

"FOR THE FIRST TIME IN THE HISTORY OF LATIN AMERICA, there's been an armed movement that has a different logic than the previous armed movements," said Bishop Samuel Ruiz, a small, confident man with a glowing smile. He met with us when we visited his human rights center.

"In the past, all military movements have said, 'Since no one's ever done justice, we will take power to do justice.' This movement of the Zapatistas has a different logic. They don't want the power. They want to get involved with the process of power, to allow other sectors to get involved in the process of power."

The Zapatistas have refrained from using old rhetoric of a "revolution of the proletariat," or any explicit Marxist dogma. Instead, their platform is one that makes sense to the *campesino* (small farmer): work, land, housing, food, health care, education, independence, freedom, democracy, justice, and peace. They have fused the energies of both indigenous resistance and protection of the small farmer's way of life; both have been key to heighten-ing popular participation and civilian support.

Combined with the armed uprising has been the nonviolent in-volvement of civilians all over Mexico. Tens of thousands march almost daily in Mexico City in support of the people in Chiapas. Citizen expul-sion of government-supported mayors in small towns has become commonplace. Non-governmental organizations (NGOs) have played a prominent role in the peace negotiations, forming a "belt of peace" to discourage any elements of violence around the talks. CONPAZ, the recently formed San Cristóbal coalition of NGOs, performs health and human rights work, education, and indigenous economic development to "complement the work of the revolution."

With the neighboring states of Oaxaca, Guerrero, and Hidalgo living under almost equal levels of poverty, government corruption, and social injustice, why was the uprising so heavily concentrated in Chiapas?

Consciousness raising by the Catholic Church, many say, provided fertile soil to shake Chiapan foundations of injustice and power. In other Mexican states, the Christian ministry has not been so deeply established and resolute about its mission and role in society.

"Our concern is to make the good news of the gospel become real to the people and not only an expectation for after death," began Vicar Gonzalo Ituarte, Bishop Ruiz's animated colleague in the diocese of San Cristóbal. "We believe that people here are not experiencing the least of the benefits of the salvation of Christ. They are not treated, especially the Indians, as human beings. This is one of the few dioceses in Latin America that has spent so many years in the work of consciousness raising—34 years."

Father Jorge Rafael Diaz Nunez is a priest in Ocosingo; his parish is the largest in all of Mexico. Diaz spoke more specifically about the process of conscientization. "Pastoral praxis here is rooted in local poverty, violations of personal integrity, and institutional injustices. Through this pastoral practice over many, many years, consciousness of local Indians has risen dramatically.

"This has been carried out by thousands of lay catechists, who are unpaid, who go out to their Indian communities and work with a reflective process through which Indians learn to express their word and feel themselves to be persons. We call it the Tijwaneh Method ["pointed" or "spicy" in Tzeltal]. If the church can be accused of anything, it is of this: of having contributed to the conscientization of the indigenous peoples," he explained.

It wasn't exactly a silent conspiracy of conscientization, either. Father Ituarte explained, "The 'prophet of bad news,' Don Samuel [Bishop Ruiz], for 34 years has been telling us, 'Something is going to happen. These people are suffering. Please do take this problem seriously,'" said Ituarte.

LAND—OR THE LACK OF IT—IS PERHAPS the most critical issue for Mexico's rural population and a central demand of the Zapatistas.

A Mayan's identity is bound up with the land. Vicar Ituarte underscores this: "For the Indian, the land is the mother. For example, when they are starting to prepare the harvest, they ask permission to the land. They give offerings to the land, to the Earth—mother Earth. And then they give thanks for the products. It's a sacred relationship. They include nature as part of their lives.

"For us, it's business. And now with the new Mexican law, they are invited to buy and sell their mother."

The "new Mexican law," as Ituarte phrased it, is the Salinas-backed, NAFTA-inspired reform of Article 27 in the Mexican Constitution, the article that guaranteed communal lands—*ejidos*—for *campesinos*. The reform, enacted in 1992, allows the *ejidos* to be divided, bought, and sold. Eugenio, a work-worn community leader in Chalam del Carmen, told us, "As indigenous people we see these articles as being won by the flow of blood during the Mexican Revolution. But now they are being taken away."

Land evictions have displaced indigenous people for many years. Ever since the government opened the Lacandón Rain Forest for habitation 25 years ago, landless and desperate *campesinos* resettled in the jungle, slashing and burning much of the forest for farming. "During the 1960s came the conquest of the jungle," Father Diaz of Ocosingo explained. "We call this the exodus, because it was the farmhands, the servants, and the sharecroppers who left the slavery of the farms to populate the jungle."

These new agricultural settlements spelled disaster for the already endangered species and the mammoth mahogany trees of the jungle, many of which had been growing before Columbus arrived on the American continent. Seventy percent of virgin rain forest intact in 1970 plummeted to only 20 percent in 1990. Population in the jungle region is expected to double by the year 2000 to almost 500,000 inhabitants.

In Morelia, a town once surrounded by the Lacandón jungle, the local catechist explained the dilemma: "We know that we should not cut down the trees. We know this not because people tell us, but because it is something we have learned from our own ancestors. From the stories of our ancestors, we know of the damages to ecology. But how are we going to eat? There is a limited amount of land."

MANIPULATION AND CONTROL OF THE POPULATION by local authorities in Chiapas is also a chief root cause of the uprising. Our delegation's experience in the small city of Las Margaritas provided a parable of the power structure in Chiapas.

The Chiapas governor was planning a visit, and it was the talk of the town. Las Margaritas had been occupied by the Zapatistas for a few days, and now with 8,000 war refugees crowded into this little city a big audience was expected for his speech.

Many refugees told of receiving messages from the municipal government that they must evacuate their outlying communities because they were not safe anymore. Transportation into Las Margaritas was guaranteed by the municipal president, as was food, medicine, and shelter in the camps until the fighting ceased. Though many cited fear of guerrillas as reason to leave their communities, few had actually encountered any guerrillas passing through to threaten or forcibly recruit them.

As the crowd began to gather in the town square, groups of indigenous refugees were led to the front of the stage. Several held large signs with messages of support for the governor and a continued military presence in Las Margaritas. Those carrying the signs said they had neither written the messages nor understood what they meant. One refugee held his sign for all to see—upside-down—for the entire event.

Applause interrupted the governor's speech countless times, led by a man on stage who drew the response of the sign-holding refugees. Three introductory speeches to the governor (including one from a member of the local Presbyterian church) offered support for government policies and pledges to maintain a military presence in Las Margaritas.

About 15 minutes later, a group of a hundred people began to gather around the Catholic church; they soon made their way to the front door of the municipal building. A short woman with a strong voice led the gathering.

"Don't stay quiet!" she shouted. "The people must rise up!" A petition signed by 600 people demanding the removal of the municipal president was pressed into my hand as I approached this new gathering.

"We want freedom of expression. But look above there. They are filming us," the woman continued, gesturing toward the balcony where two men pointed video cameras at the crowd. "We want to express how we feel. But the whole town is afraid to speak out for fear of the municipal president."

Was she fearful of the Zapatistas?

"They don't give us fear because they say what we are saying. We are all people struggling, struggling against injustice. I do not want blood. But I want peace; peace with justice."

ANY EFFORTS AT REFORM SEEM UNLIKELY without a fundamental shakeup of the local power structure. "Chiapas functions more like a ranch than a state. Everything is completely controlled," Mario Tejado Busarol, a

Mexican social anthropologist told me as he described his 10-year work experience in the state. Chiapans, like other Mexicans, don't differentiate much between PRI as a political party and the government; PRI *is* the government.

While liberation is the driving force of the local Catholic theology, a different brand of theology in many Chiapas evangelical churches often feeds the region's power structure. (Chiapas has the highest concentration of evangelicals in any Mexican state—16 percent of the total population and nearly 25 percent of the indigenous population.)

Louis Scott, academic dean of the Centro de Estudios Superiores de Integración Cristiana in Mexico City and author of *Salt of the Earth*, a study of evangelicals in Mexico, explains that the large Pentecostal and Presbyterian churches have taught a fundamentalist dispensational theology. He writes:

> Classic dispensationalism teaches that during the church age the world will become worse and worse, and consequently the church should withdraw from political involvement in order to remain pure and to wait for the Lord's second coming. . . .The mission of the church is similar to that of a lifeboat used to save a few individuals before the ship [society] sinks.

There are also the *caciques* to contend with, the local term for the town's wealthy, land-owning civilians. The *caciques* have a mass of economic, political, and fire power and a long history of corruption in Chiapas.

Oscar Guillen, a tall, light-skinned man with gold chains, a red pickup, and shiny cowboy boots, sat behind a large desk and described his ranch, which was being occupied by the Zapatistas outside of Ocosingo. "There are no *latifundios* [large landholdings] in Chiapas, and there doesn't exist any more land to divide up. Two hundred hectares is sufficient to take care of only one family." (Many Indian families we observed lived and farmed on little more than one-half hectare.)

"This [the uprising] is a mystery," Guillen said. "We don't know the cause of their fighting. Indians live happily, they are not marginalized. They have corn and tortillas; that's all they need."

PEACE TALKS WITH THE ZAPATISTAS have resulted in rapid, far-reaching government concessions never seen before in any Latin American guerrilla movement. Autonomous forms of indigenous government have been discussed. Housing, hospital and road construction, electricity, and potable water will be developed in the indigenous communities from which the Zapatistas arose.

Amazingly, EZLN rebels have been allowed to keep their weapons until national reforms are met to their satisfaction. The Mexican government has also agreed to review for a 90-day period the effects of NAFTA on the indigenous population. With the indigenous flavor of the uprising calling attention to the Mayan people, their longstanding traditions and unique way of life may be able to help shape the direction of the country.

And yet on March 24, Luis Donaldo Colosio, predicted future president, was assassinated—causing political turmoil and bringing the peace talks to a standstill. The kidnapping of a Mexican billionaire has heightened the feeling of uncertainty.

In the face of all these events, the issue of violence arises, and our group struggled with it. Had it not been for a violent uprising, would we even be here calling attention to these problems? If Indian peasants hadn't resorted to the language of violence for the government to hear their claims, would their communities be on the verge of receiving housing, health clinics, electricity, and clean water? Would NAFTA's effect on the poor even be spotlighted?

Undeniably, the foundation of church-based conscientization work, the nonviolent efforts of thousands of Mexicans, and international pressure have turned a regional guerrilla conflict into a national plea for justice. Genuine democratic participation has proven to be a driving force in swaying the path of the country. If allowed to continue, Mexico may soon see its first fair elections in 70 years—despite Colosio's absence. Optimism must be tempered with realism. The peace-negotiated development projects initiated in some indigenous communities are a good beginning. However, if the system that deprived the communities of these basic necessities in the first place is not addressed, such development is a short-lived panacea and will only lead to further marginalization and desperation. Within the new political space, the continuous, nonviolent efforts of civilians will be crucial.

The Zapatistas lit a fire under neoliberal economics; they exposed its neglect of the poor for all to see. The Chiapas reality demonstrates that economic growth—the yardstick of success in the neoliberal minds behind NAFTA—can no longer be the exclusive measure of progress. The costs of making poor people self-supporting and protecting the splendor of the environment may create "unfavorable" short-term financial results. Yet if the neoliberal model endures unabated, Chiapas will certainly not be the last site of guerrilla uprisings or full-scale armed revolution.

With cautious hope, Mexico treads carefully toward a new chapter in its history.

JEFF SHRIVER was in Mexico from February 3-15, 1994, along with a group of human rights lawyers, church representatives, and journalists. The group's visit was coordinated by the Ecumenical Program in Central America and the Caribbean.

Reprinted from *Sojourners*, 2401 15th St. NW, Washington, DC 20009. Subscription: $30/year.

FROM YALE TO JAIL

DAVID DELLINGER'S QUEST FOR JUSTICE

by GEORGE HOWLAND, JR.

from NEW AGE JOURNAL

In the fall of 1940, David Dellinger, then a twenty-five-year-old seminary student, refused to register for the draft on moral grounds and was sentenced to a year and a day at Danbury federal prison. It was the first time that Dellinger, the Yale-educated son of a well-to-do Boston lawyer, had been incarcerated for his beliefs, but it certainly would not be the last. As Dellinger recalls in his revealing recent autobiography, *From Yale to Jail: The Life Story of a Moral Dissenter*, his treatment at the hands of the prison authorities—meant to break him of his rebelliousness—only served to confirm the direction his life had taken.

Locked in Danbury's "hole," a dank and lightless punishment cell, after refusing to observe the prison's rules of racial segregation, Dellinger realized that "if you fight clean and hard, people can kill you, but they can't hurt you. They can do terrible things to you—and probably will—but they can't hurt you unless you do it to yourself." At that moment, he recalls, he made a promise to himself: "From now on, no one will ever frighten or control me, no one will stop me from living to the full and loving to the full, loving everyone I know and everyone I don't know, fighting for justice without seeing anyone as an enemy."

For a remarkable half a century, Dellinger has kept his vow. Sustained by rich spiritual resources, a contagious love for people and for life, and a fifty-two-year marriage to Elizabeth Peterson, he has fought "clean and hard" on the pivotal issues of our time, traveling the globe in defense of civil rights, nuclear disarmament, peace, and social justice. Along the way he has joined forces with the likes of Martin Luther King, Jr., Abbie Hoffman, A. J. Muste, Barbara Deming, and Dorothy Day. If Dellinger was ever a household name himself, it was as one of the Chicago Seven, the man who, when facing the club-wielding police outside the Democratic National Convention, calmly told the crowd to "stay where you are. . . .This is being done for the whole world to see"— words that would later become the famous chant "The whole world is watching." In the assessment of actor and activist Martin Sheen, Dellinger is "one of the most important and bravest nonviolent revolutionaries of the twentieth century." And he may also be one of the most underappreciated.

Today, Dellinger, seventy-nine years old, lives with his wife in Vermont, writing (his six books include *Vietnam Revisited, More Power Than We Know*, and *Revolutionary Nonviolence*); lecturing; and still fighting for his beliefs. At long last, with the publication of *From Yale to Jail*, the influence of his life's work is becoming more widely known. "Before reading this book, I knew and greatly admired Dave Dellinger. Or so I thought," comments social critic Noam Chomsky. "After reading his remarkable story, my admiration changed to something more like awe."

DELLINGER WAS BORN IN WAKFIELD, MASSACHUSETTS, the second of four children. His parents embodied contradictory impulses: His father was a conservative Republican, yet he exuded an egalitarian ethos in his daily life; his mother was a society matron, but led her son to the passions and eternal questions contained in the world of literature.

When Dellinger is pressed for an explanation of how he moved from an upper-middle-class childhood to the front lines of social change, he invariably returns to Wakefield. "In junior high I made the mistake of falling in love with a poor Irish girl and becoming best friends with a poor Italian boy," he explains. "Ever since, I have been an advocate of doing away with the race and class divisions that plague our society."

Along with his developing social conscience came a similarly iconoclastic spiritual awareness. "In junior high, although I hated church, I had looked up some words of Jesus and had been very impressed by them," he says. "On the other hand I realized that there were a lot of things in the New Testament that I didn't really agree with. You know, hell fire and damnation, and the idea that we were somehow born sinful." The young pacifist soon discovered a religious figure who would have a more pronounced influence: Saint Francis of Assisi. "Frances had gone out and kissed the leper, expressing his belief that inside the wasted body of the person was something very lovable," he says. "Frances's famous call for peace is something I have always believed in very much—reconciliation, love, and not using violence to settle one's disputes."

The natural world also became a source of inner strength and renewal. Contemplation of nature revealed to Dellinger the unity of all things and left him "full of unity, or, as the Buddha says, empty of divisions and separations."

Dellinger has spent his entire life trying to realize this mystical insight in the material world. "My life is an attempt to bring together the internal and the external," he explains. "I may feel all kinds of spiritual exaltation at the drop of a hat, and yet, somehow, if I don't go out and meet the problems, especially the problems that are making other people feel less happy than I do, then it becomes distorted."

THOUGH THE ROOTS OF DELLINGER'S PACIFISM can be traced to his childhood, the crucible that would help him work out his pacifist politics and nonviolent tactics was World War II. In 1940 Congress passed a conscription law in anticipation of U.S. entry into the war. At the time, Dellinger was a student at the Union Theological Seminary, in which he had enrolled, he quips, "to learn more about the heretics." Dellinger could have received a religious deferment, but he regarded that as little better than a bribe. Together with seven colleagues, he refused any special status, didn't register for the draft, and was sentenced to Danbury.

"My opposition to World War II was probably the most controversial stand that I have ever taken," Dellinger writes. Being a conscientious objector to America's "good war" forced him to wrestle with difficult questions of conscience, but the philosophy of pacifism that emerged has remained consistent throughout his life. "I believe that all war is evil and useless," he argues. "Just as it would be stupid to plant weeds and to try to harvest vegetables, so it would be stupid to encourage the lies, conscription, and murder of war and to hope to produce democracy, freedom, and brotherhood."

Soon after his release from prison, Dellinger met someone who shared his devotion to pacifism. "Nothing else ever happened to me as important as meeting Betty (now Elizabeth) Peterson," says Dellinger. When they met in late 1941 at the national conference of the Student Christian Movement, Peterson "was opposed to the draft, wanted to live in a commune, and had been working the previous summer with Mexican migrant workers." A month later they were married by Peterson's father.

Financial concerns were never the guiding force in their lives. Says Peterson, "We just believed strongly enough in what we were doing that we always found a way to survive." In 1947 Dellinger, Peterson, and four other couples formed Glen Gardner, an intentional community in rural New Jersey. Over the next twenty years Glen Gardner was home for the couple and their five children. The family survived through a combination of subsistence farming, Peterson's teaching, and Dellinger's work in Glen Gardner's cooperative print shop. "It was very difficult, and one never knew where the next dollar was coming from," Peterson recalls. "It seemed like whenever there was an absolute emergency or need, something came from somewhere. So I really believe in casting your bread upon the waters and it will come back to you when you need it."

Not that being a family of nonviolent revolutionaries was easy. "Looking back, I wonder about some of the chances that I took when we had small children," Dellinger observes. "I'm not going to now justify or feel guilty about what I did, but I have to say I wonder a little bit: Was I being fair to them? What would have happened to them? There were times when I felt I had been away too much and my kids suffered and my wife suffered."

The civil rights movement and protests against the Vietnam War gave Dellinger the opportunity to practice his politics on a much larger scale. In the '60s, Dellinger was co-chair of the Spring Mobilization Committee Against the War (the Mobe), which organized demonstrations attended by hundreds of thousands, most notably the October 1967 nonviolent siege of the Pentagon and protests outside the Democratic National Convention in 1968.

At the Pentagon siege, Dellinger managed to acknowledge the energy of his young colleagues without backing down from his belief in nonviolence. "I remember Jerry Rubin and a bunch of those guys struggling very hard against Dave, trying to turn the thing into a violent assault against the soldiers," recalls writer and activist Grace Paley. "I remember him standing up to all of these people with . . . a totally stubborn nonviolence, a very tough kind of pacifism." At the Democratic convention, Chicago's Mayor Richard Daley dispatched his city's finest, and a police riot ensued. The five-month conspiracy trial that followed—described in fascinating detail in *From Yale to Jail*—became yet another forum for Dellinger's civil disobedience, with the defendants (there were actually eight) using various non-violent protest tactics and legal procedures in their strategy of "putting the government on trial."

Dellinger's outbursts and actions—at one point he placed his body in front of U.S. marshals as they aggressively seated Bobby Seale, receiving a knee in the testicles for his trouble—led to his repeatedly being cited for contempt of court. "It was Dave, of all the defendants, who was the Rock of Gibraltar," recalls William Kunstler, one of the attorneys for the defendants. "Everybody else was up and down, had good moments and bad. But Dave had his principles. He believed in them and did not deviate from them." Dellinger—ironically portrayed as the architect of the violence—was convicted along with four others of inciting to riot and was sentenced to five years in prison (a verdict later overturned on appeal). It was, he now says, his "fifteen minutes of fame."

Indeed, Dellinger notes, "all that temporary fame and adulation threw me off balance more than I knew." When the United States pulled out of Vietnam, Dellinger extricated himself from the spotlight and returned to grassroots activism. Through the '70s and '80s he continued to teach, write, and carry on campaigns of nonviolent protest—including a 1987 action in the Washington, D.C., Rotunda against the United States-sponsored contra war in Nicaragua. Dellinger, Peterson, and five others were subsequently arrested, tried, convicted, and sentenced to community service. ("When I asked [the judge] what community service meant," Dellinger recalls, "he said, 'Just keep on doing the things that you are doing every day anyway.'")

MORE RECENTLY DELLNGER HAS BEEN LENDING his support to prisoners both famous (antiwar bank robber-turned-fugitive Katherine Ann Power) and unknown, and helping select a new editor for *Toward Freedom* magazine, whose board Dellinger co-chairs. His recent writings include an article published in *Covert Action quarterly* titled "Hope for the Nineties." In it, Dellinger argues that these days "there is much more rebellion and experimentation with positive ways of relating to our fellow human beings than meets the casual eye or is made clear in the mass media."

When asked where he finds the strength to continue his political work, Dellinger seems a little chagrined. "To be honest, I had just a little twinge of uncertainty, like maybe I should feel guilty because I don't feel discouraged. I think it's just because I get so full inside from . . . well, I'm looking at a tree out the window now," he says. "I think of what Albert Einstein once said: 'There are only two ways to live your life. One is as though nothing is a miracle. The other is as though everything is a miracle.'"

Perhaps because his spiritual work has proved so central to his politics, Dellinger is critical of those who would separate the two. "I'm thinking of a meditation center I've been to a few times. It seems like people come there and have a thrilling experience becoming centered, and then they go about their normal greedy lives of trying to rise higher than their fellows. I contrast what I have observed in some [spiritual] retreats with what I have observed in Southern churches during civil-rights days, how the church services were among the most inspiring I've ever been in, with laughing and *amen*ing and praying and just a wonderful participation by just about everyone there. And when it was over they didn't say, 'Oh, how wonderful that was. I'm going to come back next week to do it again.' Instead, they opened the doors and we went out to face the police dogs and the water hoses and the clubs and all the rest of it."

Dellinger remains, however, unwilling to set himself up as some kind of infallible authority. "Now that I'm an elder, I think that elders have as much to learn from younger people as younger people have to learn from them," he says. "I think that one always has to listen as much as one talks and to learn from people of different attitudes." He reluctantly imparts a few pieces of advice for today's political activists. "Never become arrogant or think that we have all the answers. . . . Be willing to experiment and make mistakes. Trying to be perfect is a very restrictive thing. One has to strike out and take actions that fit the best that one sees and understands and intuits, but realize in the process that one may make mistakes."

Though Dave Dellinger may be an extraordinary person, nothing would distress him more than to have ordinary people decide that his life is too exceptional to provide an example for anyone else. Dellinger knows that change is brought about not by exemplary individuals acting alone, but by thousands of regular folks working together.

GEORGE HOWLAND is a freelance writer living in Seattle, Washington.

Reprinted from *New Age Journal*, 42 Pleasant Street, Watertown, MA. Subscriptions: $24/year. For subscriptions call, (815) 734-5808.